UNITED
PARTICIPA
KOREA

ALSO BY PAUL M. EDWARDS

Combat Operations of the Korean War:
Ground, Air, Sea, Special and Covert (2010)

Between the Lines of World War II:
Twenty-One Remarkable People and Events (2010)

Small United States and United Nations
Warships in the Korean War (2008)

The Hill Wars of the Korean Conflict: A Dictionary of Hills,
Outposts and Other Sites of Military Action (2006)

UNITED NATIONS PARTICIPANTS IN THE KOREAN WAR

The Contributions of 45 Member Countries

Paul M. Edwards

McFarland & Company, Inc., Publishers
Jefferson, North Carolina, and London

All photographs courtesy Center for the Study of the Korean War.

LIBRARY OF CONGRESS CATALOGUING-IN-PUBLICATION DATA

Edwards, Paul M.
   United Nations participants in the Korean War : the
contributions of 45 member countries / Paul M. Edwards.
      p.   cm.
   Includes bibliographical references and index.

   ISBN 978-0-7864-7457-8
   softcover : acid free paper ∞

   1. United Nations—Armed Forces—History—Korean War,
1950–1953.   2. Korean War, 1950–1953.   I. Title.
DS918.E366 2013
951.904'24—dc23
                                                2013030191

BRITISH LIBRARY CATALOGUING DATA ARE AVAILABLE

On the cover: Hawker "Sea Fury" Fighter is catapulted from the
British light fleet aircraft carrier HMS *Glory* during Korean War
operations circa June 1951. This aircraft bears the number "VR-943"
(official Royal Navy photograph, from the All Hands Collection,
Naval History & Heritage Command).

Manufactured in the United States of America

*McFarland & Company, Inc., Publishers
   Box 611, Jefferson, North Carolina 28640
      www.mcfarlandpub.com*

To Charles Christenson,
a Minnesotan with a sense of humor

Table of Contents

Preface

This is a book about a forgotten part of a war that has been vastly ignored. The Korean War neither captured the American imagination nor required the best of the American spirit. The newspapers from that era are strangely missing long or detailed stories about the war. According to the historian Gary Huey, it was "by every measure used in public opinion polls, the Korean War was one of the most unpopular wars ever fought by the United States."[1] Perhaps that is because it was a war that demanded very little from the American people; few but the troops involved suffered. There was no sense of unity like that expressed during World War II, no carpooling, no victory gardens, no rationing. Troops needed for the war were called up individually, and so there were no communities with mass involvement.

President Harry S. Truman, aware that his nation had just emerged from a period of restrictions — rationing, shortages, and taxes — determined that this time there would be both "guns and butter," and bought the war on credit. For the American people, unless they themselves or loved ones were involved, it was not a particularly significant event, certainly not a traumatic experience for those that did not participate. When it was over there were no celebrations, no victory parades, just relief.

Much has been made of the fact that the Korean War was a United Nations war, but little has been said about the nations that decided to fight, and then fought, that war. This book is about those nations whose participation has long been overlooked in the narrative histories. These contributions ranged from their political influence wielded during the hot debates of consideration and the tensions of voting at the United Nations, to participating in small unit actions of front line troops. The American involvement is included for balance, but in such limited detail as to be but general information. For those interested in the American effort, I would recommend one or two of the many excellent histories of the war, including Clay Blair's old but still excellent *The Forgotten War: America in Korea 1950–1953* or the view from British historian Max Hastings in *The Korean War.*[2]

My interest in this war and the many nations that fought in it came early in my life. During my brief and un-noteworthy involvement in Korea I remember with the amazement of a nineteen year old the first meetings with soldiers from so many other nations; I saw the best and worst of them and marveled at their simple involvement. No better informed than I, they knew little or nothing of why they were there or how their small involvement affected the movement of nations on the world stage. They came with their strange customs, unique uniforms, incomprehensible languages, and yet they were very much like us. Few could have explained why their nation sent them or what the various countries expected to get from their involvement, and yet they were there and they knew what was expected of them. It is a cliché worn dull by its many uses, but the great discovery was that their blood ran the same red as that of my comrades. My understanding was limited, the arrogance of my age unmatched, but my appreciation for these international representatives has never wavered.

Most narrative histories of this event, obviously written by members of the predominant nation, rarely mention the troops of other nations involved in the struggle. The slight is even more exaggerated in those works concerned with reporting the air and sea war. The classic *The Sea War in Korea* by Commanders Malcolm Cagle and Frank Manson makes little or no distinction between nationalities when discussing the naval involvement. But, the individual nations have not done a lot better. The British have done the best in accounting for their participation and to a lesser extent the Canadians, Australians, and New Zealanders, but there is surprisingly little, in English, of the prime involvement of the Republic of Korea, or the significant contribution of say the French, the Dutch or even the small but feisty nation of Luxembourg. Even some of the more significant reference works, dictionaries, almanacs, and encyclopedias are amazingly stingy with their coverage.

And yet, around 1950 the United States and the United Nations were pleading for the involvement of every member nation, pulling out every diplomatic, economic, or military tool they could find to expand forces. In 1950 America was looking for friends.

This war was, among other things, the baptism by fire for the still untested United Nations, and the response of so many nations was essential if the body was to enter this war with the authority of international interest and concern. The United Nations, having first decided not to locate in North Dakota, had not yet finished the building to house its many delegates, yet it sought to function as fully as possible. At a time when most people could not tell you what a Cold War was, previous allies were maneuvering for ideological commitments. In the political arena, the war in Korea was the premier event in the clash between the ideological factions trying to control international affairs following World War II. Historian William Stueck goes so far as to suggest that the Korean War was a "substitute for World War III,"[3] an insightful analysis that emerged from his awareness of the many forces at work at the time. The line between the Soviet Union and its followers and the Western allies was being drawn, and this war, among other things, was essential in identifying those lines and determining on which side many of the nations would settle.

Despite its long identity as the "forgotten war," I am more comfortable with the term "ignored war," for that seems to be a better evaluation. The scholarly community, however, has not forgotten Korea. Some remarkably good work has been done, particularly in the last decade. And yet, because of the long sleep during which the American people, as well as the rest of the world, chose to ignore the war, much about it is still unknown; vast areas of the war have yet to be considered. Even in his collection of studies that explore the war in more realistic terms, William Stueck in *The Korean War in World History* fails to have an index entry for many of the involved nations other than the big four. The same is true of *Rethinking the Korean War,* an insightful consideration of the complexities of international support. This is not a slight against William Stueck and his fellow authors, for they have accomplished some remarkable work, but rather an effort to point out that these contributing nations have not yet receive the attention they perhaps deserve.

The Korean War veteran has not been as outspoken as some of his colleagues. There are few reunions and gatherings, and the Graybeard — the Korean War Veterans' Association — has only a minuscule percentage of veterans as members. But they would agree, I believe, with historian Bevin Alexander's comment in his unfortunately misnamed book *Korea: The First War We Lost*: "The Korean War became the arena for fateful clashes of national wills, in which leaders at all levels made decisions ranging from remarkable sagacity to desolating error. Korea is thus a human story of mortals in high and low places acting in crisis as their individual lights directed them."[4]

Since the Communist nations involved in this conflict continue to safeguard their archives, a real balance of the reporting on the war will not be achieved. But there is little reason for us to avoid consideration of nations that participated and which, with some little effort, can be identified and understood.[5]

Rest assured it is not the author's intent to overstate the case. Surely the bulk of the demands of this war fell on the American military and for that they must receive the most attention; but they did not do it alone. Any understanding of what happened in Korea, or why it happened, must include the story of those nations who invested their political agendas, their cash and commodities, and the lives of their men and women, in the outcome of this international conflict.

Introduction

If there is any necessity for Congressional action I will come to you. But I hope we can get these bandits in Korea suppressed without that.

— President Harry Truman

On a large field of green at a place called Tanggok, not far from the port city of Pusan, South Korea, lie tracks of white crosses, row after row, bearing the names of men who died in the Korean War. On each cross is embossed the symbol of the nation under whose flag they came to fight. In this immaculately kept and astonishingly beautiful area one finds the remains of soldiers from nations all over the world, and markers over the graves that bear religious symbols ranging from the Christian cross to the Crescent and Star of David. And yet, when recalling this bloody war, few remember the great variety of nations that fought together under one flag in this international conflict.

When author George Orwell first introduced the phrase "Cold War," he most likely did not envision how quickly the suspicions of nations would turn the conflicting ideologies of their governments into a series of hot exchanges — limited but nevertheless deadly encounters. Among these clashes and responses, the outbreak of the Korean War was perhaps the most significant because of how quickly it became a test for nations. It was a time when the Cold War teams were identified, a time to stand up and be counted.

When, in the early morning of 25 June 1950, Captain Joseph R. Darriog of the Korean Military Advisory Group (KMAG) was awakened by gunfire, he was most likely unaware that the nature of the modern world was about to change once again. He was there with his small unit of military advisors because it was always feared that such a thing would happen, but neither he nor the governments he represented had adequately prepared for it. Some few continued to make the claim that the Republic of Korea (South Korea) was

5

responsible for initiating the war, and saw behind it a conspiracy in which the United States played a significant part. But the general consensus was that the Communist led aggression[1] was provoked by the government of North Korea with the goal of reunification.

The North Korean invasion of the Republic of Korea became an international crisis both because it tested the resolve of the United Nations and because it forced many countries to consider and reconsider their willingness to take sides in the growing Cold War that was slowly encompassing the world. Of the fifty-three nations that supported the UN decision to intervene, more than forty nations were eventually involved in the conflict, many sending their young men and women to fight and die in this small, isolated nation. At the peak of its strength the United Nations forces in Korea numbered 932,964 men and women. This number, which included the troops of the Republic of Korea, fought as a united body under a unified command; they were the United Nations.

Of all the places the involved nations could have chosen to create this test, Korea must be one of the most difficult. While a beautiful nation with a long history of cultural achievement it is also a vastly rugged place that suffers the extremes of heat and cold. In summer the heat and humidity bogs down human activity, and in the winter, with the winds blowing down from Siberia and funneling along mountain valleys, the temperature drops to forty below zero or colder. In the 1950 the land possessed few paved roads and travel was limited to the north and south, while crossing the peninsula meant going by boat. Few cities existed and the hundreds of little villages were often cut off and unaware of what was happening to the rest of their nation. The people, while intelligent and capable, had few opportunities, and many were terribly angry at the division of their country and the line that had been drawn that separated them from family.

The quick-tempered and outspoken President Harry S. Truman by-passed the United States Congress and took his concerns over Korea to the newly organized United Nations.[2] Operating out of Blair House and surrounded with military and diplomatic advice, he was seeking a multi-national response to the Communist aggression. In emergency session the deliberative body met and passed United Nations Resolution of 25 June 1950 that declared the invasion of the Republic of South Korea by the Democratic People's Republic of Korea to be a "breach of the peace." It called on the government of North Korea to execute an "immediate cessation of hostilities." It was a futile plea and had little to no effect on the government of North Korea. The Truman administration's concern over the attack and its determination to support South Korea was reaffirmed by UN Secretary General Trygve Lie, who believed it would be a disaster if the UN failed to forcefully respond to this, its first real challenge.

Most scholars date the beginning of the Cold War with the Czechoslovakian *coup d'état* in Prague in February 1948,[3] and that is as good a date as any. But the tense situation had been building for some time before that. Even before Germany surrendered Joseph Stalin was showing signs of going it alone. The military, represented in this case by the boisterous General George Patton, thought that it might be necessary to turn armies to the East. The shadow of Soviet intentions had begun to affect the attitude of nations. Responding to pressures created by the Soviet Union's growing influence and with serious concern over the expansion of Communism, the Truman administration had established the Truman Doctrine, which at first had provided aid to Greece and Turkey. But the doctrine quickly turned into a policy of containment, and in the years following Winston Churchill's Fulton, Missouri, speech in 1946, it seemed to be working.

Having completed World War II and presided over the return of U.S. troops from their foreign assignments, the president might well have expected an easier time. But the world of Harry Truman was, in 1950, not an easy one. Communist expansion in the East was raising serious questions about possibility of future peace. Ever since World War II, the basic antagonism between capitalism and communism, remained. As well, the balance of power was taking on a new tint. The "old powers" of Great Britain, France, Italy, Germany, and China had lost much of their influence in the struggle, their economies weakened and their manpower decimated, leaving the United States and Russia with the burden of power. New alignments were needed. Even Japan, as that beleaguered nation was rising from the destruction of World War II, was experiencing anti–American riots in the streets. America, realizing that it was unable to police post-war Europe, decided to try and rebuild it, launching the Marshall Plan in 1947. The immediate Soviet response to the Marshall Plan was the organization of the Communist Information Bureau (Cominform) in September 1947 and later the Warsaw Pact. It was to put Communist pressure on France and Italy, to make a failure of the Marshall Plan, and to weaken nationalism in Central and Eastern Europe. Within a year the bureau had removed all non–Communists from the governments of Poland, Hungary, Romania, and Czechoslovakia and pressure on Finland and Norway. Moves to suppress Yugoslavian nationalism led Tito to break with Moscow, but the struggling nations were never all that far away.

The Berlin Blockade, initiated by the Soviet Union without warning, had tested the West's determination and was countered by an airlift that provided needed commodities to the city, carried out by a host of nations.[4] Then the Russians exploded their first atomic bomb, a complete surprise that made Russia a player. In Asia from India to China there was discord caused by Communist uprisings focused against colonial rule, with the Malaysians fighting the British and the Indochinese the French. In the spring of 1950 the People's Republic of China decided to lend assistance to its Communist allies in Indochina, and Washington watched unsure of what to do other than to send additional aid to France. The world was ripe for a war, and one can only wonder if things had not worked out as they did on the battlefields of Korea, if the same Cold World struggle would not have transpired in Vietnam.

In Washington, the Republicans, many still holding on to their isolationist tendencies of an earlier day, raised their objections to Truman's theory of containment. They had made significant gains in the political arena and were able to thwart many of Truman's social policies and to prevent any conscientious extension of Franklin Roosevelt's New Deal. Walter H. Judd, of the House, and spokesman for the China Bloc, was constantly urging the State Department to provide full support, suggesting even military support, to Chiang, which he assumed would prevent the "Communization of Asia."[5]

Senator Joseph McCarthy made his first charges against the State Department in February 1950 and unleashed a campaign of fear and hate nearly unparalleled in American history. The effect would not only destroy many careers and weaken the personnel available to deal with the situation in Asia, but damage the morale of the diplomatic branch of government. The diatribes led by the Republican senator and supported by opportunists in the government, all based on unsupported charges against much of the American public, led way to concerns over conspiracies and dovetailed beautifully with the charges emerging from the Chinese bloc in Congress.

Right or wrong, President Truman and the Democrat Party were facing an opposition party that was determined to accuse them of being soft on Communism and blaming the administration for the fact that China had fallen to the forces of Chairman Mao Tse-tung. There had been no way for the United States, despite its aid and long diplomatic trips made by General George C. Marshall, to stop Chinese Generalissimo Chiang Kai-shek from the fate he had so surely crafted for himself. Years of unparalleled corruption and mistreatment of his people, as well as his misuse of billions of dollars in American aid, had finally led to his defeat against the Communist forces on the mainland. The Red Chinese, as many Americans identified them, had beaten the slowly dispersing army of the Nationalist leader, and his government had, in 1949, withdrawn to the island of Formosa. This came as a blow to the American people who had always considered China an ally, and saw this Communist victory as one part of a larger world-wide conspiracy managed by the Soviet Union. This was a major defeat and the loss of a friend. Historian William L. Neumann wrote that it was "an even greater disaster for American policy than Pearl Harbor,"[6] and while that may well be an exaggeration, there is no doubt that the Democrats who were blamed suffered from it. There was a strong China lobby that believed America had a significant future in China with its potential for massive markets and political alliances and, as a result of the administration's mishandling, it had now been lost.

As it turned out, while a tragedy in their own right, the events in Korea may well have been seen by Truman and his administration as an opportunity to prove to the opposition that they were not "soft." It may have been, as Dean Acheson commented, that "Korea came along and saved us."[7] He was not, obviously, expressing pleasure at the events in Korea, rather he was simply acknowledging that in a year of unparalleled political tragedies — from the loss of China to the Communists on the one end and the discovery that Soviet spies had penetrated the American atomic research program on the other end — this was something to hold on; something to deal with.

Upon hearing the news of the North Korean invasion, President Truman flew back to Washington from his home in Independence, Missouri. He had called ahead for a meeting of his closest advisors at Blair House the following day. He was surprised at the events and he was worried about the larger implications. Neither he, nor John Foster Dulles, appeared to house any doubts that this was an act of Communist aggression and felt that it required an immediate and aggressive response. At this time there was no evidence to support such a belief, but the president had come to the conclusion, fairly quickly, that the Soviet Union was somehow involved, though he was wise enough not to make that accusation at the time.[8] It was an evaluation on his part but Truman believed that the invasion in Korea was primarily a softening up operation, the first move on a timetable of world aggression that would, if not opposed, inevitably lead to violence in Europe and then to World War III.

While the last of the American presidents not to have a college degree, Truman was a serious student of history as well as a veteran of World War I, and he was starkly aware that the British and French appeasement of Nazi Germany had brought disastrous consequences on the world. His memory of that, and what it had meant to the world, was often on his mind. He was not going to allow such an appeasement to occur again, not with Kim Il Sung, and not on his watch.

Truman's belief that the Soviet Union was somehow directly involved in this invasion of South Korea vindicated many of the assumptions made in NSC 68, a top secret National Security Council report of 1950. Believing as they did that North Korea was totally controlled by Moscow, the president and the National Security Council[9] assumed that the puppet state would not have acted without direct instructions from Stalin. The best thinking of the National Security Council was focused on the intentions of the Soviet Union, having determined that they were the prime enemy facing the United States. The memorandums from the intelligence community informed the administration that the Soviets, in choosing Korea, were challenging the "U.S. specifically in an effort to test the U.S. toughness in resisting Communist expansion."[10]

At least at first it seemed that Truman had made the right choice. The American people were supportive of his decision and, for a while, there was a patriotic response, even some excitement. Not interested in another war, but with the natural patriotic fervor of a people whose security had been challenged, they responded with support. General Douglas MacArthur reported from Japan that the government of that country was greatly relieved, believing that this could be seen as strong evidence that the U.S. would defend them against Soviet aggression should it occur. Averell Harriman, special assistant to the president on national security matters, reported that Europe had been afraid that the U.S. would not make a forceful response to the challenge, and were relieved when it did. Lester Pearson, Canada's foreign minister, was pleased with the response, as was Great Britain, for both thought that the loss of Korea in this manner would damage Western prestige. It was a political high point for the president.

However, there were other voices speaking. Both George Kennan and Charles Bohlen, Soviet experts with the State Department, expressed the need for caution, believing that the administration needed to be careful about putting too much reliance on the policy compacted in NSC 68. The document was too rigid. Early in 1950 the Truman administration had started working on a document with the National Security Council that would outline American policy toward the Soviet Union. The top secret document that resulted[11] identified the Soviet Union not only as an enemy to the United States, but painted it with the multiple colors of evil to the point that it suggested war was inevitable.[12] The two experts believed that when working with the Soviet Union it was far more important to consider the nation's intentions rather than its capabilities. Given both its tendency to threaten as well as to exaggerate its abilities, some thought more attention needed to be given to just what the Soviets could accomplish. And, at the moment, the intentions of the superpower were not all that clear. However, Kennan told the British ambassador, Sir Oliver Franks, that "the president and his advisers were convinced that, even if the Communist invasion did not signal Moscow's readiness to risk all-out war with the United States, it represented a challenge to the will of the non–Communist world that had to be met."[13]

Truman was, as this unfolded, also very concerned with the role of the United Nations in the first real test of its potential. Considering himself a father of the international organization, he was deeply aware of how fragile it was. In a serious moment he would explain to General MacArthur that one reason America was fighting in Korea was "to bring the United Nations through its first great effort in collective security and to produce a free world coalition of incalculable value to the national security interest of the United States."

After listening to his advisors, Truman made his decision concerning the events in Korea. He would later suggest in his memoirs that he found this decision to be even more difficult than the one he had to make that led to the dropping of the atomic bomb on Japan five years earlier. And, while his decision may or not have been totally legal, Congress did not challenge him. As it played out, the firm reaction earned him some limited renewal of congressional and public support; his approval rating rose above 40 percent one of the few times during his presidency.[14] This, and the corollary affirmations, were far reaching decisions made quickly; many have argued far too quickly.

While apparently few could see that far ahead, Truman's decision to go to the aid of South Korean President Syngman Rhee, and perhaps as important, to dispatch the Seventh Fleet to the Formosa Strait to neutralize Taiwan, were decisions which altered the course of history and turned what might well have remained a civil war into an international crisis. But, believing that he was looking at the larger picture, he felt that the protection of Taiwan was essential and related to the overall question.

In February 1949, at his request, the Joint Chiefs of Staff had investigated the situation on the island and assessed that a Communist takeover of Taiwan would be highly unfavorable to the United States because it would allow for the domination of the sea routes between Japan and the Malay area, as well as extending control to the Ryukyu Islands and Philippines.[15] Nevertheless, the move to guard the Straits of Formosa had other repercussions as well, for it forced the People's Republic of China to call off its plans for the invasion of Taiwan, and put a damper on its prospects for an East Asian revolution. As well, it focused international attention on the newly formed government in China and spotlighted its control of the mainland.

While there is considerable evidence that President Truman would have gone it alone in Korea, he saw the great value in any reaction being portrayed as a response of all nations to the problems of one. Thus what the UN did was important and Truman was determined the UN needed to be involved. Believing that the UN's long association with the problems on the Korean peninsula gave it unique authority, the United States provided a proposal that would identify North Korea as the aggressor and demand a withdrawal. The UN agreed. Certainly the absence of Jacob A. Malik, the Soviet delegate who had walked out of the body, made passing the resolution much easier. The fact that Stalin failed to return his ambassador with the purpose of blocking the vote at the United Nations that allowed an international reaction to the invasion of Korea has never been completely understood by historians of the war. Certainly the question of the admission of Communist China played a part that, in itself, is not fully understood. In their work *Uncertain Partners*, Goncharov, Lewis and Xue make two suggestions. One is that Kim's plan for the invasion of the South and his promise to have the war over in five days would mean that the fighting would be over before the United States or its allies could interfere. There is evidence that Kim made such a promise on the belief that the Communists in South Korea would rise up and greet him, but this seems like a long shot. But given the thinking at the time, it might well be an explanation.

The other seems to be a better explanation. If the resolutions passed and the United Nations became the force involved in the conflict, then the Soviet Union would be relieved from putting into effect the clause of the Sino-Soviet mutual defense pact that protected against military interference by the United States. If the forces involved marched into Korea under the flag of the United Nations, then Stalin was free to help in whatever way he considered best, but was not forced into action by international treaty. Stalin did not seem to care what flag the participants would be using.[16]

In her timely and significant investigation of the Soviet archives, Kathryn Weathersby did not find any evidence to support these two suggestions but believed the documents she uncovered did in fact support the idea that the Soviet's believed Communist China would enter the conflict if the integrity of North Korea was threatened. And, on the other hand, that Stalin was not willing to risk damage to his relationship with China by ending the boycott and thus suggesting that Russia was not standing behind its insistence on Communist China being seated as the proper representative of the Chinese people. Weathersby also offers another possibility, that a return to the UN on the eve of the attack would suggest that the Soviet Union had some prior knowledge of the pending attack and was returning to prevent UN action.

What were the reasons then behind Joseph Stalin's behavior? One reason may well lie in his belief that the Communist victory in China left Mao with troops free to support the Korean nations if necessary. This victory also indicated to Stalin that the United States was weak and was not willing to extend itself to prevent the takeover. He must surely have believed, as well, that the recently completed mutual defense treaty that he had worked out with the PRC would make the United States somewhat more hesitant in starting any trouble with China. Besides, it is believed, he was viewing American action throughout the world and interpreting the mood of the American people as uninterested and unwilling to interfere.

And so the resolution that basically set up the situation for a United Nations war was passed. A good many nations raised objections, but when it came time to make a decision, they voted in favor. The opposition of Yugoslavia's Ales Bebler was not strong enough to prevent a 9–0 vote in favor of the resolution. Two days later UN Security Council Resolution of 27 June 1950, drafted by the United States, went even further and called upon its members to assist South Korea in repelling the North Korean aggression. The draft resolution was supported and passed without amendment just before midnight on the 27th. It called on its members to provide whatever was necessary to "restore international peace and security in the area." Once India had come on board in support of the resolution, and Ales Bebler had voted his opposition, Secretary General Lie addressed the members urging them to provide the aid called for in the resolution.

In this action the United Nations stood firm in its position as a body of international responsibility. Some twenty years before, the much weaker League of Nations had failed to stand up to either Japan or Italy, and in doing so had contributed to the outbreak of World War II and the demise of the league. Just how much this memory contributed to the collective decision is difficult to measure, but it played some role.[17] By the end of the week, 33 of the 59 member states of the UN would express their support of the resolution and another 20 would eventually endorse it. A large number who did so were also members of NATO.

According to White House advisor George M. Elsey, writing in July 1950, the world reaction to the American decision was overwhelmingly favorable. That may have been a little on the optimistic side, but the first responses appear to support him. French Foreign Minister Robert Schuman agreed that the action taken by the U.S. was the only proper one available to the body. The Belgian foreign minister expressed satisfaction with the vote, as did the British Prime Minister Clements R. Attlee, whose support was applauded by the House of Commons. The Dutch foreign minister, as well as Luxembourg Foreign Minister Joseph Bech, felt that the Soviets would be surprised at the firmness of President Truman's views and supported the decision. The same view was expressed in one way or the other by the Norwegian foreign minister, as well as dignitaries from Costa Rica, Nicaragua, Panama, Chile, Peru and Colombia.[18] Not all nations were supportive, of course, and although Lebanon, Syria, Jordan and Iraq all managed to issue vaguely worded expressions of support for the UN action in Korea, Egypt could not bring itself to do even that.

In retrospect the response of the membership seems overwhelming. To the amazement of some, the deliberative body had addressed the issue and taken action. In the next few months, nearly forty nations made a contribution of some kind, ranging from troops to commodities. Rallying along far different and varied lines from those that had united the allies in World War II, nations large and small weighed up their political positions, their international goals, their limited resources, and invested in both the promises of the United Nations and in the expectations of their own futures.

At home much of the wrangling was subdued for a moment and the U.S. Congress acted less than a week after the intervention decision was made when they backed the president's efforts by quickly passing the Deficiency Appropriations Act of 29 June 1950. This act expanded the size of aid going to support the Republic of Korea (ROK) Army. Then, within a short time, it passed Truman's requests for money to fight the war in two defense appropriation acts. For a brief period the American people seemed interested in the war, and support for the president and his decisions were acknowledged.

While many more nations would end up promising more than they actually provided as help, the initial response had been good and was, in the main, supportive of United States initiatives. But the job of keeping the multinational support of the General Assembly was no small matter. The West was in a minority when it came to votes in the General Assembly and as the war extended and became increasingly bitter, there was growing criticism about the means by which America was fighting the war, especially the seemingly unlimited use of air power. The nation that appeared most likely to upset the American expectations from the war was India, and the United States was afraid that it would use its power and influence to get the UN General Assembly to condemn the American handling of the war. That is all a part of the story.

Sources and Acknowledgments

Without a doubt, a book of this nature relies on the good services of a broad band of colleagues, associates, and research librarians, and I want to acknowledge my debt to the many that provided such remarkable service. Among the extended list, special thanks must go to the highly professional staff of the Joint Services Command and General Staff College Library at Fort Leavenworth, Kansas, where the United Nations documents are located, to Dr. Mike Devine and the staff at the Harry S. Truman Presidential Library and Museum in Independence, Missouri, and to Gregg M. Edwards, the director and his staff at the Center for the Study of the Korean War, in Independence, for the use of their significant collections. Because there is so little available, either in primary or secondary documents, about these "other nations" it was necessary for librarian and archivists, as well as the staffs of historical departments of various nations, to greatly exceed the normal requests for help. Thanks also to veterans who shared their stories either in person or through their archives — Jim Schultz, Wayne Funmaker, Alma Blair, Hap Harrington, Paul Wolfgeher, Don Sutton, William St. Clair, and others.

Secondary sources are surprisingly limited, as few books turned up about the military and commercial aid provided by many of the member nations. For some nations the contribution to the war in Korea was a very small period in their national histories, and historians, even those with national interests, have not written much on this involvement. With the exception of France, most significant contributors have written something about their participation but these are both hard to locate and usually not translated. There are two exceptions to this situation. I need to express my special appreciation to Gordon L. Rittman, whose excellent *Korean War Order of Battle: United States, United Nations, and Communist Ground, Naval, and Air Forces, 1950–1953*,[19] is the most comprehensive and reliable source for information on the armed forces of the involved nations. His efforts have produced a remarkable resource and great thanks are extended. The second is the work of William Stueck. *The Korean War: An International History*[20] is one of the few efforts that really digs into the complex international situation produced by the North Korean invasion. William Stueck as done as much as anyone to try and untangle the complexities of multi-nation influences, and I have relied heavily on his insights. A third source needs to be mentioned as well. The work by Kathryn Weathersby, both translations and analysis, has made clear so many of the unanswered questions about the war that just about any study is indebted to her; as of course am I.

Appreciation must also be expressed for the researchers and public relations persons of those nations that responded to inquiries about their national involvement. And yet, some surprise must be registered by the fact that several of the nations involved are now, for reasons of changing political climates, not willing to discuss their contribution or to provide materials relating to it.

To my wife of many years, Carolynn, continued thanks for encouragement and appreciation for understanding the obsession with putting it down. Also thanks and appreciation to Gregg Edwards, stalwart compatriot, Michael Pearlman, a colleague with a sense of humor, and Greg Smith, all who make their mark on whatever I do.

Who to Include

One of the first items of business in considering this work was which nations should be included in this study. One would think that now, more than sixty years after the conflict began, that all those facts would be out and well known. But that is not the case. In March of 2010 the government of South Korea was "uncovering" still more information about those nations that came to its aid during the war. The additional nations that they are now considering include Brazil, Bolivia, Nicaragua, Austria, Myanmar, Japan, Taiwan, and Vietnam. In November 2010 the South Korean ambassador, speaking at a Veterans' Day parade, announced that Haiti had been one of the first nations to come to the aid of South Korea when the war broke out. He gave no details as to what the aid involved, nor have there been any additional comments.[21] Some of these nations, obviously, were involved at one level or the other, and have been included. But until more evidence is discovered, this announcement has not been taken seriously.

Casualty and Involvement Figures

Of the many unanswered questions that still haunt those studying the Korean War, perhaps the most disconcerting is the difficulty in getting accurate information about the number of troops involved and the number of casualties suffered. Just about every account, official and otherwise, differs in some fashion. During the confusion of any war, such an accounting is very difficult; the rapid movement early in this war meant that many records were lost. The varying accounts are sometimes the result of the management of information by the nations involved as some seem to have been interested in upgrading, or downplaying, the cost of their involvement. Getting a proper account of casualties is also hampered by the lack of a clear definition of "casualty"; is a man killed in a jeep accident on the way to a battle considered killed in action? War is a hazardous business and deaths from all sorts of accidents can be numerous. Some nations, even those friendly with the United Nations, failed to give consistent numbers when reporting their dead and wounded. Some nations involved — Italy, India, and Japan, as examples — are generally not listed on casualty reports even though they had personnel in the war zone. So, we operate on estimations.

It is estimated that nearly 95,700 UN troops were killed and 200,000 wounded. It is estimated that 46,000 ROK soldiers were killed and more than 100,000 wounded. The Pentagon estimates that the Chinese lost over 400,000[22] killed and 486,000 wounded with more than 21,000 captured. The North Koreans lost an estimated 215,000 killed, 303,000 wounded and more than 100,000 captured or missing. But these figures are subject to change. Individual nations tend to report low figures.

Following the end of combat, the North Korean government returned some remains of those declared missing in action. In the years since the war, the Department of Defense Prisoner of War and Missing Persons Office continues to try an account for those listed as missing in action or as non-repatriated prisoners of war. More than eight thousand missing in action still have not been located. The casualty numbers given in this account are taken from "official" sources and every effort has been made to make them as reliable as possible.

Other Data

Redundancies: In several cases the nations being discussed fall into more than one category. When this happens they have been considered in each. In these cases every effort has been made to see that information is not repeated. The fact that some nations asserted their unwillingness to be involved and then became involved is but one more of the complexities of this difficult period.

Language: Many locations in Korea are best remembered by their Japanese names since that is how they appear on the Japanese developed maps used by many United Nations units. When possible the more proper Korean name is used. In reporting Korean proper names they are given as spoken, last name first. It is helpful to remember that in Korean *chon* denotes a small river, *do/to* means island, *gol/kol* a village or gorge, *nae* a stream, *namdo* signifies Northern provinces and *pukto* the South province. It is also true that while *ri* means village and *do* means island, the common usage includes both; the name of the location and the descriptive term.

For the lack of any other collective name I have used the term "other nations" throughout to mean those other than the United States and the Republic of Korea who were participating.

Time and Dates: There is always some disagreement about dates. This can be accounted for by the fact that various reporting units used different methods for identifying dates and as well, and had different identifications for actions taken. It is also aggravated by the fact that the time zones between the United States and Korea are a half a day apart. Insofar as it can be achieved, the dates in this volume are recorded as they are listed where the event is taking place. For example, the officials in Washington, D.C., may appear to have heard about the invasion before it occurred.

1

A Brief History
of the Korean War

It wasn't a small war. It was a major war confined to a small area.
— Admiral Arthur D. Struble

The partition of Korea in 1945 was one of those totally unfortunate actions that appeared to make some sense at the time but would later become a disaster. In the Cairo Declaration, in December 1943, U.S. President Franklin Roosevelt, British Prime Minister Winston Churchill and China's Generalissimo Chiang Kai-shek promised Korea, among other things, that it would be granted independence in due course. In the meantime Korea would be divided. When called upon, Americans Colonel Charles Bonesteel and Dean Rusk, equipped with a small *National Geographic* map, drew a line at the 38th parallel, apparently with little to no respect for political or geographical boundaries. They took no notice of the agricultural or industrial components of the nations, nor the political construct that remained from pre-war years. Besides, as was noted, the line passed "through more than 75 streams and 12 rivers, intersected many high ridges at varied angles, severed 18 small cart roads, 104 county roads, 15 provincial all weather roads, 8 better-class highways, and 6 north to south rail lines."[1]

At the big-powers conferences held at Cairo, Tehran and Yalta and finally at Potsdam, it was made abundantly clear that Japan would not be allowed to keep any of the lands that it had taken as the result of military conquests since 1895. This obviously included Korea. The many other areas and colonies that were freed would be returned to the determination of their host nations.

Among the other things on the minds of those agreeing to the division of Korea was the realization that the Russian Army, already on the move in

Manchuria and physically close to Korea, might once it got started drive all the way to Pusan and from there lay claim to the whole of the country. While Russia had not given any indication that this was its plan, there was value in drawing a line at which it was expected to stop; it was the same ploy that had been used in Austria, China and French Indochina. If anything, it was a product of Roosevelt's fear that colonial people were not able to rule themselves and the need to have friendly troops in control.

A good many excellent volumes have been written about why war broke out on the Korean peninsula in June of 1950 and a simple account here can at best give you information; not sound reasons. The nation of Korea was divided by the Allied powers in order to accept the Japanese surrender and, at least for America, to limit Soviet expansion. The long promised independence of Korea was put off once again as the nation was subjected to vast international pressures. American leaders were afraid that at this point in time the Koreans, who have been occupied for nearly half a century, were not ready for self-rule. The tensions that were quickly growing between the United States and the Soviet Union were immense. One way this soon became apparent was in their attitude about their occupation of Korea. The Soviets, who did not declare war on Japan until the final days, but moved south out of Manchuria until they reached the 38th parallel, wanted a part of peace arrangements and a foothold in Korea. The United States, which brought its forces from Okinawa to occupy the southern portion, arrived late and found the Soviets already entrenched in the north. The nation, so easily divided, would begin decades of struggle for some form of reunification.

When it became evident to the United States that the Soviet Union did not intend to work out a unification arrangement in Korea, the United States turned to the United Nations in 1947 hoping that it might be able to bring about some kind of settlement. The United Nations called for free elections in Korea in 1948 but the Soviet Union refused to be involved. So, with no alternatives apparent, South Korea held an election and a government under Syngman Rhee was put in place. This was soon followed by the formation of a Communist government, under the Russian trained Kim Il-Sung, in North Korea. The result was that the Korean people were divided into two politically opposed governments, neither of which seemed to be open to compromise, and both of which distrusted the other. In the north the Democratic People's Republic of Korea under the young Communist Kim-Il Sung and in the south the Republic of Korea under expatriate Syngman Rhee were both determined to bring about the reunification of the country by any means available.

Following up on their mutual agreement, both the Soviet Union and the United States pulled their troops out by 1948. Then, in the summer of 1950 after months of border clashes and political wrangling, the forces of the North

Korean People's Army moved south across the parallel and unleashed a war for which the Republic of Korea was totally unprepared.

President Truman responded immediately and by the second day authorized General MacArthur to aid American and friendly nations' dependents. With the support of the two UN resolutions, Truman moved forward. Using American air power MacArthur first defended the evacuation of dependents and then was told to provide a show of force. Creating a unit from occupation troops, primarily untrained and armed with World War II weapons — Task Force Smith, as it was called — moved into Korea in July 1950. The hope, apparently, was that a display of American troops would stop the North Korean advance. But neither this small force nor the army of the Republic of Korea was strong enough to control the forward movement of this well trained and highly disciplined North Korean army. Within days the Democratic People's Republic of Korea (DPRK) had moved south to take Seoul, then crossed the Han River and moved toward the port city of Pusan.

Fighting across the breadth of Korea, the American and Republic of Korea (ROK) forces were driven back by a steady and continuous attack. By August the advancing North Korean forces were threatening the UN holdout at the Pusan Perimeter, a stretch of about twenty miles that was the last stand before evacuation.[2] In a long and intense series of battles, the UN, under General Walton Walker, held on to its small stronghold as men and materials began to arrive from Japan and the United States to support them. The badly stretched military was pulling men and material from everywhere they could be found, fighting the war with left-over World War II equipment and re-treads.

As North Korea's logistic lines increased and it was getting more difficult for the DPRK to supply its troops, and the United States accumulated men and supplies at the heavily defended harbor of Pusan, the tide of the battle slowly changed. Forming X Corps, General Douglas MacArthur made a surprise and ambitious amphibious attack at Inchon on the west coast. There, supported by ships of a task force that included vessels from Australia, Canada, New Zealand, France, the Netherlands, Great Britain, and some secretly drawn from Japan, UN troops landed. The move was to drastically alter the situation. After landing on 15 September, American troops of Tenth Corps under General Edward Almond moved toward Seoul.

At the same time, Eighth Army under Lieutenant General Walton Walker was breaking the North Korean hold at Pusan and began moving north. Fighting against an army whose morale was dropping and whose supply line was getting longer and longer, he was able to move at a steady pace. His now stronger force turned the tide and began pushing somewhat isolated DPRK forces back toward the 38th parallel. After a determined move up the peninsula, General Walker and the Eighth Army was able to join forces with Almond and X Corps, and recaptured the ROK capital. Recognizing that logistics were playing a key role, air interdiction continued; bombing missions over North Korea caused massive damage and slowed the movement of supplies. The naval blockade of Korea was maintained.

The war might well have ended at this point, and many will argue that it should have, because as the army of North Korea was driven from the Republic of Korea, the United Nations mandate had been fulfilled. North Korea had been expelled from South Korea. However, the rules of the game were about to change.[3]

Despite the disapproval of many of the nations involved, the Truman administration and eventually the United Nations, by resolution, made the decision to push north to the Yalu and bring North Korea to its knees. The fight in Korea was no longer just an issue of preserving South Korea, but now the idea of a reunification under control of the UN loomed large.

In a second planned amphibious operation, this time against Wonsan on the east coast, members of the Tenth Corps were committed to moving north against North Korea along an eastern corridor while Eighth Army moved up the west coast, pushing the remnants of the DPRK Army before them. Following a couple of airborne assaults to cut off the retreating enemy, Eighth Army moved rather steadily toward the north. The new goal was the Yalu River.

The Chinese government under MaoTse-tung, however, was not willing to let that happen. The newly formed People's Republic of China was both afraid of the arrival of American troops on their border, and perhaps even more important, were aware of the necessity of strengthening their own national identity. Through the good offices of the Indian ambassador they had warned the United Nations that if American troops crossed over the 38th parallel, the PRC would enter the war. For reasons still being argued the United Nations Command paid little attention and did not take the presence of Chinese volunteers captured earlier seriously. First the ROK and then UN forces crossed the parallel in pursuit of the North Korean Army. The advancing force took the North Korean capital and moved forward. As General Walker's Eighth Army approached the Yalu River on the west, General Almond's Tenth Corps moved north of the Chosin Reservoir. As they advanced they came upon a few, then a lot, of Chinese soldiers who, when captured, identified themselves as volunteers. It seems incomprehensible that the intelligence community failed to discover evidence of the movement and supply of more than 130,000 Communist soldiers. It seems hard to believe that without any of the advantages enjoyed by a modern army — little communication equipment and almost no mechanized resources — they could have pulled this off. By the end of November 1950 Chinese volunteers, having hidden and waited for the UN

Commanding General Walton Walker (center, facing) and staff by a Texan T-6 observer plane.

command, entered the war in force.[4] Contrary to the best intelligence that MacArthur could muster, hundreds of thousands of Chinese volunteers, many of them veterans of the Chinese Civil War, poured over the border and challenged the UN.

Immediately it was a new war and even MacArthur could see it. His "home by Christmas" offensive was stopped in its tracks and he called for a withdrawal. His forces were caught off guard and his units poorly prepared for what lay ahead. With the Chinese involvement came increased Soviet activity, as more weapons and apparently some military personnel — especially pilots — participated. On the east, Tenth Corps, caught by surprise along the Chosin reservoir and facing an overwhelming number of Chinese troops, had to move back. The longest and most deadly retreat in American history had begun. Walker's UN forces, in the west, had no alternative but to retreat as well, stopping occasionally to allow troops to be evacuated by sea.

The Army and Marines of Tenth Corps fought a brave and orderly retreat from the Chosin Reservoir to the port city of Hungnam. There the military, with more than two hundred vessels from a dozen nations, evacuated 100,000 troops and just about the same number of civilian refugees. The evacuation, the greatest in American military history, saved X Corps to fight again. On the west Eighth Army moved rapidly south until they were once again driven back across the 38th parallel and the capital city of Seoul had changed hands once more. At this point in the war serious consideration was given both to the use of atomic weapons and to the total evacuation of Korea: a withdrawal to Japan. Both possibilities were considered, both were discounted. Nevertheless, the war had reached a critical stage. At this point, in late December 1950, the Eighth Army's commanding officer, General Walton Walker, was killed in an automobile accident.

Walker was replaced as the Eighth Army commander by General Matthew Ridgway. General Ridgway was a strong and popular officer who was able to revitalize the failing troops and launch a series of well planned and executed campaigns against the Communists. Once again the UN forces began to move north. In time he was able to retake Seoul. But he was not fighting a war just about territory; he believed that the most successful tactic was to plan missions with the purpose of killing as many of the enemy as possible. Nevertheless, he moved forward and established a series of lines that ran roughly along and slightly north of the 38th parallel where the UN dug in.

Behind the scenes, however, the Truman Administration was undergoing a change in thought. More and more it was becoming evident that the war in Korea might well be unwinnable and Truman was determined to prevent it from expanding into World War III. He opted for a negotiated peace settlement. What he wanted was a peace agreement at a reasonable cost. The goal now seemed to be a cease-fire and the war itself took yet another turn.

Partly as a result of this change in thinking, partly because of charges of insubordination, and the recent return of a longstanding disagreement that was coming to a head, President Truman sacked General MacArthur in April of 1951. The move came theoretically for insubordination, but the decision was far more complicated than that and was not unheralded by many of the allied nations who had grown leery of the general's behavior. By this point the war in Korea was becoming increasingly political and the assignment that was given to the new commander, General Ridgway, was a far different one than had been given MacArthur. An end to the war was sought but it was clear that even if the Communists were willing to negotiate, it did not necessarily mean peace, for any solution was a long way off.

The decision to negotiate obviously meant that political considerations took on a larger and more immediate role. For the men and women fighting the war it was a significant change. The conflict dramatically transitioned from the highly mobile war of 1950-51 to the more stagnant period that became known by the positive as the Hill War and the negative as the Stalemate. The massive movements that had characterized the early stages of the conflict were gone and both sides toughened up their positions and set in for the long haul. Bunkers and outposts were built and multiple lines established as defensive measures.

The war was to be fought in small pieces. Unit action larger than a company required the permission of higher headquarters, and any movement of battalion size needed authority from Japan. The blockade continued and the air war, though more restrained, was maintained. Lines changed only fractionally as one side after the other fought small battles, mostly for isolated hills or individual outposts. The talks dragged on and on as the lines hardened. The main line of resistance was at nearly the same line that had divided the nations at the beginning of the war.

With established lines guarded by isolated bunkers and outposts and long communication trenches, the war took on something of the look of World War I. The fight was harsh and violent but movement was considerably restrained. Political considerations meant that most military assignments were designed to match the progression of the armistice talks. Both armies suffered considerably from the extremes of weather and from the constant fighting for limited accomplishments. The goals for involvement became increasingly blurred and morale was low.

A series of Eighth Army commanders came and left and men rotated in and out, units were exchanged and the war continued with no real signs that victory was possible or defeat inevitable. Haunting the battlefield and the negotiations table was the constant fear that the situation would get out of hand and lead to a third world war. Fighting these concerns and with diminishing support on the home front, as well as lessened support by the allies, the United States was limited to the stagnation of a holding action. Without a formal declaration of war, and fighting in an unfamiliar country with no traditional friendships or at home no large Korean immigrant population, it was getting harder and harder for the U.S. to focus any interest in a war in this distant land. Hamstrung by the lack of an overall military goal, and restrained by increasingly complex international and domestic necessities, the war became a quagmire of small assaults, rebuttals, and new assaults fought with exhausted and often disillusioned men. Some hills, like Pork Chop Hill, changed hands five and six times as political justifications were mapped out at Panmunjom, and the main line of resistance moved back and forth sometimes by no more than a few yards.

Hung up over the American demands for voluntary repatriation, and the Communists at face-saving, the talks were off and on again, determined primarily by the mood of the delegates and the latest victory or defeat on some small insignificant hill. Then after a long dry spell at the negotiation table and shortly after the death of Joseph Stalin — and in good measure because of it — the armistice talks took a more serious turn. President Truman had been replaced by Dwight D. Eisenhower. Ike, as most called him, had gone to Korea as promised in his campaign and he swore to bring it all to an end. With peace talks and more saber rattling, an agreement was finally worked out. The long-argued issue of prisoners of war was solved in America's favor and the location of a demilitarized zone (DMZ) established. In Little Switch and Big Switch prisoners were exchanged and bodies collected. The agreement was not what either side wanted, nor did it bring the war to an end; it provided only an armistice that might be broken at any time. The South Korean government did not attend the agreement nor sign the armistice. Nevertheless, at 2100 hours on 27 July 1953, the sounds of guns all along the front were silenced. Men hesitantly came out from the bunkers and stood safely under the evening sky. The warring nations faced one another along a line that very nearly approximated the line where it had all begun. The firing had stopped but the situation that had given birth to the conflict was not resolved.

The war had never been popular at home. Truman, both because of the war and the firing of MacArthur, had lost much of what little support he had, and had chosen not to run again in the face of such opposition. While thousands of American troops would remain in Korea stretched out along the DMZ, the war itself was widely forgotten almost as soon as the firing stopped.

2

The Role of the United Nations

The only reason I told the president to fight in Korea was to validate NATO.
— Dean Acheson

When John J. Muccio informed Washington of the attack on South Korea, it had, for America at least, all the serious characteristics of a full scale war. This was more than another of the many border clashes it had endured. The attack, seen as both unprovoked and unexpected, was really neither. Military confrontations along the border had been going on since the separation of the nations, and Syngman Rhee had been behind them as much as Kim Il-Sung. Bad blood and agitation between the two had been going on for some time and it should have come as no surprise to anyone that both voiced, and anticipated, that a war designed to reunite them had finally arrived. As far as being unexpected it is true that neither the fledgling Central Intelligence Agency (CIA) nor Army Intelligence had given the South Koreans any immediate warning. Military intelligence had made some effort and General MacArthur had received reports from his intelligence section that suggested the North Koreans were planning an attack, but MacArthur did not think so.[1] The CIA at least was caught off guard and the broader intelligence community was no better informed. The limited number of agents[2] and poor sources available in Communist North Korea were offered as excuses. As a result of perceived CIA failures, Truman fired the director, Roscoe H. Hillenkoetter, and replaced him with Walter Bedell Smith.

To add to the lack of expectation was the lack of preparation. Despite the presence of KMAG (the Korean Military Assistance Group), the ROK was simply not prepared for a prolonged fight. And, since the United States personnel had taken their heavy equipment with them when they left, fearing that Rhee would use it to attack the North, the ROK had no tanks or heavy artillery. Admittedly, the ROK officer corps was poorly trained and some military commands were still being granted in return for political or economic favors. When the attack occurred, many portions of the ROK Army, who should have been on guard, were at home helping with the harvest. If Rhee's government had received any sign of the coming attack he did not act on it.

From the beginning both Dean Acheson and President Truman turned to the United Nations when they thought of a reprisal. The Republic of Korea had already made such a plea. So, as Truman was gathering his think-tanks about him, the United States had already asked for an emergency session to discuss the situation.

The Moral Question

The actions of the United Nations involved military, political, economic, and even some sociological considerations. But, while not often considered, there were also legal and moral questions behind the involvement of the nations who participated, as well as for the UN itself. Was, some have asked, the UN involvement in Korea the same bullying that it was created to prevent? Selected governments of the world, many battered and bruised by the violence of World War II, sought to establish the means by which the disagreements among nations could be settled by discussion and debate rather than by war. That security for one nation depended on the security of all nations. Not all, of course, were so inclined; not all joined. But many believed and adopted a body — taking the name from those victorious nations of World War II — in which they invested their hopes and perhaps their future security.

Few, it is suspected, would have believed that this body, so dedicated to peace, would in such a short time call upon its member nations to amass an army for the express purpose of going to war. Some would wonder if this was the proper action given the arguments for its creation.[3] True, many nations had witnessed the great trauma that resulted when ignoring the understanding that "all that is necessary for evil to prevail is for good men to do nothing." And while some governments wanted to avoid war altogether and others viewed the UN's role as being more restrictive, the majority apparently subscribed to the Niebuhrian principle[4] by which President Truman abided: "evil in the defense of good is no evil." While the phrase is often voiced by men far less moderate than Niebuhr, it nevertheless fosters a concept of a *just* war. In the minds of many involved, all over the world, World War II had been such a war. This view stood in variance with the idea, proposed most adequately by such men as George Patton, and apparently subscribed to by President George W. Bush, of *preventive* war.

The UN, and certainly the U.S, was not thinking in these later terms, even though the language of the National Security Council Document No. 68 might make one wonder. Today, the UN mandate, self-changed would adopt the view that it was somehow legitimate to "interfere in order to prevent," but that was not the case in Korea. They were facing a live action invasion. At this time the UN apparently believed, or at least a majority of members did, that an attack on any member nation was an attack on all nations. But, of course, neither North Korea nor South Korea were members of the body.[5] Thus some have wondered on what authority members of an organized group had the right to interfere in the political and military affairs of non-member nations. Obviously, the UN believed that its concern for the members' security depended on it taking an interest and furthermore an action in the affairs of non-member nations. Who, other than members themselves, made them the determining judges of a nation's behavior, particularly of nations that had chosen not to join them?

This, of course, is beyond the question of the morality of individual nations. Truman's anguish over the decision to go to war in Korea may be some evidence of his concern, but he does not elaborate on that in his memoirs. For some nations, like India, we are well aware that it was a concern. The rush to judgment and the judgment rendered, by those participating, set the tone for years and decades to come. It is a tone that was not then, and is not now, accepted by all nations.

The Resolutions and Who Supported Them

When considering the role played by "other nations," we are inclined to forget the ongoing battle of ideologies at the United Nations. In a series of resolutions and proposals, the nations of the world fought a parallel war during which the implications of the Korean conflict came to the forefront. In this on-going and often heated discussion, the United Nations considered several highly significant and long-lasting issues. The more important ones are addressed here briefly.

The United Nations resolutions, which provided the legal base for involvement in Korea, were short and simple. The first was drafted by the United States and was the first diplomatic response by the UN to the North Korean invasion. It was preceded by immediate disagreement first of all about what the attack meant and second how it should be considered. Among those most upset were the United Kingdom, France, Egypt, Norway and India, all of whom interpreted the outbreak of hostilities as another phase in a long smoldering civil war. In addition, there was some question about the integrity of South Korean President Syngman Rhee and consideration of how much he could be trusted to portray the situation adequately. They wanted more information or, as in the case of some of the unaligned nations, more delay. The key issues were as follows.

25 June 1950. When the Security Council met at the request of the United States to consider the North Korean invasion of South Korea, the members were the Republic of China, Cuba, Ecuador, Egypt, France, India, Norway, the United Kingdom, the United States, the Soviet Union, and Yugoslavia. The Soviet Union was embarrassed that its long time resistant nations had been elected to the Security Council, but for other reasons was not in attendance. The resolution that was proposed called for the immediate end of the hostilities. It was adopted by a vote of 9–0. In the background the Soviet Union was playing it cool with little mention of the conflict either in its newspapers or in its diplomatic talk among nations. It maintained that the conflict in Korea was a civil war started by the Republic of Korea and that the North had interfered simply to put down the fighting.[6]

27 June 1950. Within two days the U.S. was back, this time sponsoring a resolution that called for UN action against the aggression. The same basic membership was in place at the time. The resolution was clear and straightforward. Because it was so significant to the war it is recorded here:

> Having Determined that the armed attack upon the Republic of Korea by forces from North Korea constitutes a breach of the peace,
>
> Having called for an immediate cessation of hostilities, and
>
> Having called upon the authorities of North Korea to withdrawn forthwith their armed forces to the 38th parallel, and
>
> Having noted from the report of the United Nations Commission for Korea that the authorities in North Korea have neither ceased hostilities nor withdraw their armed forces to the 38th parallel and that urgent military measures are required to restore international peace and security, and
>
> Having noted the appeal from the Republic of Korea to the United Nations for immediate and effective steps to secure peace and security,
>
> Recommends that the Members of the United Nations furnish such assistance to the Republic of Korea as may be necessary to repel the armed attack and to restore international peace and security in the area.

The resolution, despite wide and serious concern over its effect, passed seven to one; Yugoslavia posted the only serious argument and voted no. Egypt and India abstained. The Soviet Union was still absent from the chamber.[7] It was boycotting the Security Council meetings on the pretense it was a protest over the failure to seat the People's Republic of China as the rightful representatives of the Chinese people.[8] When the second resolution was called for a vote, India and Egypt had not received instructions so did not vote. After waiting unsuccessfully for these nations to receive instructions, the body adopted the resolution without amendment. India later supported the resolution.[9] The single opposition vote was delivered by Ales Bebler of Yugoslavia.

The legality of the vote was, and always would be, in question, at least to the Soviet Union. It stood by the argument that the vote was invalid not only because the PRC had not been seated, but because the UN Charter specified that in order to be adopted, resolutions on non-procedural matters required seven affirmative votes, including the concurring voices of all five permanent members. The response provided by the body was that earlier, during the Soviet boycott, the Security Council had adopted the principle that the Soviets' failure to vote constituted an abstention, not a veto.

17 July 1950. As the South Korean, American and British forces were trying to hold back the tide of the North Korean advance, the United Nations met again, this time to establish a unified command in Korea to conduct the war. They also placed the administration of the war in the hands of the United States as executive agent for the UN. In effect it united all member nations participating under a single command structure. Because it provided no specific guidelines for running the war or reporting on its progress, it left most of the decisions to the American government. The U.S., as least on most military matters, turned to the Joint Chiefs of Staff (JCS). The United States had earlier rejected the secretary general's proposal that because the war was being fought under the banner of the UN it should be directed by a committee of co-ordination for the assistance of Korea. This view was supported by Great Britain, France and Norway. It was the U.S. position that since it was paying for the war and sending the most aid, it should retain control. The UN was not blind, however, for politicians, military personnel, as well as refugee workers, provided reports back to the UN that often challenged those of MacArthur.

7 October 1950. While in the background several nations were making efforts to bring about a cease-fire, the military advances of the UN forces revived the question of whether the UN should pursue the North Koreans into their own territory. The Offensive Across the Thirty-Eighth Parallel Resolution authorized the United Nations Command (UNC) to cross into North Korea and, in effect expand the war an additional two years. Both MacArthur and the Republic of Korea were in favor of this action, believing the ultimate goal was the unification of the peninsula. Others expressed concern that it would bring China and maybe even the Soviet Union into the war. Warren R. Austin at the UN supported the decision by questioning, "Shall only a part of the country be assured this freedom? I think not."[10]

This move should not have come as a surprise to anyone. When asked about crossing the 38th, Truman had told a press conference earlier that the question was still open for discussion and on 17 July he had asked the National

Security Council to prepare a recommendation for the possibility of crossing the border and destroying the North Korean Army. All during this discussion the British and Indian governments opposed any movement into North Korea, but they acknowledged that the military momentum in Korea was quickly outstripping their political activity to prevent it.

10 November 1950. At the first evidence the Chinese were involved, the British made a proposal that would halt MacArthur on the Hungnam-Cheongju line and create a DMZ from there to the Yalu River. The British were afraid that if the UN forces got too close to the Yalu River there would be an all-out war. The proposal recommended the North Koreans would lay down their arms and the area would be administered through a UN Commission that would consult with China on any issues of security. Both France and Italy favored the plan but Secretary of State Dean Acheson did not, and asked for a delay in its presentation. The British decided, while the U.S. stalled, to consult with China but received no response. While it was considered briefly by the State Department, the military disagreed and sided with MacArthur. The general was upset even by the suggestion. He argued that the appeasement of the Chinese by giving them a strip of North Korea was reminiscent of Munich in 1938. He went on to say, "Indeed, to yield to so immoral a proposition would bankrupt our leadership and influence in Asia and render untenable our position both politically and militarily."[11] The proposal was finally turned down by Washington.[12]

As the war moved ahead and the situation became more dangerous there were further considerations given to the bombing targets on the Manchurian side of the river; authority to bomb the other end of the bridges was what they wanted. President Truman, Dean Acheson, and General Marshall, as well as the Joint Chiefs of Staff, all believed that it was necessary if the PRC involvement was to be contained, and if planes that were attacking UN bombers were to be silenced. On 13 November 1950 the State Department sought the reaction to this idea from other governments. It was not permission the State Department was seeking, it was argued, only reaction. Unexpectedly the reaction was swift and decisive and in this case at least the allies played an important role.

The United States had sought reaction in London, Canberra, Ottawa, Paris, Ankara, New Delhi, Wellington, The Hague and even Moscow. What it got was a wholly and unanimously adverse reaction. Many took the position that it would lead to the very things they were trying to stop: expanded hostilities. Still others saw it as a unilateral move to extend the war. Several nations though it might well bring the Soviet Union into the war. The Dutch government suggested it "would afford the basis for a Soviet charge that the UN was only a front for the U.S."[13] The plans for air strikes on targets in Manchuria were dropped.

The British made it clear that their fear of the conflict expanding to all of Asia was so significant they were willing to make some concessions to the Chinese in hope of a cease fire. There was, as well, a growing possibility that other member nations would make cease fire proposals that the U.S. would find politically unacceptable. America had already rejected the December 11 resolution proposed by the Asian states because it did not provide for a limitation on the increase in Chinese supplies and men at the front, thus providing problems if the cease fire did not hold. As it was, however, it was becoming evident that the United States' support from its allies in the UN was becoming more significant than the swings in domestic criticism and opinion might suggest.

14 December 1950. The UN took action again, this time creating a Cease Fire Group. As early as July 1950 Jawaharlal Nehru submitted a proposal for ending the war. This was but one of the many proposed by delegates representing the Arab-Asian block. Their efforts became more aggressive in December 1950 and continued, largely out of sight, until the end of the war. At the peak of their influence they not only had built a strong consensus with the anti–Communists but also on occasion with an individual rebellious American ally. It was this group that called on the president of the General Assembly to create a committee of three persons to consider what the basis would be for a satisfactory cease fire in Korea. The group consisted of Nasrollah Entezam of Iran, Lester B. Pearson of Canada, and Sir Benegal N. Rau of India. By the 15th it had identified the terms that would be acceptable to the United Nations Command but could not get a response from China. The Chinese continued to insist that any consideration of a cease fire also had to consider the seating of a PRC delegate at the UN and the question of Taiwan.

30 January 1951. In a meeting of the UN Additional Measures Committee, the United States argued that the PRC was engaged in aggression and requested the appointment of a group composed of the UN Collective Measure Committee to consider additional ways to meet the aggression. The group was composed of Australia, Belgium, Brazil, Britain, Canada, Egypt, France, Mexico, the Philippines, Turkey, the United States and Venezuela.

The governments of Britain, France, Canada and India were particularly anxious about the U.S. expectation and were afraid that they would force through a resolution that condemned the Chinese. These countries were aware that it was America's intention to sever diplomatic relations with China and impose new trade and financial restrictions as well as blockades. The fear of the consequences also led several Asian and Latin American countries to speak out rather clearly that a conflict with China would not be supported by their governments. In the face of this the U.S. softened its position on any possible war with China and withdrew its hope for the severance of diplomatic relations, accepting instead a selective economic embargo. Expressing some of the arrogance with which the other member nations had to deal, Admiral Forrest P. Sherman, the chief of naval operations, suggested that while an embargo by the UN would be good, "it might well be time for the U.S. to take unilateral action on their own." Such an idea was dismissed, in time, because of the realization that without UN support, especially Great Britain, an embargo would be ineffective.

1 February 1951. This was a resolution proposed by the United States, despite many objections, that would condemn the PRC as the aggressor in Korea. The United States wanted such a resolution on record. The Truman administration believed that failure to do so would have lasting effects on the home front and eventually on the stability of the UN itself. But its allies were not all that supportive. At this point few were willing to identify China as the enemy. Great Britain had considerable doubt about the wisdom of such a movement. It was more sensitive to the Asian position and sympathetic with India's views. Beyond that there was the fear that once again such an action might lead to an expansion of the war beyond the confines of Korea. The U.S. moved quickly to assure the members this was not true. All were not convinced. Canada thought that such a resolution needed to wait to see if a negotiated settlement could be reached. France voiced its disagreement with the resolution. Indonesia was against such a move at this time and India quickly voiced its disapproval.

On the other side of the discussion it was believed that under pressure from the U.S. the Arab-Asian bloc might support the resolution. Both Australia and New Zealand feared that breaking with the United States on this issue might adversely affect its hope for a defense treaty, and so planned to vote with the U.S. Several attempts were made to block the resolution but they were not successful. When the Israelis suggested a more conservative resolution, the Arab delegates became upset. Then when the body passed the motion for a forty-eight hour adjournment by a vote of 27–23–6, including support from several of the NATO nations, the U.S. thought it had lost.

However, when a compromise arrangement by the U.S. assured the body that General MacArthur would not be given anymore authority, and that no recommendation would be sent to the General Assembly until further peace efforts were tried and failed, the U.S. resolution moved forward. On 30 January the First Committee approved the U.S. proposal by 44–7–9, and two days later the same vote passed it in the General Assembly. Among those for whom the vote was not assumed, only India and Burma voted against it, while Lebanon, Iraq, and Iran voted in favor.

This was a victory for the United States. It strengthened the hand of the State Department. The failure to pass this resolution, Acheson had written

Bevin, would be the end of the United Nations. The British saw this as a part of the American effort to impose a stiff embargo against the Chinese, which had failed before, and they were against it. Their efforts among the Commonweal nations to oppose the American resolution brought the relationship between the two countries to a new level of tension.

Nevertheless, and despite the fact that Communist China had announced that any attempt by the UN to name it the aggressor would eliminate any chance of a negotiated armistice, the UN moved toward such a resolution. The First Committee rejected the so-called Twelve Power resolution and accepted the amended U.S. resolution by a vote of 44–7–0. India was terribly upset by this action and in one instance suggested that the action had engendered "a feeling in this part of the world that the growing issue is one of Asia against the rest or the East versus the West."[14]

At one point the French government, worried about the direction the war was going, sought a UN resolution designed to assure China that UN forces would not attack its territory. Their proposed resolution would make it clear that the UN would not bomb the Yalu River power installations, and that the Chinese border would remain inviolate. The U.S. felt that this resolution was too restrictive and left open the possibility that the Chinese could attack UN forces from behind its border. The resolution went nowhere.

A paper written for the Canadian Department of External Affairs suggested that "the cost of preserving the appearance of unity [within the West] has been great."[15] And the concern was valid. Several of the allied nations had given public approval to U.S. policies that, in their better moments, they realized were not always well thought out, and sometimes even considerably dangerous. These nations lacked, or had not sought, sufficient help from other nations to provide any reasonable alternatives. Many Korean watchers had recognized that there had been a change in the attitudes, at least among the European and some of the non-aligned nations, an attitude that now reflected more concern over the possible extension of the war and less about establishing victory in Korea.

7 May 1951. The United States continued in its effort to expand the selective embargo against China. The resolution passed with the Soviets abstaining. In effect it was another American victory at the UN, but it did not greatly change the situation since Australia, Canada, and Great Britain had already been conforming to its provisions. The action was not without its dangers, however, because China's resources were limited and its ability to overcome such an embargo fairly weak. There was the very real possibility that it would respond with military measures. In this discussion Ambassador Philip C. Jessup recommended to the National Security Council that the U.S. avoid announcing any unilateral trade embargo, or the freezing of Chinese assets, because the action would have little effect on China and would simply antagonize governments that had proven friendly to the United States.

8 October 1952. When the peace talks broke down in the fall of 1952, after the United States called for a suspension, several more efforts were made in hope of reestablishing negotiations. The General Assembly took up a plan submitted 2 September 1952 by Luis Padilla Nervo, the Mexican ambassador. The Mexican POW (Prisoner of War) Settlement Proposal suggested that those soldiers who did not want to return to their host country would be able to enjoy temporary asylum in the territory of a UN member nation. The U.S. gave the idea some serious consideration but the Soviets made it clear that they did not trust the Mexicans and would not support it. The Mexican POW settlement really offered little other, perhaps, than a chance for delegates to save face, as in this plan the real decision about prisoners would be settled after the armistice. In the end the UN turned to the Menon plan.

October 1952. This concerned the Twenty-one Power UN Resolution. It was an effort by President Truman to get the UN to stand firm on the conditions of the truce talks, particularly agenda item four, and the repatriation of POWs. The secretary of state wrote to the president of the United States, "The outstanding political fact of the Assembly thus far has been the domination of the proceedings by the Arab-Asian group, which has been successful in every major effort up to this point. The Arab-Asian block has been exceptionally skillful in allying themselves with Latin Americans and Soviets on particular issues, obtaining majorities which could not be countered by votes of Western European and Commonwealth members."[16] Many of America's allies urged Washington to compromise on the demands for repatriated prisoners but none had as yet spoken out against it publically. In October 1952 the U.S. was able to convince twenty nations to co-sponsor a resolution that would require voluntary repatriation. However, when the Menon plan began to obtain more support, the consensus broke down.

3 November 1952. The Peruvian POW Settlement proposal called on the appointment of a commission that would take whatever steps necessary to ensure that the prisoners were repatriated in accordance with their wishes, and that those who resisted would be offered protection in a disclosed neutral zone. It was rejected immediately by the Soviet Union as unworkable and the Truman administration rejected it, unhappy with the prospect of neutral nations being involved.

17 November 1952. The Menon POW Settlement Proposal seemed to be more acceptable. After a series of other draft resolutions from Indonesia and Iraq, the efforts began to center on a plan offered by V. K. Krishna Menon. This proposal, set forth by the Indian representative, was designed to break the stalemate at the negotiation table that had festered about the question of repatriation for two years. The Chinese demanded forceful repatriation, as was required by the Geneva Convention of 1949.[17] The U.S., on the other hand, had adopted a principle of voluntary repatriation which, in fact, violated the Geneva Convention. Many of the allies opposed the American position, finding it an unnecessary hindrance to a cease fire. At first the U.S. rejected the idea, as did the Soviet Union, which was suspicious of India's intentions. But with pressure from Canada and Great Britain the United States agreed to give the Menon proposal priority over its own Twenty-one Power proposal. The U.S. was aware that while it had managed to put together twenty nations to co-cosponsor its resolution, it was also true that many of these allies still were unhappy with it. The gap between the two plans was not all that wide. The Menon plan called for a cease fire, an exchange of willing prisoners and the establishment of a four nation Neutral Nations Repatriation Commission to supervise the rest. However, once Acheson managed to get an amendment approved that called for a four month limit on how long the POW could be held, he supported it.

3 December 1952. Many nations were much relieved when the General Assembly adopted the resolution. The entire Soviet bloc voted in opposition. Nevertheless, as time passed the proposal provided the framework for an eventual agreement.

The push for an armistice continued and as the delegates to the negotiations balked over wording and disagreed over protocol, the fighting went on. Most would agree that the war was going on too long. Even after the death of Stalin in March of 1953, America's allies, who were very anxious to see the war end, feared America was not seriously seeking a cease fire arrangement. The demands were too high and the Communists would never agree to them. When in May 1953 it looked like the United States might be altering its position, even though it had given tentative agreement to the Menon Plan, there was an uproar of criticism from the governments of Australia, Belgium, Burma, Canada, India, Italy, and New Zealand. In May 1953 Ohio Senator Robert A. Taft made a speech that expressed something of the nation's frustration over these criticisms. He said that given all the opposition that the U.S. was facing, it "might as well abandon any idea of working with the United Nation in the East and reserve to ourselves a completely free hand." It was not well accepted and President Eisenhower quickly responded, assuring the allies that they were very much needed and concluding that "we have to have that unity in basic purposes that comes from recognition of common interests."[18]

7 May 1953. Seeking a resolution to item 4 of the cease-fire agenda, the repatriation of POWs, the UNC gave tentative approval to a settlement proposal. The idea had come from the Communist delegates and suggested that

Top: Korean girls riot as part of Rhee's effort to halt the Armistice Treaty. *Bottom:* Multi-national honor guard for General William Harrison (center, second from left) and Colonel James Murray (next to General Harrison) at Panmunjom.

A Neutral Nations Repatriation Team checks troops before leaving Korea.

the non-repatriated prisoners of war be sent to a neutral state following the armistice. There they could be addressed by their home state with an idea of convincing them to return. After more consideration the "other nations" found fault with it because the proposal did not allow for the release of the prisoners after the period of explanations, nor did it name the neutral nation to be considered. The Communists returned with a new eight-point proposal. This created a timeline of two months after all the POWs desiring to be repatriated would be. Those who remained would be transferred to the Neutral Nations Repatriation Commission made up representatives from Czechoslovakia, Poland, Sweden, Switzerland, and India. The disposition of those still holding out after four months would be determined at a political conference three months after the cease-fire agreement. This plan was not far off that of the UN resolution of 3 December 1952 that both North Korea and China had rejected.

27 July 1953. A week after the death of Joseph Stalin the United Nations, the North Koreans and the Chinese accepted a cease fire agreement. Despite Rhee's effort to sabotage the arrangement by releasing nearly 27,000 prisoners in his control, the agreement was signed. President Eisenhower, who had promised to end the war, was furious over Rhee's behavior and considered implementing Operation Everready, which would have removed Rhee from office.[19]

After Rhee's unilateral action the Communists suspended negotiations. They accepted the UNC's hasty assurances that it was not behind what had happened, nor did it support the action taken. The Communists agreed to return to the table when, and if, the United States could provide evidence that it could control Rhee's actions. They also returned to the battlefield. Sending a message, they focused their assaults against primarily ROK targets, but also directed one probe against the UN forces on Pork Chop Hill, driving them off. On 8 July the Communists indicated that they were ready to resume the talks, and the talks continued toward the armistice agreement.

The necessary control of Rhee had been accomplished by a mission headed by Assistant Secretary of State Walter S. Robertson who, with a series of stick and carrot diplomatic actions, worked it out that Rhee would accept the armistice in return for massive economic and military concessions.

Removing Stalin from the scene appeared to be significant to the outcome of the armistice effort; just how much is undefined. The evidence coming out of Russia via the work of Kathryn Weathersby suggests that the Communist leader was not all that sure North Korea would be able to win the war, and when Eighth Army reversed the scene and began moving north toward the Yalu, he is reported as saying, "So what? If Kim Il-Sung fails we are not going to participate with our own troops. Let it be. Let the Americans be our neighbors in the Far East."[20]

After China's entry and success, however, Stalin took a hard line on the question of an armistice; such a stand made sense for many reasons. Not the least of these was that the continuation of the war was a significant drain on the resources of the United States, so significant, in fact, that it pretty much prevented the U.S. from making military moves anywhere else in the world. It was, as well, an excellent place to try out and expand weapons and technology and a never ending source of intelligence about America and its military.

Ten days after Stalin's death, the new premier, Georgi Malenkov, marking a new period of history, indicated that the difficulties between Moscow and Washington could be settled with mutual understanding and by peaceful means. His immediate actions indicated that he would be taking a somewhat softer line with the Western powers.[21]

The final arrangement called for a political conference to follow that would consider the unification of Korea. After a final argument about how to sign and exchange the document, a long and heated discussion of what amount of press coverage there would be, and a new door cut into the south end of the building thus allowing the UN delegates to enter from the south, it was signed. Syngman Rhee had forbid the representative from his nation to attend. According to the plan, senior delegates were to sign the armistice at Panmunjom at ten in the morning of 27 July. They did. The military was given twelve hours to stop fighting. After years of conflict and haggling, a cease fire was established.

Despite the relief of the cease-fire, many people realized that there was a down side to the approval of an armistice. The State Department did not see this as an end to the East-West struggle at all and anticipated that if the pressure was relieved in Korea, the Communists might well extend the struggles by taking action in some other trouble spots: Indochina and Burma were the most alluring but Yugoslavia and Iran were also possibilities. A part of this concern that would later prove to be highly significant was the belief that if the French lost control to the Communist in Indochina, that Malay, Hong Kong, Burma, India, Siam, Pakistan, Iran and large parts of the Middle East would become Communist. The worst scenario, however, might be a letdown of American willingness to maintain a high profile military.

President Truman, always willing to speak his mind, later commented about the armistice President Eisenhower accepted, saying that if he had tried to pull it off the Republicans would have drawn and quartered him.[22]

Structure and Command

The United Nations Command that ran the Korean War was basically of the same structure as the U.S. military during World War II; it was a policy of unified command. The idea of "unified command" was adopted during the world-wide involvement of American troops fighting in many theaters during World War II and remained in place after the war. While it worked fairly well, it also displayed some difficulties and had not been fully implemented, particularly in the Pacific, where command decisions were divided between army and navy personnel.

In February 1946 the chief of naval operations, Admiral Chester Nimitz, complained that the existing arrangement was ambiguous and unsatisfactory. The Navy wanted a unified command over all forces in a theater. The other services were less inclined to agree and the argument continued as service rivalry mounted during the period of military reduction. The compromise that was worked out was called the Outline Command Plan and was approved by President Truman in 1946. It created seven areas of command and missions. Those created were Far East Command, Pacific Command, Alaskan Command, Northeast Command, Atlantic Fleet, Caribbean Command and the European Command. The forces in Japan, Korea, the Ryukyus, Philippines, and the Marianas were under Far East Command, and they were responsible for occupation duties, security and preparation for general emergencies in the area. Later action removed South Korea from this alignment. The Joint Chiefs of Staff would exercise strategic direction and would assign forces as needed.

The outbreak of war in Korea put the Far East Command to the test. Under presidential authority, General MacArthur as Commander-in-Chief Far East (CINCFE), was given responsibility for the initial reaction. With commitments still coming in and the limited forces in South Korea suffering significant withdrawals, the UN Security Council resolution of 7 July 1950 assured a unified command of UN forces gathering in Korea. It asked the United States to name a commander and Truman appointed General Douglas MacArthur.[23] Therefore, on 10 July 1950 General MacArthur established the United Nations Command (UNC). He assumed the position of Commander-in-Chief United Nations Command (CINCUNC) while maintaining his responsibilities as CINCFE. His primary responsibility as CINCFE remained the occupation and defense of Japan.[24]

Under the Far East Command that directed the war in Korea, there were component commanders for the Air Force and the Navy, but General MacArthur kept the Army components himself. Thus he was wearing another hat, that of Commanding General Army Forces Far East (CGAFFE.) His headquarters staff was essentially made up of Army personnel, much of which had been with him for a long time. The only exception was the Joint Strategic Plans and Operations Group (JSPOG) that had Air Force and Navy representations. There was, as well, a decided lack of military representatives from the "other nations" involved in the fighting. After MacArthur had left the theater, the Far East Command was more fully staffed with other service representatives and placed on a par with other component commands.[25]

The occupation of Korea had not been one of America's great achievements. Once in country the primary goal of the occupying force had been to remove the Japanese from power and conclude their surrender, but a strong secondary role was to contain the political and military influence of the other nation. That had not gone so well. To begin with, the U.S. Army was apparently not prepared and still had its occupation force, 23rd Corps, located in Okinawa some 600 miles away and loading on ships. It was 9 September by the time the Americans reached Seoul. By then a lot had happened.

The second disaster was placing the occupation in the hands of Lieutenant General John R. Hodge as Commanding General U.S. Forces in Korea. Hodge was a fine soldier with an exemplary record as a combat commander, but he was in no way a diplomat; if anything his personality worked against his assignment. The primary problem seemed to be that he saw no distinction between the Koreans and the Japanese people, nor did he understand the deep hatred the Koreans had for the Japanese. Being short-handed and without having the support of trained administrators, he reverted to retaining many of the Japanese in many key civil and police positions, even to allowing some Japanese soldiers to remain armed. When even Hodge realized the extent of the problem and asked Washington for trained and experienced administrators to be sent, it was too late. And, when replaced with American civil servants it was with people who did not understand the culture or maintain even a basic grasp of the Korean language.[26]

To add to the problem, General Hodge was not sympathetic to what had happened in his delay and he identified the Korean People's Republic, the government that had been set up by nationalists after the surrender and before the arrival of the Americans, as being illegal. In time he supported Syngman Rhee, and in 1946 the South Korean interim legislative assembly was established. Efforts were being made to move South Korea toward a democracy. Hope of unification had faded with the Soviet refusal to be involved in national elections.

The movement from occupation to the divided governments in Korea is a long and terribly complex story that is well considered by Bruce Cumings, Allan R. Millet, and Jin Chull Soh, and no wide discussion is necessary.[27] But

ROK President Syngman Rhee and Mrs. Rhee with UN Command team.

Top: Communist soldiers refuse to wear UN clothes and sit stripped before a prisoner exchange. *Bottom:* A Communist Chinese negotiation team, with American interpreter, at Kaesong.

Admiral John Daniel leaves with a signed agreement for Operation Little Switch.

needless to say, the role of Syngman Rhee and his rise to power in South Korea was both an essential and a contributing part of the road to international crisis. Both Asian specialists and State Department officials were leery, if not downright afraid, of Rhee. He had made few friends in the State Department and was outspoken about his differences with the United States. In addition he was not respected by leaders in other Asian nations who had seen evidence of his heavy-handedness.[28] Despite their concern, there were still those in

Washington who supported Rhee and saw him as the best hope for some form of democracy in Korea. As well, the arguments of the Department of Defense, supported by the occupational commander General Hodge and the area commander General MacArthur, was that supporting Rhee would do a great deal to relieve the United States Military Group in Korea (USAMGIK) from the stain of being pro–Japanese, and would support many of the reforms they were pushing as well as bringing the various factions of the independence movement into a government.

And so it was that with MacArthur's support the expatriate Rhee was greeted in Seoul on 16 October at a high profile press conference where Hodge and others pledged their support of Rhee and his Korean Democratic Party. Rhee's movement toward control of Korea was aided by the Moscow Agreement of 27 December 1945, in which the U.S-Soviet Joint Commission, the body with the responsibility of directing the occupation, would develop plans for a provisional government established through national elections.

While the Korean people welcomed the Americans as an occupying force — most anything was better than the Japanese — it was but an obstacle to the long-dreamed-for Korean independence, thwarted by people representing themselves as friends. The Cairo Conference had considered independence but had made the rather arbitrary decision that the Koreans were not ready to govern themselves. The Koreans were well aware that the Allies did not consider them with the same respect as they did Europeans. One British official, when asked his opinion of Korea's future, wrote, "Korea is not worth the bones of a single British grenadier.[29] And a good many of those who were coming into power believed that the United States had betrayed them in their earlier dealing with the Japanese. This is the position taken by American historian J. E .Witz and his argument is well supported.[30] Despite the arrangement made with the Soviet Union, there was some disagreement over the final decision to remove the occupational troops. When it came time, Dean Rusk warned against it, saying that the Koreans were not ready. However, ambassador Muccio refused to support his position and the troops left.

Once America left, however, it tended to lose interest. Many suggest that this obvious lack of interest was instrumental in the North Korean decision to invade. Dean Acheson has been much maligned, as many blamed him for opening Korea up to invasion when he spoke to the National Press Club on 12 January 1950. The evidence is that he was not to blame. The Acheson speech was carefully constructed and he weighed his words. Speaking well within the policy as it existed at the time, he addressed three items. He was interested in outlining the difference between American interest in the conditions in Asia, which he defined as being an agent for the growth of freedom and economic well-being, and the Soviet position, an interest better identified as neo-colonialism. He also wanted to assure the Asian nations that the United States maintained an interest in their welfare and that any attacks against them would be matched by a responding action by the United Nations and the civilized world. And last, that the United States was unable to provide for nations the loyalty of its people, but that for those loyal to their own governments the United States was there to help. While it was true that he did not focus on Korea or include it in the area of immediate concern, he did not withdraw American interest.

Nevertheless, America was involved. So when General MacArthur took command in Korea, he was authorized to use the UN flag in all military operations. It was designed to be a United Nations effort and its authority stemmed from collective influence of that body. As suggested earlier, the lack of well-defined provisions for reporting meant that the war was primarily left to the Joint Chiefs of Staff.[31] MacArthur himself seemed critical of the lack of United Nations supervision of the war,[32] though he made very little effort to keep them apprised of his activities.

For many, the early year of the war was in fact MacArthur's war, and volumes have been written, both supportive and highly critical, about his conduct. He is certainly subject to criticism for his own actions but he is often blamed for difficulties that were not his responsibility; intelligence, for example. And, he did manage to unify his command to the point that the nations involved could function as a body. The control of forces became complete on 14 July 1950 when Republic of Korea President Syngman Rhee placed all of the ROK troops under UN Command. Considering Rhee's personality and the nationalistic agenda he maintained, it was an obvious indication of the desperation of the situation.[33] At 0001 hours on 13 July 1950 Lieutenant General Walton Walker was given command of Eighth Army that had been selected for responsibility for the ground war in Korea.[34]

While every fighter was welcomed and appreciated by the UN command, the difficulties caused by the unification of fighting men from twenty plus nations were often close to overwhelming. As more and more soldiers from member nations appeared, the problems magnified. Not only were there the difficulties of language (sometimes within individual units) but of different weapons, different diets, different clothing requirements, diversified training methods, and the infringement of national commanders, but the UN command also faced the peculiarities of individual units based on their culture or religious background. There were as well deeply entrenched differences and disagreements among participating members. The job of keeping them congenial was sometimes difficult. Even the Commonwealth forces, with their common language and traditions, experienced difficulties growing out of an excess of nationalism. Some nations, as was the case with Australia and Turkey, had been bitter enemies during previous wars (in their case World War I) and yet the managed to come together in this often hazily defined cause.[35]

Those fighting under the Commonwealth were operating under political considerations that, in some ways, made them a sub-command. First of all there was considerable tension among the nations who shared a traditional bond but not necessarily the same agendas. The British were very concerned how their troops would be used. For example, the commanders of the First Commonwealth Division were required to report to their government on any orders they received that appeared to place their forces at undue risk. This loophole, which became known as "waving the paper," provided the Commonwealth commander with a sense of independence and, in most respects, allowed the forces their own areas of operation. Nevertheless, the Commonwealth managed to hold together under the stress of the Korean War.

The British Commonwealth land forces were operating under the functional control of the UN Command which, in the main, was staffed by American officers. While this worked out better than might be expected, there was often tension. There was also some remarkable cooperation as, for example, cases in which British officers served willingly under American officers they outranked.[36] In some cases, however, they were not under the direct command of the United States. When involved in the Commonwealth forces, the individual national distinction "Royal" was excluded from the title. All Commonwealth naval forces served under the U.S Naval Forces, Far East. In this book each of the Commonwealth nations are considered separately.

At least three perceivable problems, with command in the long run affected the nature of the war: the failure of the Joint Chiefs of Staff to control MacArthur, the political and sometimes personal conflict among the various commanders, and the inability to use the forces of the "other nations" to the best advantage.

First, the Joint Chiefs of Staff seemed incapable of guiding and directing General MacArthur. Or, lacking that, they appeared to be unable to control him once they had given him instructions. There were occasions when he ignored or downright disobeyed them. General Ridgway, it is reported, once asked his friend and fellow officer Holt Vandenberg, "Why don't the Chiefs send orders to MacArthur and tell him what to do." The answer apparently was, "He wouldn't obey."[37] The question of his original appointment, a man in his mid-seventies, is one of those still without answers. General Eisenhower was reported as saying he preferred a younger general for Korea, rather than "an untouchable whose actions you cannot predict and who will himself decide what information for Washington to have and what he will withhold."[38] Historian Fehrenbach wrote that MacArthur was perhaps the best choice for a holy war, "but in Korea, in 1950, the United States was not fighting a holy war. Momentarily and at MacArthur's urging it had lost sight of its original goal and proceeded into the never-never land."[39]

Despite misconceptions to the contrary, General MacArthur was not involved in the decision to cross the 38th parallel and unleash the UN forces into North Korea. This was a Truman administration decision made somewhat earlier and reinforced on October 7 by UN resolution. Many analyses of the war treat MacArthur as reckless, arrogant, eager to expand the war, righteously and unduly optimistic that the Soviets would not retaliate, and indifferent to constitutional and legal restrains on the military. Some of this may be true, but it is not a fair picture when looking at the successes in organization that he obtained.

Second, serious consideration must be given to the capabilities of the local commanders involved. Certainly Matthew Ridgway was well received and came out of the war about as appreciated as any of the command. But General Walker, the feisty commander who served with Patton in World War II, is open to question. His handling of Eighth Army was questioned even before Inchon and his breakout at Pusan, and MacArthur's men leveled criticism at him for his command arrangement, the slowness of his progress, and the heavy casualties that his units took. There had been talk of his removal since the initial retreat.

As well, the leading commanders simply did not agree and on some occasions found themselves in open opposition. Lieutenant General Walton Walker did not get along very well with Major General Edmond Almond, whom MacArthur put in command of X Corps and who, by most every account, was a difficult man to work with. Nor did Major General Oliver P. Smith, the Marine commander, place much faith in Almond's ability to command. He believed that Almond was unfamiliar with air-ground warfare and often pushed his delay of orders to the point of insubordination. The degree to which personalities played a part is hard to define but just as hard to ignore. The experience in corps and divisional commands has not been well investigated but evidence of incompetence and command disagreement and misunderstandings is obvious.

And third, it appears that the United Nations Command did not consider the "other nations'" contingents as either necessary or serious contributors nor were they well used. Far too often they were assigned to cleaning up guerrilla locations or guarding supply, communication and transportation lines. Some units, as well trained as the divisions they were supporting, were assigned weeks of training because local commanders did not know how to use them. Because of their size many contingents were not seen as capable of acting on their own, and yet their assignments to other units made them, often, the "gofer" unit, with better assignments given to new or replacement troops.

The Response of Nations

The Truman administration, reacted and the United States fostered involvement so rapidly, American foreign policy in regards to Korea was not well spelled out. It would be difficult to locate any policy in the archives of the National Security Council. Over the years there had not been a great deal of love lost between the two nations and the period of American occupation had not played out as well as either the United States or the United Nations had hoped.

President Rhee had learned at an early age that the U.S. was not to be trusted to always act with the best interests of Korea in mind. Rhee had gone to the U.S. in 1904 seeking its good offices to intervene in the Japanese annexation of Korea, citing the provisions of the Treaty of 1882,[40] and the U.S. answered using the slimmest of excuses to avoid taking any action. Most State Department officials had written off Rhee, and had less than serious concerns about Korea and how it fit in their sphere of interest or concern.[41] The Joint Chiefs of Staff, presided over by Generals Omar N. Bradley and J. Lawton Collins, along with General MacArthur, were primarily responsible for shaping the case for Korea. With cuts in the available ground forces and a slipping budget for operations and the up-keep of weapons and equipment, they did not want any American troops in Korea and, at best, to provide only limited military aid to the Korean government.

The second UN resolution, by calling for aid, required an answer. At first it was generally positive and affirming, but also many of the responses were far more political than they were potential. As Secretary General Trygve Lie pushed for members to commit themselves, the responses slowly began to come in. Given both the suddenness of the situation and the political strains immediately put into play, they might have been expected to vary widely, but they were unusually similar. Most confirmed their support of the action and accepted the moral implication of the Security Council's resolutions. At the same time, many nations also felt the need to provide some up-front limitation on what they could, or in some cases would, do.

The impact of the responses was slowed by an early memo circulated from the Secretary of Defense on 14 July 1950, which considered the conditions and means by which help would be accepted from other nations. With a certain amount of arrogance, the memo informed interested nations that military help would be accepted primarily on the potential efficiency of the units offered and their availability and suitability for early employment. It also spelled out that logistical and transportation considerations had to be met by the host nation, and included additional and rather vague criteria such as "the likelihood of such units being employed profitably in Korea."[42] Admiral

A. C. Davis, at the direction of the Joint Chiefs of Staff, suggested that no requested units should be taken from the Philippines, Italy, Turkey, or Saudi Arabia. The Joint Chiefs apparently had decided that "these countries may have urgent need for their own use of all of the forces which were available to them."[43]

As might be expected, the Commonwealth nations were quick to respond with Great Britain and Australia sending token military aid immediately. In Europe, France hailed the resolutions as the initial application of the principles of collective security, attested to their necessity, and then informally agreed that a French naval vessel would be sent to the trouble zone. The little nation of Luxemburg welcomed the decisive and courageous steps of both the United States and the United Nations, and promised to provide whatever help that it could. Sweden expressed its nation's full agreement with the determination of the resolutions, accepted that the People's Democratic Republic of Korea had committed a violent breach of the peace, and promised that "while it could not make forces available it was considering other means of help."

Latin America was an area from which much was expected. But, in all truth, the Latin American nations were primarily unaffected by the war coming to Korea; most considered it too far away to be of any real significance. A large portion wanted to support United States as well as the United Nations, and two Latin American nations — Cuba and Ecuador — were members of the United Nations Security Council, and had been critical in the passage of the U.N. resolutions.

Nevertheless, while hardly a unified area, the South American and Central American countries had a great deal in common. Among them was the feeling, most likely justified, that while the U.S. had maintained strong relations with them during World War II, it had neglected the region since then. America, they witnessed, was providing huge amounts of economic aid to Europe, but little aid was available to their countries. They were tired, and resentful, of being taken for granted. Besides that, many of these nations were grievously poor, and the amount of money involved in providing military assistance was simply prohibitive. The assumption on the part of the U.S. that participating nations would be reimbursing them for expenses incurred during deployment created a heated controversy. Other nations were disappointed in what the U.S. was suggesting as an acceptable size for their contributions.

The nations of Chile, Brazil, Uruguay and Mexico were particularly upset with this ruling. They saw the size restrictions imposed by the Joint Chiefs of Staff as an effort to keep them out. No South American nation, other than Brazil and Mexico, had any tradition of sending troops for involvement in the wars of other nations, nor any real understanding of what that would involve. Most of the Latin American armies were small, poorly trained, and with improper weapons. Argentina, which had the best military in the area, had been feuding with the United States for the past decade and was not inclined to support the U.S. in this case. Brazil was willing to offer a substantial military contingency but expected large economic aid in return and then, later, backed out in the face of increasing domestic opposition to their involvement. The same was true for Chile, Mexico and Uruguay, which found that they could not get enough domestic support to justify their involvement in this foreign war. International historian William Stueck perhaps explained the attitude best when he wrote, "They hedged when asked to provide cannon fodder for U.S. crusades in remote lands."[44]

Nevertheless, as some point, Argentina, Bolivia and Brazil all expressed their affirmation of support for the UN resolutions and agreed to meet the request with whatever means were at their disposal. They were willing to acknowledge the need to fulfill the responsibilities imposed by Article 49 of the UN charter, but were not all that quick to suggest how they would do so. Venezuela announced its support of the endeavor and said it would fulfill all "obligations deriving from its membership." The Dominican Republic informed the UN that it was in complete agreement with the resolutions on Korea, and as far as its resources would permit it would provide assistance in maintaining the independence and peace of the Republic of Korea. Ecuador supported the resolutions and said that it "is prepared within the limits of its resources to assist in re-establishing" the order that has been disturbed in Korea. The nation of Guatemala said that it was in agreement with the measures adopted by the Security Council and would lend all possible cooperation.

Costa Rica quickly endorsed the resolutions and promised support, but at the same time made it clear that there was little it could do "in view of the fact that the Costa Rican constitution forbids a standing army and since the economy of Costa Rica is very limited."[45] The island nation of Haiti gave full approval and agreed to provide cooperation and moral support. Honduras announced that it was prepared to furnish such cooperation as was within its power with a view to the restoration of peace in Korea. The government of Mexico reported to the United Nations that it would faithfully fulfill the obligations incumbent upon it as a member. It too was prepared to cooperate within the limits of its resources. Nicaragua responded that it was prepared to provide assistance and would even be "prepared to contribute personnel when deemed advisable." Paraguay, Peru, Panama, and Uruguay were outspoken in their support of the United Nations but equally hesitant in what they would provide.

Despite the responses, however, the United States was not satisfied with the collective possibilities of its neighbors. It called for a meeting of the Organization of American States in hopes of persuading member nations to make larger contributions, but many nations delayed responding and it was not until March 1951 that they met. Even then no formal commitment was made for troops to Korea. The meeting's primary success was an agreement on maintaining the flow of strategic materials and commodities from Latin America to the factories in the U.S.

At the time, early July 1950, it also appeared that the United Nations anticipated some hope of general Islamic support. Moroccan nationalists appeared more sympathetic to the cause than anticipated, but the general response, while affirmative, was not a lot better than Latin America. By mid–July 1950, Turkey, which proved to be one of the strongest allies, responded that it supported the UN Charter with all its "strength and sincerity" and that it was prepared to fulfill its obligations under the charter. Iraq announced that it intended to consult with other members of the Arab League to consider a reply to the appeal, and even Iran strongly affirmed the United Nations decision. Yemen took note of the resolutions but made little commitment. While representing an entirely different perspective, the newly emerging state of Israel vigorously supported the actions taken by the United Nations. The country of Afghanistan confirmed the resolutions "but due to existing anxieties about the unsettled position in Pashtunistan wishes to be excused from giving any help to the Korean Republic."[46]

The African country of Ethiopia, which had suffered more than its share of foreign invasions, fully supported the decision and immediately withdrew any and all assistance to North Korea. It also "endorsed the efforts of states in better immediate position to render assistance to the ROK." The Union of South Africa promised to give careful and sympathetic consideration to the United Nations' appeal for support.

The Burmese prime minister was greatly encouraged by the stand taken by the UN and expressed his nation's support. The government of Indonesia appeared to be entirely sympathetic to the position taken by the United Nations, but felt that since it was not a member of the body that it could not come out in definite support of its actions. The Philippines were slow but eventually succeeded in providing a vigorous approval of the action that was seen to be in support of the growth of democracy in Asia. The small island nation of Iceland reported that it fully agreed with the actions of the United Nations, and would support it in any way that it could, but "for obvious reasons will not be able to furnish military or economic assistance."

According to George Elsey, State Department specialist on the Communist nations, even the Yugoslav delegates to the UN had informally told members of the United States mission that their country privately understood and supported the Security Council's resolutions, but that it was unable to give public support because of its ongoing ideological war with the Soviet Union.[47] India's Prime Minister Nehru did not like the United States' policies on Formosa and Indochina and, was not an energetic supporter of either the United States or Great Britain. He never made his position completely clear. He was not comfortable with the fighting that had broken out in Korea. He considered Asia to have a special relationship with India, and sought to minimize the issues of the war through a non-aligned policy during the Cold War. He indicated that while his nation did not originally vote on the 27 June 1950 Security Council resolution, the nation had accepted it two days later and supported it. However, his nation would not be able to provide any material assistance. He further clarified its position by pointing out this decision by his government did not suggest any modification of their foreign policy.

One or two nations used the situation to register their own protests against United Nations action. One was Egypt, which refused to support the Security Council's resolutions. It voted for the 25 June resolution only because its representative, Mahmoud Fawzi Bey, acted without instructions from the capital. Once he received instructions from his government he abstained on the resolution of 27 June most probably to register an Arabic objection to previous United Nations actions with respect to conditions in Palestine.

As the war went on there were two points in particular at which the many nations involved responded to what they saw as American led, and highly unwarranted, actions. The first was the crossing of the 38th parallel, the point many saw as the end of the United Nations' commitment. The second was when President Truman made it known that he was considering the use of atomic weapons.

In the first instance the allies were, almost to a nation, willing to grant their tentative support to the United States, but they were nevertheless unhappy with the decision to cross over the 38th parallel and push north. This was more than they had signed on for. They were frightened of Chinese reaction and convinced that failure to consider a responding intervention by the Chinese was little less than arrogance on the part of MacArthur. His insistence on carrying on with his "home by Christmas" offensive despite the strong evidence that Chinese troops were already involved in force would lead to what political scientist Jonathan Pollack called "the most infamous retreat in American military history."[48]

Just why this decision was made is the subject of much discussion. Traditionally it is believed that the successes at Inchon encouraged the military and the Truman administration to support further action. But the argument among historians about how much MacArthur's victory at Inchon provided the military euphoria to encourage further action has been challenged by James Matray, who discredits this view with well-made arguments.[49] Nevertheless, General MacArthur favored the idea. And despite their concerns, the Western allies held firm.

Once it was obvious that the decision had been made to cross the 38th parallel, the Truman administration became involved in the big sell both domestically and to its allies. President Truman, addressing the American people by radio, suggested that "Koreans have the right to be free, independent, and united" under the United Nations.[50] At the same time, diplomatic efforts were being made to test the view of the allies, and the administration believed that most nations, despite their hesitancy, would be willing to give affirmative reactions. A total victory, with the corollary effect of uniting Korea, would be most impressive to the Asian nations and would send a strong message to the Soviet bloc about American intentions and expectations. Behind this maneuvering of course was the constant fear of any action that might draw either the Soviet Union or the People's Republic of China into an expanded war.

In the second instance the response from the Commonwealth nations to President Truman's seemingly off-handed remark about the use of atomic weapons was swift.[51] Percy Spender, the Australian foreign minister, gave a grudging support of the United States' position if it became necessary, but affirmed that the use of any such weapons had to be preceded by widespread consultation. Great Britain, which made few efforts to hide its disagreement, or its belief that the expanding crisis in Korea was the result of MacArthur's mismanagement and aggression, were so upset that they sent Prime Minister Clement R. Attlee to Washington, on 4–8 December, to discuss it with Truman. Once again the British urged Washington to consider the status of Taiwan and the PRC at the table so that negotiations on the Korean War might come to an end. But apparently the primary mission was to discourage the use of, or the threat of using, atomic weapons. In this sense the mission failed, for the prime minister did not get anything but an oral promise that they would be consulted prior to the use of such weapons.

When Attlee came to the United States to consult with Truman he came with the opinion and agreement of most of the non–Communist world. India's response was decidedly negative and suggested that it was necessary to keep in mind that the primary goal of the war in Korea was to prevent, not expand, the spread of hostilities. It used this point, as well, to suggest the necessity of linking the question of Taiwan with that of a Korean armistice in order to prevent any possibility of expanding the war through the use of atomic weapons.

The reaction from most allies was restrained but in the end supportive. The delegates from the European nations of Greece and Turkey support the United States' position, if it became necessary, as did the nations of Afghan-

Prisoner of war camp at Koje-do guarded by a multi-national UN force.

istan, Saudi Arabia, and Liberia. But most of the Asian nations registered their shock that the use of atomic weapons was being considered, once again against an Asian nation. A large portion of the Latin American nations supported the president's 30 November statement, but expressed the need for caution and for wide consultation.

As the war progressed the relationship between the United States and Third World countries did not improve greatly; the war effort did not secure many new friends. In the first place American support for the corrupt government of Syngman Rhee proved hard to defend to many nations that still questioned the ultimate goals of the war. But beyond that, while it is hard to define in less than a separate volume, the problem seemed to center on the American failure to offer an appropriate response to the growth of nationalism.

As long as the U.S. maintained a Europe-first attitude, it would always be more interested in nurturing new alliances there, and many Third World nations were well aware of that. In addition, the fact that many of these new emerging states had strong Communist elements, or at least leanings, also limited the U.S. willingness to help. The misunderstanding among American planners about what constituted a Communist government would come back to haunt the nation later.

In perspective, sixty years or more later, the economic growth of both the Republic of Korea and the Nationalist stronghold of Taiwan have provided a valuable comparison between the ideologies of capitalism and communism for other nations in the area to consider.

3

Who Is to Fight?

If the best minds in the world had set out to find us the worst possible location in the world to fight this damnable war, politically and militarily, the unanimous choice would have been Korea.

— Dean Gooderham Acheson

Just what the involvement of each nation should be might have been clear to the military mind, but the complexity of the behind the scenes bargaining was ongoing. The balance between military necessity and individual national agenda was early tipped one way or the other by both national ambitions and external pressures. There were all sorts of things going on besides the composite of what military teams might be available. William Stueck,[1] spells out the vast array of national issues, from pride to aggrandizement, which lay behind both the desire to participate and the decision not to. The involvement of these forces was a bifurcation with the military and the department of state taking different views and roles.

On the one hand the military, represented by the Joint Chiefs of Staff, wanted military units that could eventually contribute to the victorious outcome of the war. Some nations, which for a variety of reasons desired to be included, were not seen as being particularly helpful. The military concerns went beyond the front line and involved consideration of language, size, equipment, training, and even religious and dietary considerations. As noted earlier the military had high expectations for what it wanted. The smallest unit that would be acceptable would be an infantry battalion, about 1000 men. Each man was to be fully equipped and have a reserve supply for sixty days, and the parent nation must promise reimburse the U.S. for money spent on equipment, food, and commodities provided. It was a wholly unrealistic concept. Besides, the U.S. State Department thought the military was missing the point; this was far too stringent and ignored the larger value of having many nations involved. And so the State Department challenged this view.

President Truman was convinced that the war in Korea — alas the Cold War as well — was to be viewed as a struggle not between the Soviet Union and the United States but between Communism and the free world. To do this he needed the authority that came from a multi-national effort and on this assumption the State Department requested that the military use as many national contingents as were willing, with particular significance being directed toward Asian and Latin American nations. Their military significance might necessarily be a second consideration in their involvement.

The argument over the acceptable size of the units was not just a matter of fighting strategy, it had to do with costs and administrative difficulty. It took just about as many persons and about as much paperwork to record the assignment and disposition of five trucks as it did of five hundred. When negotiating the financial arrangements, and billing the nations involved, it required as much time and money to negotiate the financial dealing for five million dollars of equipment and service as it did for dealing with 50 million dollars. The best that can be said is that the dealing with smaller nations and the policies and procedures that were established, would come in handy as the UN became involved in more such actions all over the world.

As the confusion contested and in some cases delayed the movement of troops, the commander in chief, Far East, recommended that the UN be billed on the basis of the overall average cost per man, per day, as evaluated on the basis of costs experience. It could be easily modified for those nations that were covering part or all of their individual costs. Another suggestion, proposed in March 1951 by G-3, suggested the various UN contingent forces should be increased to division size and fully equipped by the U.S. The argument was that then American forces could return to the U.S. without their equipment. The idea was not well accepted by G-4, which believed any such concept would leave America terribly vulnerable and without weapons. There was always the danger that the transferring of weapons to foreign units was dangerous, for that would leave them unavailable to be deployed to other areas of action if needed. The problem throughout the war was that while the U.S. was supplying weapons to other nations, it was also necessary to supply weapons for the U.S. troops as well.

There was some belief, particularly in the American Congress, that the allies were not pulling their weight. Just what Congress expected is unknown. But they bemoaned the fact that "the American boys who are fighting and dying on the battlefields of Korea today, with their backs to the sea, do not have a single nation we have helped so much, there in Korea fighting alongside them."[2] In July 1950 the *Denver Post* and the *Kansas City Star* ran articles suggesting that "this was the UN show and others should be sending their soldiers and equipment to fight in this police action."[3]

Much of the effort to draw in troops took a turn as the UN began to pull out of Pusan and advance toward the Yalu. In late October of 1950, the UN advance against North Korea bred optimism, and General Charles L. Bolte[4] advised the Joint Chiefs of Staff that the contingency of troops other than those from the U.S. and ROK was growing too large. He advised consideration of a reduction and requested that troops from Belgium, the Netherlands, France and New Zealand might be withdrawn. At one point this was taken seriously and troops already underway were halted. For example, Greece was asked to unload ships full of men and supplies that were about to leave the dock, suggesting that they were not needed. This same situation was repeated when the first efforts at peace talks were considered. Believing that it was more important to build up the South Korean strength, General Ridgway took the opening talks at Kaesong as a point to recommend that the contributing UN nations not be materially increased until the situation became clearer.

Despite these moments of optimism, in early January, after the Chinese intervention and the retreat of Eighth Army, the cry went out for additional troops. The first thought was that Australia, Canada, Greece, New Zealand, and Turkey would be able to send additional battalions. General Maxwell Taylor, in his evaluation of the need, felt that Turkey, Greece, Great Britain, the Philippines, Argentina, Brazil, Mexico, Australia, and New Zealand could all, if they so desired, come up with a force of division size. Acknowledging the fighting performance of the Turkish Brigade, it was felt that another brigade from Turkey would be a particularly significant addition. In an effort to set this up, the deal with Turkey was sweetened with promises of financial aid and the agreement to support Turkey's early application for NATO membership.

The Joint Chiefs of Staff considered other potential sources. They approached the government of Iran suggesting that its involvement would provide its troops excellent experience and training. Using the same argument, they approached the nations of Israel and Egypt. They also suggested that such a move would be seen as a gesture of Western confidence in their military capabilities. Seeking troops from Pakistan, the UN made an approach on somewhat the same basis, suggesting that it might lead to the eventual peaceful resolution of the ongoing question about ownership of the Kashmir. On the other hand, General Ridgway did not want additional troops from either the Philippines or Thailand since he considered them to be something of a liability.

The requests were not producing much. Robert Lovett, acting secretary of defense, complained on 31 March 1951 that everything was not being done to press member nations to send more troops. What he wanted were experienced, trained and equipped soldiers, not token gestures from states that might otherwise make significant contributions. He pushed indiscriminately on as many nations as he could. As it was, the State Department's very insistence might well have been in some cases, the source of their reluctance. The United States, some had concluded, was too pushy and was taking too aggressive a position. Some who were more than willing to fight for South Korean independence were not as willing to be seen as joining the United States in a confrontation against Moscow.

Admittedly, several nations continued to hedge with their promises. Despite the effort to obtain troops ready to go on line, many of the contingents arrived with far less training than they needed, and time and money had to be spent in additional training before they were ready to fight. Other forces were simply unprepared for front-line duty and were assigned to security roles guarding communications and rounding up guerrillas. Admittedly some UN members were far more talk than fight, dispatching large headquarters organizations to oversee the operations of few combat troops, making far more of a show than a contribution.

Nations Involved but Not Participating

Several nations on the world scene were significantly involved in the outcome of the war but did not participate in-country. In some cases their involvement was so dubious in nature or so politically sensitive as to be virtually useless. For large numbers their precarious positions made them anxious to avoid showing too much support one way or the other. Nevertheless judging their involvement carefully, one can see that they played significant roles in trying to influence the outcome of the war.

There were several sides to the conflict, but three in particular stood out: the Western Nations, the Communist Bloc, and a loosely defined body of countries that identified with the Non-aligned Nations. There was as well the ill-defined Arab-Asian group that often swung in their loyalties. The Western countries, particularly in Europe, tended to support the U.S. but were by no means puppets; they moved forward with their own agendas. Just as obviously the Soviet Union and those who were in their camp were not going to support the resolutions, or the war, and in fact objected significantly. Disagreements at the beginning, and the continued arguments that reflected the progress of the war, produced a mix and match of nations that is often difficult to explain.

On one other side of this debate lay the sometimes unpredictable Communist Bloc which, as the war debate emerged, consisted of East Germany, Poland, Hungary, Bulgaria, Czechoslovakia, Romania, Albania, and sometimes Yugoslavia. They tended to be more unified in their support, although the variations of the Communist ideology were already beginning to show. The nation of Albania had fallen to Communist control and became the People's Republic of Albania in 1946. Bosnia had been a member of the United Nations since 1945 but since had come under Communist domination. Czechoslovakia fell under the Soviet influence and despite fierce fighting by those seeking democracy in 1948 its government was taken over by the Communist Party of Czechoslovakia. Hungry became the People's Republic of Hungry in 1947 and voted consistently with the Soviet Union. East Germany had never been out from under Soviet control. Rumania had followed the same path.

Yugoslavia was perhaps the nation with the most difficult decisions to make. A close ally of the United States during World War II, it was in a precarious situation at home with plenty to keep its own troops involved as border tensions with Hungry, Bulgaria and Romania remained. It faced the constant danger of Soviet's subversive activities as well. During the Korean War it remained on friendly terms with the United States and on several occasions consulted sympathetically with the U.S. In the end there was simply too much pressure from the Soviet Union to commit troops.

The long suffering nation of Poland, a member of the United Nations since 1945, nevertheless fell under Soviet control, and following a questionable election in January 1947, it began the transition from a democracy to a Communist state as the People's Republic of Poland. It appears, from the number of times it was identified as the source, that it was the nation through which the Soviet Union leaked information it wanted the West to consider. On 17 March 1951 Poland attacked the U.S. in a long speech at the UN and then proposed a Four Point Plan that called for an immediate cease fire and the repatriating of prisoners of war "in accordance with international standards." It called for the withdrawal of all U.S troops two to three months after the armistice was signed and the unification of Korea by the Koreans themselves and under the auspices of nations that had not taken part in the war. The U.S wanted to counter this but was not sure it had the votes needed to block the proposal. After behind-the-scenes discussions, it convinced Colombia, Honduras, Uruguay, Nicaragua, Thailand and the Philippines to co-sponsor the response and the proposal was blocked.

As many as thirteen Arabic and Asian delegates to the UN sometimes banded together in their efforts to influence the situation in Korea and bring about a cease fire as quickly as possible. And while that goal was not achieved as they wished, they did use their influence to prevent the United States from forcing through the UN ideas that they believed were too strong even for an anti–Communist consensus. As a result of their activities, the General Assembly passed the 14 December resolution calling for the creation of a member committee to "determine the basis on which a satisfactory ceasefire can be arranged."[5] Again, their effort proved unsuccessful, but the majority of this group then supported the UN resolution of 1 February 1951 that condemned the People's Republic of China as an aggressor.

India's leadership with the non-aligned nations provided another significant factor in controlling the situation. India did not want to participate but they wanted to be involved. While it is covered elsewhere[6] it is sufficient to point out here that the Indian government was involved in several efforts to establish peace. What became known as Indian Peace Initiative of 1950 consisted primarily of the recommendation that the UN seat the People's Republic of China, that the Soviet Union end its boycott of the Security Council, that a cease fire be established in Korea, and that an effort be made toward the reunification of the Koreans. The Soviets gave a non-committal response, but the United States was angry over the proposal and took the chance to reaffirm its position that it would not consider the status of the PRC in the UN as a part of their discussion of a peace in Korea. The plan was dropped.

India was also behind a plan submitted along with the United Kingdom, in May of 1952, known as the Anglo-Indian Five Point Plan, which was designed to break the deadlock over the repatriation of prisoners. The effort eventually fell apart and after the details of the plan were leaked, probably by Poland, the United States lost interest. The Indian resolution was a partial framework for the agreement on the prisoner of war issue that finally produced results.

Afghanistan maintained a reasonably sized army but according to the Joint Chiefs of Staff the army was poorly trained and inefficient. Besides that, they were Muslim, with all the problems the military believed this would cause. The nation of Syria had gained its independence in 1946 when Free French forces drove out the German occupation. However, French troops remained, and it was only after serious riots that they finally left. Syrian government officials had voted against the UN call for the 1948 elections in Korea. They were also irritated at South Korean president Syngman Rhee, who rebuffed their effort to have a more representative political system establish in Korea. When the time came to be counted they issued a vague expression supporting the UN but their hearts were not in it.

Egypt had what was considered a large army of nearly 57,000, but at the same time it was seen as ineffective. The question of religion also came up again, as the military seemed to believe it would create logistical problems.

But it was a moot point. While Egypt had voted in favor of the 25 June resolution condemning the invasion, it was as far as they were willing to go. Egypt presents a good example of the U.S. failure to understand the dynamics of emerging Third World nations. Circumstances were such that it might have drawn Egypt much closer.

Great Britain had exercised considerable power there, but that power was declining and Egypt was concerned about Soviet moves in the area. It needed friends. Turkey was willing to step in to aid them, but the U.S. were more interested in Turkey as the location of air bases; the close borders with the Soviet Union made that a decided advantage. When Egypt found itself in a disagreement with Great Britain over the Suez Canal, the U.S. backed its ally. The U.S. had not forgotten that Egypt had been unwilling to vote in favor of its stand on Korea.

Israel was a fledgling nation with a tiny population and it was, despite its obvious Western leanings, surrounded by hostile nations. By no accounting was it in a position to commit ground troops. Iraq also had a comparatively large army but felt considerable pressure created by Soviet interests in the Persian Gulf. The United States was particularly interested in Pakistan's involvement, but that nation already had political problems that were on the UN agenda, and its price for cooperation with the United States was too high. The nations of Belarus, Croatia and Macedonia had all been members of the United Nations since 1945 but for reasons of instability did not feel they were in a position to be involved. The same situation was replayed in Serbia, Slovenia, and Ukraine, all charter members of the United Nations.

The nation of Sweden supported the American position and it became evident that there were some elements emerging within the government that wanted to send a military contribution to join the UNC. These same elements also wanted the nation to seek admittance to NATO. However, the dominant Social Democratic Party focused pressure on Sweden to maintain its long tradition of armed neutrality, as was the case in World War I and II. Japan, while centrally concerned with the outcome of the conflict in Korea, was not in position to indicate support or disagreement, nor were they able to openly provide troops for what they believed were compelling political reasons.[7]

Until the scholarly community addresses the internal forces at work in these many countries, it will never be clear at what point the decision was made to identify them with either cause in this Cold War showdown. But the assumption that seems to come too easily is that because they were not involved in the fighting, they were not involved in the outcome. This is just not true.

During 1951 the U.S. still considered itself at a military disadvantage in Korea but the war so far had galvanized the U.S. government into action. The

U.S. armed forces, especially the Air Force, was rapidly increased and modernized. Effort on building the hydrogen bomb increased. Air fields were constructed in Morocco, Libya and Saudi Arabia. Also, the number of American divisions in Europe had risen to six. Eisenhower had taken command, and Greece and Turkey were asked to join. The U.S. completed a series of defense agreements with Australia, New Zealand and the Philippines in September 1951, and concluded the Japanese peace treaty against Soviet objections.

4

Nations Providing Fighting Forces

Whatever was sufficient to get us to this point is insufficient to get us any further.
— Darian Cobb

Once the commitment was made the secretary-general, on 29 June 1950 all the member states were asked to respond and to provide clear guidelines on what assistance they could provide. The process of identifying support was in difficulty right from the start. Despite its status as the executive agent the U.S. was not prepared for, or interested in, going it alone. On 13 July the U.S Defense Department made it known the United States should not be expected to carry the whole burden of the war, although no such assumption had been made. The U.S indicated that the needed help and they wanted more than token assignment. The U.S. maintained high, perhaps even elevated, concepts of what support might be available. Expecting troops at least as well trained and equipped as America was providing, it specifically named Great Britain, New Zealand, Australia and Pakistan as examples.

Under pressure from Secretary of State Dean Acheson, the Joint Chiefs of Staff (JCS) agreed to accept company size offers. Secretary of Defense Johnson reinforced the belief that forces should be accepted "to the maximum extent practicable from the military point of view."[1]

But what did that mean? How was this to be interpreted by nations willing to contribute? Not all of the member nations had strong or well identified armed forces. Fewer still maintained modern air forces or combat navies that were available. And what made a contribution practicable?

The agreement to participate was not just a decision made; involvement was complicated and straining. Many of the larger nations that responded were in the final stages of downsizing following World War II. Their military systems if not weakened most certainly were focused on peace. Their troops, even those who had been put in reserves, were scattered, the officer corps restructured, the training lessened and standards reduced. Their equipment, after years of hard service was in disrepair and worn out, and much of it growing obsolete. The military budgets, most pushed to extremes, were depleted. Their people, rebuilding their lives after years of hardship, were exhausted and reluctant to see war return. Providing another military source would not be simple.

For the smaller nations it was perhaps even more difficult. Among them few, if any, had any military tradition of international involvement and they were not sure what had to be done, or how to do it. Troops had to be located or, at least, separated from recognized commands. Often the military has to be pacified. For most nations volunteers had to be located — some truly volunteers and some a variety of mercenaries — to fill the need. Did they want to send the cream of the crop or was it sufficient to fulfill their obligations with those who were willing, even if not their best? Arms had to be collected and supplies, even if limited to immediate needs, had to be located from local sources. Medical services and inoculations had to be provided. English speaking officers had to be located and transportation found and arranged. Communication with the UN, still making its own adjustments, was difficult and involved. Liaison with the U.S. and eventually with the United Nations Command had to be worked out for assignments and acceptance to be arranged.

Australia, Great Britain, Canada, New Zealand, and the Netherlands offered naval support. South Africa and Australia provided early air power. The only nation that offered ground troops was Nationalist China on Taiwan. Chiang Kai-shek said he could provide three full divisions, nearly 33,000 men. On 1 August, General MacArthur formally turned down the offer on the grounds that the Nationalist troops were not well trained and had no attached artillery.[2] Other offers of ground troops came more slowly, but by 23 August, the UN had identified and accepted forces from seven nations, a commitment of nearly 25,000 men. But the gap between those offering fighting units and those delivering them was much broader than anyone had anticipated.

From the U.S. side the reception of troops would not result in the fighting forces that had been envisioned. There was the immediate problem of logistics. It was understood that troops sent from outside the United States would need immediate supplies and equipment and that these needs were immense. Before the men in the field could fight they had to be clothed and fed, and armed with weapons, equipment, and ammunition. But supplies were limited. The U.S. in its rush to return to civilian life following World War II had severely limited its ability to procure and maintain military hardware. What was available was mothballed or, in most cases, allowed to rust in the field. There simply were not enough military supplies to provide what some nations needed. Nothing had been worked out about how these procurements would be achieved and how the costs would be covered. Later a system was worked out so that in return for providing what was needed, and maintaining the soldiers in the field, each contributing nation would pay the U.S. $14.70 per man per day with the exception of Canada, which for some unexplained reason, paid $16.50.[3]

These costs were added to the resentment toward the United States' role. Once it was involved, the U.S. had moved ahead with its usual "can do" attitude, leaving some nations feeling unjustly pushed and reluctant to put their troops completely in the hands of the Americans. Nevertheless, the first order of business, even while fighting a retreating action in Korea, was to form a cohesive military force. It was necessary to find as many common denominators as possible, some means of simplifying and centralizing the support of the troops in the field. No matter what the various governments promised, the contingents that arrived differed vastly in their training and their general readiness for combat. For example, there was considerable unhappiness among the British, who traditionally wore and preferred their brutally heavy black "ammunition boots." When they were supplied with American boots they found them totally unsuitable.

Determining the size of the contributions of these "other nations" is difficult. All of the nations involved maintained the practice of rotating men and units, with many of them rotating whole battalions at a time. Because of this, the number offered as "total contribution" generally means the largest number involved at any one time. For example, Canada's highest number of soldiers sent to Korea is given at 21,940. But there were rotations and roll-overs of contingents and the actual number who served might be considerably more.

From the beginning the number of nations involved, and the troops they provided, was not meeting expectations. Secretary General Trygve Lie and those who followed him made numerous efforts to persuade nations to participate. Even those who had volunteers available for service were not sure how they could be accommodated; the distance between what they wanted to do and what they had the capacity to do could not be overcome.

Apart from the military, economic, and political problems involved there was growing concern over the manner in which the United States was conducting the war. The availability of troops was often reflective of the state of UNC success on the battlefield. Others, putting their faith in the potential of a cease fire, delayed, unwilling to send troops it they would not be needed. After the Chinese volunteers entered the picture the reluctance to send troops increased. General George C. Marshall, turned diplomat, was openly aware that after the initial commitments had been made the hope of getting more troops from the less committed nations was limited. And as the war went on this fear was made evident. But, despite these concerns, in the end some three-quarters of the members of the UN participated in the war and supplied about five percent of the troops not from South Korea or the United States.

It is a significant act when a nation decides to send its young men and women into battle, especially when its unclear how it relates to their nation, and when the cause is murky and the final outcome undefined. Not only were these governments putting their young people in harm's way, they were cementing relationships in a potentially long and costly Cold War. Some nations found the decision simple, even traditional, and the deployment uneventful, while for others it reflected a compromise of some considerable magnitude. For some it was as much a moral decision as it was political. How ever the decision was reached, the following nations sent their men and women to fight in support of the United Nations.

Australia

Australia lies in the Southern Hemisphere and is made up of the mainland, the island of Tasmania, and several smaller islands in the Indian and Pacific oceans. A member of the Commonwealth of Nations, it often took its lead in international affairs from Great Britain. It had been involved in the events in Korea from the beginning and had served as a member of the United Nations Commission for the Unification and Rehabilitation of Korea (UNCURK) in 1947, while a member of the United Nations Temporary Commission on Korea. At home, when the war broke out, it had been in the process of demobilizing much of its armed forces prior to reorganization and was not in the position to make much of a commitment. Besides, Australia's interests did not lie in Korea.

Shortly after news of the North Korean invasion was broadcast, the Australian government issued this statement: "Communist aggression stressed the possibility that the Communist guerrilla campaigns in Malaya and Indochina might be intensified as a result of the developments in Korea." But it did not go much further. Following the end of World War II the Commonwealth of Australia had little deep interest in the problems in Asia. Its attention was more focused on providing the nation's part in the protection of the Middle East should the anticipated war with the Soviet Union break out. Less than two weeks before the fighting started on the Korean peninsula the Australian Imperial General Staff had urged the government to be prepared to commit its forces in the Middle East.[4]

Nevertheless, in response to the United Nations' call to action, Australia's Liberal prime minister, Robert Menzies, quickly committed his nation to participation. He was supported in this decision by the opposition Labor Party and by most of the nation. Australia believed the UN had a major role to be played in the strengthening of international security and was committed to mutual security. Ambassador Percy Spender encouraged sending ground troops because he believed it would have long term benefits to Australia and help encourage the U.S. to sign a defense treaty with them. The government feared that the weakening United Kingdom, on whom it had counted for years, would be unable to provide aid as it had before.

For the Australian people, however, the initial interest in the war was low, and even as the government sent out the first destroyers to support the UN, the event hardly made the news at all. For those Australians who were closer to the problem, their concerns were with the potential advance of Communism and the fears of what would later become known as the "domino theory." Australia, because of its long friendship with the United States, was also eager to support it as well as the United Nations. Minister Menzies was also anxious to maintain the strong military ties with the United States that had been built up during World War II. However, despite what was going on in government, it was not until troops were called up for service that the public began to take much notice.[5]

When the invasion occurred Australian forces were already in theater. The 77th Squadron and the 3rd Battalion Royal Australian Regiment were stationed in Japan serving with the British Commonwealth Occupation Forces. A significant number of Army and Air Force Nursing Sisters were also stationed in Korea. Australia allowed these units to be involved as soon as possible.

The nation's first commitment, however, was naval, and one destroyer and one frigate were immediately offered for the period of the hostilities. The two Australian ships already in the area were the frigate HMAS *Shoalhaven,* which was in Japan, and the destroyer that was stationed near in Hong Kong. On 29 June they were assigned to the UN and eventually to one of the task forces. They were immediately employed protecting ammunition ships heading for Korea. This role was then expanded as additional ships of the Royal Australian Navy became involved during July 1950.

During the war a total of nine Royal Australian Navy vessels were on rotation for duty in Korea. An estimated 4,507 sailors served on these ships, which included the aircraft carrier HMAS *Sydney,* which had been sent at the request of the British government, the destroyers *Warramunga, Anzac,* and *Tobruk* and the frigates *Murchison, Condamine,* and *Culgoa.* The destroyers and frigates were a part of the bombardment group at Wonsan and took part in the evacuation of X Corps at Hungnam. During their tours of duty the

Australian ships were credited with destroying 66 bridges, 7 tunnels, and 38 stretches of runway, in addition to proving air cover and strafing sorties. Each of the ships mentioned served two tours with the exception of the *Culgoa* that remained in Korea into November 1954.

The air squadron that was based in Japan as a part of the British Commonwealth Operation Force was equipped with American Mustang P-51s. They were quickly involved and primarily employed as fighter interceptors and on ground support missions. Because they were slower planes, the arrival of the Russian MiGs made them obsolete for air combat, and the Australians replaced their planes with British Meteor jets. Soon they were back flying fighter sweeps and ground support.

Australia also provided an air cargo and the transport squadron that flew C-47 Dakotas. On arrival they were assigned to the 91st Composite Wing (Royal Australian Air Force) and throughout the war flew men and supplies from Japan to Korea and back.

The first ground troops, the Royal Australian Regiment, arrived in Korea on 28 September 1950 and was attached to the 27th Commonwealth Brigade (soon to be identified as the 28th) at Pusan and moved north with the UN toward the 38th parallel. They had advanced as far north as Pakchon before the Chinese entered the war. During the resulting retreat the Australian unit served as a rear guard for the Eighth Army. By January of 1951 they were back north of Seoul, where they conducted successful actions against the Chinese at Kapyong, on the Jamestown Line. At one point the Australian 3rd Battalion captured no fewer than 1,982 DPRK troops north of Yongyu when the commander mounted a tank and told the enemy they were surrounded and should surrender. They were not surrounded but they surrendered anyway. During the war as some nations decided against sending additional troops to Korea, Australia continued to do so.

A good portion of the logistic support and supply for Australian troops came through the U.S. Army Quartermaster, but this caused little adjustment or difficulty, as the Australians, with very much the same general dietary habits, ate American food with no difficulty. One of those fighting with the Australians was Captain Reg Saunders, the first Aboriginal Australian to be commissioned in the armed forces. He was "respected for his ability as a platoon commander, particularly for his determination when leading patrols far from the battalion's main position."[6]

During the fighting the Australian casualties amounted to more than 1,500, with 339 killed in action and 1161 wounded. Among the naval forces the aircraft carrier *Sydney* reported that its planes had been damaged 29 times, and nine aircraft were destroyed. At the end of the war 29 Australian prisoners of war were repatriated during Operation Big Switch.

The Republic of Korea has erected an elaborate monument at Mokdong-ri in South Korea that is dedicated to the brave men of the Australian command who fought and died in defense of Korean liberty. In special recognition the 3rd Royal Australian Regiment was awarded the South Korean Presidential Citation for its determined defense of Kapyong in April 1951. The Australian government finally built a memorial to its own men and women who fought in Korea, at Canberra. It was completed on 18 June 2000. Remaining in Korea after the war to help assist with the defense of the DMZ, the last Australian troops left Korea in April of 1957.

Certainly it can be argued that the Australian contribution to the war effort was a significant factor in the signing of the Australian, New Zealand, and United States (ANZUS) treaty on 1 September 1951. It also transformed the Australian relationship with the United States, cementing an even stronger friendship. This did not mean that the cooperation between nations concerning Korea was always simple. Australia backed Great Britain in pressuring the United States to avoid the use of the atomic bomb. It also played a significant role as a buffer holding off much of India's criticism, and was a significant partner in preventing the isolation of the U.S. and its friends in the General Assembly. As well, James Plimsoll, the Australian representative, was a powerful ally for he was on occasion a moderating influence on President Rhee.

Belgium

Belgium is a federal parliamentary democracy with a constitutional monarchy. It is about the size of the American state of Maryland. The nation first gained independence from the Netherlands in 1830. In 1950 the population was estimated at a little over eight million. After bitter experiences in World Wars I and II, the government of Belgium was very concerned with its own national security and anxious to be recognized by the Western powers. As the host and original signatory of the Western European Union defensive alliance (1948) and NATO (1949), Belgium's leaders were well aware of the global consequences of the war in Korea. The national elections in 1950 returned the Christian Social Party to power and saw King Leopold III on the throne. National support for the move toward participation in the Korean War was so strong in some quarters of the government that Christian Party Minister of Defense Henri Moreau de Melen resigned from his cabinet position in order to join the volunteer force.

With the passage of the UN resolutions calling for military aid for the Republic of Korea, the government, led by Christian Social Party Prime Minister Joseph Pholien moved quickly to support both the United States and the United Nations, and agreed to participate in the intervention in Korea. However, under Belgium law only volunteers could be sent to fight in foreign wars and it was necessary for the government to put such a force together.

The military contribution from Belgium consisted of the 1st Belgian Battalion (*1st Bataillon Belge*) that left Antwerp in December 1950. It was made up of three rifle companies, a heavy weapons company, and headquarters company. They arrived at Pusan on the 31st of January 1951. The volunteers were a mixture of French speaking Walloons from southern Belgium, and Flemish, the Dutch speaking people from northern Belgium. The battalion was rotated throughout the war with the 1st serving until August 1951 and the 2nd and 3rd remaining through June 1955. During the war Belgian troops were allied with the British 29th Commonwealth Brigade and the U.S. 7th Infantry Regiment of the 3rd Infantry Division. The amalgamation of Belgium and Luxembourg forces formed the *Groupe de Liaison pour la Belgique et la Luxembourg,* which fought in numerous military operations in Korea. The Belgian forces were well trained and equipped and were available as soon as they arrived. The first Belgian troops arrived on 18 December 1950 on board the *Kamina,* and the last withdrew in June of 1955.[7]

During the war the Belgium United Nations Command, also known as the "Brown Berets," often fought beside the British Gloucestershire Regiment and were known for their positive attitude. "Belgium Can Do It" was plastered on the jeep of their pastor, Padre Vander Goten, and became the motto of the unit. Commanded by Lieutenant Colonel A. Crahay, the contingent entered the fight toward the last of January 1951. They immediately engaged with the offensive campaign then operational and were involved in cleaning up the area around Seoul after the capital was liberated. The move north had driven so fast that Walker had left pockets of guerrillas behind and they needed to be cleaned out before moving on. In April the unit was attached to the British 29th Independent Brigade and assigned with them to hold the center of the 3rd Division front. They were aided by the First Northumberland Fusiliers and the 1st Gloucestershire Regiment.

In their position the Belgian troops were on Hill 194 on the north bank of the Han River. It was here where the Chinese pointed their attack. As the Communist forces pushed forward they broke through in several places and cut between the brigade front and that of the Belgians and Fusiliers. The line was breaking and the Belgians were busy covering the retreat of the 65th Infantry as well as pulling back when world of the dangerous position of the Gloster Regiment was received. Once they had organized they were involved with elements of the 3rd Division in an attempt to relieve the Glosters from their isolated and dangerous position but were unable to do so; it was a serious loss for the British regiment.

Perhaps their most significant involvement came with the battle of Haktang-ni fought against Communist Chinese People's volunteers between 9 and 13 October 1951. The battle took place just north of the city of Chorwon, North Korea, and four miles ahead of the UN line held by the Puerto Rican 65th Infantry Battalion. The center of the advance was known as Hill 391 by the U.S. Army and it was called Broken Arrow by those who fought on it. More a ridge than a hill, it extended 1,500 meters running north to south with a steep rocky outcrop at the southern end. At the time the Belgian Battalion was considerably under-strength because the battle occurred during its rotation period. From the moment of its arrival on 10 October the unit was fired on by Chinese rockets and mortars. Late in the evening of 10 October the Chinese, crossing over from Hill 317, hit against B Company. While the attack was repulsed, the heavy artillery and mortar bombardment continued all during the next day. At the time the Belgian outfit was at about half strength — 500 out of an assigned 900. On the morning of the 12th the Chinese attacked again, this time along several fronts. With support from a U.S. heavy weapons company the Chinese were eventually driven back.

Hoping to restrict the Chinese artillery fire, a patrol from the detachment moved off Broken Arrow and attacked the adjoining hill (317) where they were able to destroy an ammunition dump before returning to Broken Arrow. During the day a thick fog began to cover the battlefield and the Chinese, taking full advantage, attacked in small patrols probing for weakened positions along the line. Then on the morning of the 13th the Chinese advanced in force, coming through the barbed wire and focusing their assault on the Heavy Weapons Company. The Chinese made some advances but as the fog cleared later in the morning the attack was repulsed and the Chinese were driven back off the hill. The Belgian unit moved on to reoccupy Hill 317 as well. When the fighting was over 98 Chinese dead were discovered. On orders from 3rd Infantry Division the Belgians, having prevented the Chinese occupation of the disputed hills, were pulled back the next day. For their heroic defense the battalion was awarded the citation Haktang-ni to be flown on their flag.

About the time the armistice talks began the Belgian troops joined the stalemated war and were involved in patrols and sometimes small and violent actions as the major powers moved back in forth on the battlefield and at the negotiation table. The force was remembered for its involvement in the 1951 offensives as I Corps tried to drive the Chinese north of the Yokgok-cheon River. There, the force, supporting the U.S. 1st Cavalry Division, moved out in Operation Polecharge to take Hill 348. There it set up on the defensive line Jamestown.

Almost from the beginning of the war Belgium transport planes had participated in the Pacific airlift that carried troops and supplies from the U.S.

to Korea. In April 1952, however, Belgium gave notice that it would not be continuing and withdrew two C-47s from the San Francisco–Tokyo run. Leaders had noticed that almost everything they carried could have been carried easier on sea transportation, and at much less cost. The cost to maintain these planes seemed far too high.

When the Belgian troops arrived they brought with them British-type equipment, but as the war wore down it was gradually replaced by the more available American weapons. At first the Belgians only relied on the U.S. for petroleum products, but in time that gradually expanded to cover most things. They did require some adjustment to the rations, asking that 500 pounds of bread and 300 pounds of potatoes be added to the usual 1000 man ration.

The cost of Belgium's participation in the war was high. Their government recorded a loss of 101 soldiers who were killed in action, 478 who were wounded and one taken as a prisoner of war.[8] At the end of the war the single prisoner was repatriated. To honor the Belgium and Luxembourg troops that fought and gave their lives in support of the independence of their nation, the Republic of Korea erected a monument at Tongduchto, in Kyonggi Province.

Canada

There was no doubt of Canada's willingness to support the United Nations, but the Canadian government seemed less concerned with its commitment than it was in keeping the American government in check, seeing that the war was run by the UN and not the U.S. Canada considered itself a player in the post-war world and was obligated to be involved in this international outbreak. Not a member of the Security Council, it had little power there, but with the support of the opposition Progressive Conservatives, it considered sending troops. The Canadians, who gave the appearance of being hawkish about the war, called for 7,065 young men for an 18 month enlistment.

At first when the news of the war reached the Canadian parliament it was little interested. Prime Minister Louis St. Laurent told the assembly that Canada would not be going to war against any nation and if it were to be involved in Korea, it would be through the United Nations. Defense Minister Brooke Claxton did not want his nation involved in an Asian War. So while the Canadian government agreed in policy with the actions of the United Nations, and was anxious to see the aggression in Korea stopped, it was reluctant to commit too quickly. Finally, a week or so after the outbreak, and under the influence of External Affairs Minister Lester Pearson, the government acknowledged that the West was being tested by the Soviet Union.

Pressure on the Canadian government was not only coming from the United States but from Great Britain as well, with that government offering Canada a place in a Commonwealth Division. The offer was that Canada, along with Australia and New Zealand, would form a division using British supplies and equipment,[9] but at this point Canada wanted to take action on its own. So, with the support of the majority of the Canadian people, and even that of opposition leader George Drew, on 12 July 1950 the government authorized Canadian involvement and the immediate deployment of destroyers.

Like most nations, Canada had followed up the end of World War II with a great reduction in military force and was in the middle of a planned reorganization of forces. In 1950 the armed services consisted of fewer than 48,000 men and women. Under the circumstances the naval forces were the easiest to send on short notice. Dispatched in early July, the warships arrived in Korean waters and were quickly involved. The first to arrive were the HMCS *Athabashan, Cayuga,* and *Sioux,* which were immediately dispatched under United Nations command. They supported the assault at Inchon and participated in the dramatic evacuation at Hungnan and the rescue of American forces at Chinnampo. A Canadian seaman on board one of the warships remembers that they had to scrounge everything from fuel to food to keep the ship functioning. In December 1950 he recalls they were sent to Chinnampo, where they were hoping to perform a Dunkirk-like maneuver to rescue American and British troops retreating in front of thousands of Chinese volunteers. It was necessary to take the ship 34 miles up shallow water, and miss low islands and shifting mudflats in water freshly mined by Communist sympathizers. "I remember seeing a hole blown in the side of an American destroyer and there were pieces of bodies floating in the water."[10]

These and six other destroyers would serve intermitted deployments until September of 1955. Each ship had either two or three deployments. The Canadian contingent of naval forces helped in maintaining a continuous blockade of the enemy coast, prevented several amphibious landings by the enemy, took part in the blockade of Wonsan, and supported land forces by the bombardment of enemy-held positions. It also had the responsibility of protecting the friendly islands and provided supplies as needed for those in isolated areas. All in all more than 3,500 Canadian sailors served.

Also in July 1950, the government assigned a Royal Canadian Air Force squadron to air transport duties with the United Nations in Korea. Squadron 426 (The Thunderbirds) flew Northstar C-54 cargo planes on regularly scheduled flights between McChord Air Force Base in Washington and Haneda Airfield in Tokyo. Starting in mid–July these flights continued on a regular

Canadian ship HMCS *Haida* (right) is fueled at sea from an American tanker.

basis until the ceasefire. During the war the squadron delivered 13,000 passengers and more than seven million pounds of air freight. The Canadian government did not provide any fighter units to participate in the air war, but twenty-two Royal Canadian Air Force pilots and technicians served with the American units, flying Sabre fighter-interceptors. In this service they were credited with downing twenty-nine Russian built planes.

On 7 August the government authorized the recruitment of the Canadian Army Special Forces for service in Korea. This unit was to be specially trained and equipped to meet Canada's obligations to the United Nations. After much prodding, it was decided to set up independent units of soldiers of fortune, since there were few regular army units available to dispatch. Nevertheless, this unit soon merged with the regular army. After Inchon its training status was downgraded and some thought they would only serve for occupation duty, but Chinese intervention altered that conviction.

The contingency consisted of the second battalions of the Royal Canadian Regiment, Princess Patricia's Canadian Light Infantry, and the Royal 22nd Regiment, a squadron of Lord Strathcona's Horse, the 2nd Field Regiment Royal Canadian Horse Artillery, the 57th Canadian Field Squadron, Royal Canadian Engineers, the 25th Canadian Infantry Brigade Signal Command, the 54th Transport, a company of Royal Canadian Army Service Corps, No. 25 equipped field ambulances, and the Royal Canadian Army Medical Corps. Brigadier General J. M. Rockingham was in command.

The Canadian troops arrived in Pusan on 18 December 1950 and tasted their first combat on 13 January 1951, when they also experienced their first casualties. In February 1951 the Princess Patricia's Canadian Light Infantry went on line with the 27th Commonwealth Brigade and participated in the UN advance toward the 38th parallel. In March they were moving into the Kapyong Valley as the Chinese volunteers advanced. During the Battle of Kapyong Valley, 22–24 April 1951, they participated in the defense of the route to Seoul against an estimated 10,000 Chinese Communists. In late April when the Chinese launched a full scale offensive, the Commonwealth Brigade was given the assignment of holding a withdrawal route through the Kapyong Valley. During this prolonged battle a defensive position was established at Hill 688 where the Patricians, completely surrounded during some of the fight, managed to prevail against large odds.

At the battle for Hill 355, known as Little Gibraltar, 24–27 November 1951, they successfully defended the hill against heavy Communist Chinese attacks. The Battle of Chipyong-ni, 13–15 February 1951—where Canadian troops in conjunction with those from Australia were heavily involved—was the first time the advancing Chinese had been stopped. The Canadians are remembered as well, particularly by the Americans, for three destroyers involved in the naval evacuation of cut-off American troops at Chinnampo. The Canadian units spent the summer of 1951 patrolling the area of the Imjin River and in the fall fought to protect the supply route to the Chorwon River.

As negotiations began and then dragged on, the Canadian brigade became a part of the newly formed First British Commonwealth Division. From the beginning it had been agreed that Canada would obtain rations, vehicles, laundry equipment and some of its signal corps equipment from the United States, but would use their own weapons and ammunition. It was one of only three countries that accepted American rations and supplies without adding anything to the rations or taking anything away. The Canadians preferred the British Bren automatic rifle over the American weapons and used them through most of the war. The eventual cost estimate sent to Canada was for 41.5 million dollars.

In May when the prisoners at Koje-do revolted and captured the camp commandant, the United States was in full command and thus took much of the criticism. In an effort to widen the responsibility, and probably the blame, the decision was made to provide an international force to clean up the disturbance. Elements of the Canadian unit were assigned. The Canadians were not pleased with this decision and complained at the manner of their use. So while the troops went as ordered, there was an official protest and the Canadian commander of mission in Japan was recalled and dismissed. Later military representatives said that the reaction "was an unfortunate incident" and that Canada made too much fuss over the event. But they used the excuse to indicate that somehow there had to be better communications and that they had all learned the lesson of the "necessity of prior consultation."[11]

During 1952 a system of rotations was put into effect for Canadian forces. In April Brigadier M. P. Bogert took command. In 1953 Brigadier J. V. Allard became commander until 1954. The Canadian units were normally rotated on a yearly basis.

As the hill war phase of the conflict continued, the Canadians were engaged in patrolling and ambush exercises with the object of dominating "No Man's Land" and securing prisoners when needed. During the last half of the war the Canadian troops served at a series of non-descriptive outpost and hill defenses. In May 1953 they withstood a strong enemy assault against Hill 187 and successfully defended it at a high cost in casualties.

The 2nd Princess Patricia's Canadian Light Infantry and the 3rd Royal Australian Regiment received the U.S. Presidential Citation for their defense at Hill 677. During the war 26,791 Canadians served, with an additional 7,000 participating between the cease-fire and the end of 1955. The Canadian forces began to leave in 1954 and the last battalion left in the spring of 1955.

Throughout the war, Canada, though often disagreeing with the United States, served as a constant ally. It was the Canadian minister to Sweden who would report that the message from Beijing was that the Chinese were willing to go ahead with the terms concerning the armistice even if further conferences on the subject proved unsuccessful, or if Syngman Rhee would make any effort to continue the war on his own.[12]

The military services of Canada suffered 1,558 casualties during the war, with 516 of these being killed in action. Following the signing of the armistice, 32 Canadian prisoners were repatriated. The Canadian government estimated that the war cost more than a billion dollars in direct and indirect expenses. In November 1975 the Koreans erected a memorial to the Canadian troops who fought in defense of their country. It was replaced in December 1983 with a much larger granite memorial in the shape of the Canadian flag at the Gapyeong Canadian Memorial. While it is designed to commemorate all service, it focuses on the brave Canadian stand during the Battle of Kapyong, 24–25 April 1951. The Hongcheon Area Battle Monument, built in 1957, is dedicated to Canada's efforts against Chinese forces at Yangdukwon-ri.

While the Canadian unit fit in well with the UN command and in time with the Commonwealth Division, there was always some contention because of the political directions that the unit was always to be sustained as a distinct force. This requirement meant that the unit could not be broken up, as some commanders wanted, for individualized unit assignment.

After the war the Korean veteran in Canada had to deal with the apathy of citizens, as in the rest of the West. One particular case is noted when the *Calgary Herald* in 1975 carried a four-part series on the history of the city. While mentioning the area's contribution to World War I and II, it totally failed to mention Canada's contribution to the Korean War despite the fact that one of the prime units involved, the 2nd Princess Patricia's Light Infantry, was stationed in Calgary. Only recently has the full story of Canada's participation in the war started coming out. The final battalion of the Queen's Own Rifles left Korea in 1956. The Canadian military came out of the war revived and the long planned revision of the corps, including the adoption of American weapons and equipment, was reconsidered to take a broader look.

Colombia

Colombia today is a constitutional republic but it has had a rather violent history. Located in the northwestern corner of South America along the Caribbean Sea, it had, in 1950, a population of 11.5 million. The capital is in Bogota. Relations between the United States and Colombia were rather shaky following a dispute over the Panama Canal, and again in the 1940s because of the pro–Catholic administration's persecution of Protestants. These relations improved considerably during World War II when Colombia, which did not send troops, nevertheless offered substantial support to the allied cause. Following the end of the Second World War, the assassination of Liberal leader Jorge Eliecer Gaitan in 1948 sparked what is generally called La Violencia. The violent outbreak eventually led to the rise of conservative leader Laureano Gomer, who came to power in 1950.

In response to the crisis in Korea, Colombia deployed its only frigate, the ARC *Almirante Padilla*, to Korea. The *Almirante Padilla*, the former USS *Groton*, had been purchased in 1947. Arriving on 8 May 1951, it was assigned to 7th Fleet Task Force 95. The shallow draught of the vessel enabled it to work close to the shoreline where it was involved in the activities of the partisan guerrillas based on the islands. The frigate was transferred to the east coast in June and was again involved in the interdiction at Wonsan and took part in the transportation and supply of agents to the off shore islands. The ship was involved in Operation Package and Operation Derail, designed to disrupt enemy communications along the coast south of Songju. It was eventually relieved by a sister ship, ARC *Captain Tono*, and then by *Almirante Brion*. The final ship remained on station until April 1954. During these naval tours 786 sailors were involved.[13]

The Colombians were also putting together a fighting force. On 26 December 1950 the 1st Colombian Infantry Battalion was activated. Despite the fact the nation had compulsory military service at the time, it was decided that this unit should be formed totally by volunteers. On 21 May 1951 the battalion, commanded by Lieutenant Colonel Jaime Polonia Puyo, sailed for Korea. The first 1,000 men of the Colombian Battalion (*Batallon Colombia*) arrived in Korea on 16 June 1951 and were attached to the 24th U.S. Infantry Division on the Wyoming Line. In January of 1952 they were transferred to the 7th Infantry Division when the 24th returned to Japan. The detachment, which involved 4,314 men, did not depart until 11 October 1954. Included in this number were several officers and NCOs of the Corps of Naval Infantry (*Cuerpo de Navbais Infantaria*).

They were heavily involved in the fighting but most remembered for the Kunsan offensive and at the Battle for Old Baldy. The 3rd Battalion was severely mauled in March 1953 when a Chinese division managed to overrun Old Baldy and overwhelm them. The battalion received the most casualties of any Colombian unit. Its final actions involved Operation Barbula and the defense of Old Baldy.

The United States provided the initial equipment needed for the Colombian contingent, and supplied and resupplied it as well as providing transportation. Some adjustment had to be made to the rations. For each 1000 rations issued the quartermaster had to add 214 pounds of rice and deleted about 50 percent of the dehydrated potatoes from the American allotment. The Colombian troops seemed to get along with the military from other nations, though some individuals, at least, considered them tough. Sergeant Red Harrington, 32nd Infantry Regiment, wrote home that he had warned the new men coming in to watch out for the Colombians. "Don't mess with them, I said."[14]

In April 1953 they were involved in the defense of Pork Chop Hill. Of the seemingly endless battles for this piece of land, S.L.A. Marshall wrote, "The concession would have been in the interest of line straightening and to sacrifice a dependable anchor. But national pride, bruised by the loss of Old Baldy, asserted itself and Pork Chop was held." Young Kao Yung-ho of the 3rd Company Colombians claimed that "the victory is to our company commander's credit."[15]

Colombia's involvement came at a price. Of the 4,314 who participated, the Colombians reported that 163 were killed in action and 448 wounded.

Twenty-eight men had been taken prisoner.[16] As the war ended 28 Colombian prisoners of war were repatriated. A monument was dedicated by the Republic of Korea in honor of the Columbian soldiers who fought and died in defense of their nation.

Ethiopia

Ethiopia, also known as Abyssinia, is located on the Horn of Africa and is the world's most populated land-locked nation. The capital city is Addis Ababa. In the early stages of World War II, in 1930s, the Italian dictator Mussolini launched an unprovoked attack on the state of Abyssinia in an effort to expand his empire. Selassie's plea to the League of Nations for intervention was disregarded and his nation was overrun and occupied by Italy during World War II. After the war the nation became a charter member of the United Nations. Ethiopia had learned the hard way the consequences that could result from the failure of international collective security and was willing to take action.

Ethiopia was a very poor nation under the leadership of Haile Selassie, with a population in 1950 of about fifteen million. It received full sovereignty in accordance with the Anglo-Ethiopian Agreement of December 1944. Perhaps still aware of his own country's plea for help, the emperor committed troops to the war in Korea. Conditions at home were not stable, however, and even as troops were fighting in Korea, members of the Imperial Guard made an attempt to overthrow the emperor. Calling on help from the U.S., he was aided by the U.S Army advisory group in Ethiopia in 1953.

When first considering participation, the emperor offered to send a British-trained battalion with English speaking officers, but this was soon withdrawn. The act, of course, was not totally selfless on the part of the Ethiopians, as there were suggestions that the U.S. should aid them by providing equipment for three full divisions.

The Ethiopian Battalion, which was known as the Kagnew (Conquerors), consisted of 1,200 men who served with the 32nd Infantry Regiment of the U.S. 7th Infantry Division. The battalion members were the only African ground troops in Korea, and they were seasoned professionals and all stood more than six feet tall. They arrived under the command of Lieutenant Colonel Teshome Ignetu. Prior to being deployed they underwent eight months of training and were provided American weapons and equipment. They were

Opposite, top: Ethiopian troops unload ammunition. *Bottom:* Ethiopian 30MM squad with American liaison (back row, center).

accompanied by their own surgeon and a contingent of Ethiopian medic aids and nurses. The rather large headquarters force that accompanied the unit was quietly detached and sent to the base area. During the war a total of 3,518 served in Korea.

The Ethiopian Battalion sailed from Djibouti aboard the American transport *General MacRae* and arrived at Pusan, South Korea, on 7 May 1951. It served through three rotations in 1952, 1953 and 1954 with a small contingency of Ethiopians troops remaining in South Korea until 3 January 1965. The battalion fought with the U.S. 7th Infantry Division, 32nd Infantry Regiment, through most of the war and played an especially significant role during the battles for Triangle Hill, fought in October and November 1952, as a part of the American advances. They were the prime defenders of outposts Yoke and Uncle and later took part in the battle for Pork Chop Hill.[17] Captain Marno Habtewold remembered while fighting off a Chinese advances on the hill that "they had each been given a flag and told to bring it back." He intended to do just that.[18]

John Schultz, with the 31st Field Artillery (U.S.), remarked in a letter to his mother after moving next to a group of Ethiopians, "I don't know who they are, they certainly ain't Americans, but they strike me as real fighting men and I'm glad there [sic] here."[19]

The Ethiopian Battalion was highly regarded by other troops, particularly for their tactical skills, and for the fact that they recovered every wounded and dead soldier from their battalion. No Ethiopian soldiers were taken as prisoners of war by the enemy. Just about every reference to the unit's involvement suggests that the Ethiopians fought in 235 (some lists say 238) battles during the war and never lost any of these exchanges. The Ethiopian troops became well known for their ability to conduct raids at night and to bring back prisoners when given the task.

They were also considered the "show troops" for visiting dignitaries coming to Korea during the war. They were called upon to serve as protection for Secretary of State John Foster Dulles's visit, and formed the honor guard for President Dwight D. Eisenhower when he made his promised trip in December 1953.

During the course of the war the Ethiopians lost 122 killed in action and 566 were wounded in action. No prisoners had been taken. However, the veterans paid an additional price for their service in Korea when, in 1974, a socialist government took control of the nation and set out on a plan of persecution of these veterans for fighting against an allied nation, North Korea. Among other things, they were refused hospital care.

South Korea was very grateful to the Ethiopians for their help and made several efforts to recognize them. A stamp was issued at the time of the emperor's visit and in honor of the "precious blood" that the Ethiopian spilled in defense of Korea. In May 1968 a monument was built at Geunhwa-dong and dedicated to the Ethiopian Empire that had rendered such great service to the Korean people. The United States awarded the Presidential Unit Citation to the 2nd Battalion for its action on Hills 602 and 700. The U.S. also awarded a Silver Star and eighteen Bronze Stars to individual Ethiopians fighters. Company No. 3 was awarded the ROK Presidential Unit Citation for its defense of outpost Yoke and Uncle. Two members of the contingency, Colonel Irgetu and 2nd Lieutenant Mamo Hapewold, were awarded the highest Ethiopian gallantry award, becoming Knights of the Order of Emperor Menelik. The national government awarded a Korean War Medal to those who served. The inscription on it reads in Amharic, "We support every nation's independence but we are always the enemies of aggression, Korea 1953."

In July of 2012 the South Korean government announced that it was going to pay a pension to the surviving 339 members of the Ethiopian forces who fought in Korea. Acknowledging that many of these men were living in poverty, they felt it was only fitting that they support those who had supported them.

The Ethiopians had linguistic and cultural challenges with the other forces, primarily Americans. Very few soldiers from elsewhere spoke Amharic, and Ethiopian soldiers had a basic distrust of the Western medical profession. For example, they demanded that doctors and nurses taste the drugs before they would take them. The United States provided complete initial equipment, supply and resupply, as well as transportation for the Ethiopian unit that had arrived unequipped. In order to meet their unique dietary needs, for every 1000 rations they received a supplement of 15 pounds of rice, 30 pounds of dehydrated potatoes, and 500 ounces of hot sauce.

Ethiopia provided an excellent example of the varied cultural customs of the nations and the United Nation Command's effort to respond. The tradition among Ethiopian warriors was that they returned from battle carrying their weapons with them. When the time came for them to withdraw it was discovered that American policy was that no weapons that belonged the U.S. could be taken out of Korea. Unhappy with this situation, 750 seasoned Ethiopian troops boarded the USS *McRae* for the return trip minus their weapons. The Ethiopian government requested that the warriors be allowed to have their weapons and agreed to pay for them on arrival. The UN sought to remedy the impasse and boarded more than five tons of weapons on board a C-54 cargo plane, cut the ship off at Colombo, and allowed the warriors to experience their traditional return.[20]

France

Ever since the French sent their fleet to aid General George Washington and the American Revolution, the United States and France have enjoyed a sometimes difficult but always supportive relationship. In 1950 France had an army of nearly half a million men. At the same time, it was also heavily involved in a number of military commitments of its own. Not only was it providing occupational duty in Germany, Austria and Africa, but she was involved in the bloody Communist uprising in Indochina.

When the UN called for help in the Korean crisis, the French government felt it was only able to apply economic sanctions against the North Koreans; which it did. It was not, leaders believed, capable of entering yet another conflict. The military had forcefully expressed its objection to taking on any new responsibility in Korea without receiving some considerable military and economic aid from the United States. So, at first, France's prime contribution was to apply economic sanctions against North Korea starting on 19 July 1950.

However, the French had more to gain from following the U.S. position against Communism than did many nations. They were involved in an effort to maintain their position in Indochina and were "engaged in a struggle analogous and parallel to that of the UN in Korea."[21] They were already looking for American help in dealing with the growth of Communism in that arena. So, on 23 August, following General MacArthur's request for more troops, they decided to form a battalion. The French participation was made possible by the efforts of a few French politicians and two general officers. France's military structure was still reeling from the impact of World War II, and General Blanc, chief of staff of the French Army, refused to commit any of his units that he had determined were still anemic and poorly equipped. Instead he decided it would be best to form a volunteer force, *La Guerre de Corée*. Lieutenant General Margrin-Vernerey Monclar, inspector of the Foreign Legion, was so committed to securing France's involvement in Korea that he took a substantial reduction in rank to accept command of the battalion. The French also determined to send a naval force to the United Nations Command.

The first French naval vessel to appear was the patrol gun-boat (frigate) FMS *La Grandière* (F731) under the command of Commander Urbain E. Cabanie. The frigate reached the area on 29 July 1950 and was immediately engaged in a transport and escort mission. It joined the UN Blockade and Escort Group during the blockade of Wonsan. The ship, which was integrated into Frigate Squadron Four (F-4), was under British command and a part of Task Force 90. The ship and crew received the Korean War Service Medal. It was built 22 June 1939 and decommissioned 25 November 1959.

French troops celebrate with their wine ration.

Despite the military demands in other locations, the French Battalion was quickly formed out of volunteers selected from the active and reserve French forces. On 25 August 1950 the French sent a battalion composed of 3,763 volunteers, which on arrival on 29 November 1950 was attached to the 23rd Infantry Regiment of the American Indianhead (2nd) U.S. Division. The French served with this unit for the rest of the war. It was first engaged in combat on 25 December 1950.

The French arrived with their small arms and individual gear, but the U.S. furnished all other logistic support. As small arms were consumed by attrition, the U.S. supplied the replacements. It also provided transportation for the French forces between France and Korea. In addition to the normal American 1000 man ration, 500 pounds of bread, 30 pounds of dehydrated onions, and macaroni were added. The French, well known for their love of good food, were no less demanding in Korea. The French had a particular dislike for hamburger (what they called hash meat) and a need for their daily ration of wine. The government provided each soldier with a half-pint a day in addition to normal coffee and cocoa rations. French prisoners were wisely picked by the Chinese as cooks, which meant that the repatriated French prisoners were in better shape than most.

With their contingency the French also sent to Korea the French United Nations Headquarters, a command unit that quickly interposed itself between the battalion of seasoned veterans and the American headquarters to which it was assigned. This caused a good deal of bad blood between the two nations and it was not straightened out until late December 1950. By then the French senior commander, a lieutenant general, demoted himself to lieutenant colonel in command of the battalion and led with it with great distinction.[22] The French organized their units much like the U.S. and were perhaps the easiest of the foreign troops to work with. When they first arrived some Americans described them as "half-wild Algerians." The relationship was made much easier by the fact that most of the French officers and many of the enlisted men spoke English. They were known for their ability to fight without artillery preparations and for being capable advocates of the bayonet charge. Like so many of the nations, the French replaced their men by the rotation of units.

General Walker was facing the onslaught of Chinese troops who had pushed the 8th Army back all along the line. He needed more troops and so committed the newly arrived French battalion. Realizing it was unwise to fight at that point, he began to withdraw all along the peninsula. The French forces, whose code name was "Icicle," were involved in the first and second battles of Wonju, often called the Gettysburg of the Korean War because of their significance. In this early January 1951 encounter they gained considerable fame by stopping an intense Chinese attack using their bayonets. They were also involved in inflicting heavy casualties among the Chinese volunteers over a series of railroad tunnels, called the Battle of Twin Tunnels near Chipyong-ni, and there again in February.

They repulsed the Chinese on Hill 453 using a bayonet charge, fought on Heartbreak Ridge and later held Arrowhead Ridge at Hill 282 for four days against Chinese attacks. In February 1951, and later that month, they engaged the Chinese in the highly significant Chipyong-ni area. Within a month they were a part of the unit that attacked the Communist held Hill 1037, a strong fortification about 50 miles east of Seoul, an attack remembered in part for the fact that it was conducted in minus 22 degrees F.

During the spring of 1951 the battalion crossed the parallel and moved into the Hwachon region, where they again were involved in slowing a new Chinese offensive. In May of 1951 the battalion's pioneer company fought to the death. In the summer of 1952 they were involved in the Battle of T-Bone west of Chorwon and fought on White Horse and Arrowhead, where they stopped the Chinese attack on Hill 2181. In the battles of Heartbreak Ridge, what the French called Crèvecoeur, they suffered heavy casualties. Lieutenant

Jacques Grisolet remembers only that "it was bitterly cold. We blew down the enemy forces again and again but they were also popping up again and again."[23]

The French contribution did not come without costs. The nation, already recording heavy losses in Indochina, reported that of 3,421 French soldiers who saw service in Korea, 287 were killed, 1,350 were wounded, and seven were reported as missing in action. Twelve were held as prisoners of war, and after the signing of the armistice all twelve were repatriated.

The French fought hard and were recognized by other troops for their determination and skills. General Ridgway reported that the French "measured up in every way to the battle conduct of the finest troops."[24] For their services the French Battalion was awarded Five French Citation of the Order of the Army, the French Fourragère, two Korean Presidential unit citations, three American Distinguished Unit Citations, and 1,898 French War Crosses. Major Jean-Louis of the French Medical Corps was one of the two men for whom statues have been raised as memorials in Korea. The "Protective God of Korea" was honored in the spot where he was killed in Hong Chon on 8 May 195. At Daejang-dong, Wonju, in Gangwon Province, the South Koreans have built a monument in memory of the troops, including the French, who fought in this significant battle. Following the successful defense at Chipyong-ni, Paul Freeman of the Twenty-third Infantry Regiment praised the French troops and referred to them as the "crazy fools," and provided them with special congratulations on their determined and heroic stand.

France did not agree with the decision to cross the 38th parallel and push to the Yalu River; the action raised considerable criticism. In 1952 an anti–American movement began in France with many of the protesters blaming General MacArthur's policies for the poor showing in the war, and exposing the world to the possibility of a third world war. Slowing down their involvement the French turned to a policy of neutralization. For the soldiers, the eventual withdrawal from Korea provided no relief. On 22 October 1953 the French Battalion left Korea and headed for Indochina, where it joined forces in the battles already going on there.

Greece

Despite their recent bloody civil war that ended in 1949, the Greeks responded positively to the UN call. This small nation had been identified as a United States ally in 1947 by the inauguration of the Truman Doctrine that pledged that the U.S. would provide military support to combat Communist threats in Greece. The Marshall Plan and the provision for locating military

Ralph Olivette (left, American) and Phil Plouf (Greek) at base camp, 1952.

bases on Greek soil after World War II had strengthened the ties with the United States. This was also true of its desire to joint NATO, which it did in 1952. The Greek government felt a considerable debt to the U.S. and an obligation to support it in this effort.

When considering the American involvement, President Truman said that "Korea is the Greece of the Far East," seeing the situation there very much as he had faced it in the 1940s. The U.S. had taken over the role of protector in 1947 when Great Britain felt it could no longer assume that responsibility.

The Greeks, who had their own troubles with the Communists, were nevertheless willing to commit to the fight against this expanding ideology. But it was also interested in siding with the United Nations and the United States as a part of their drive to be included in a mutual defense agreement and gain membership in NATO.

The Greek contribution consisted of a reinforced infantry battalion and a Royal Hellenic Air Force flight of transports. Flight 13 was made up of seven C-47s and 67 officers and other ranks from the 355th Transport Squadron. These men were highly experienced fighters, having taken part in World War II and the Greek Civil War. They arrived on 3 December 1950 and were

Plane (C-47) from Greek Air Cargo command.

assigned to the 21st Troop Carrier Squadron (later the 6461st) at Taegu. From May 1951 to May 1955 it was based at Kimpo Air Base.

The original Greek plan had been to send a brigade as well, but because of the state of the war at the time the decision was made, it was suggested a battalion would be enough. Later in the war the Greek government offered additional troops. The offer was declined on MacArthur's instruction since, at the time, he thought the UN was winning and the war would soon be over.

The ground forces were called the Sparta Battalion, under the command of Lieutenant Colonel Georgos Koumanakos, and they arrived in November 1950. The battalion was composed of 849 men in three rifle companies, including machine gun platoons, and a headquarters company. All the men were specially selected volunteers from the Greek 1st, 8th, and 9th Divisions, and had considerable experience. In August 1951 the Greek component was expanded to 1,063 men and finally to 2,163 men. They were attached to the U.S. 1st Cavalry Division as the 4th Battalion, 7th Cavalry Regiment. The Royal Hellenic Army was, at first, encumbered by an Expeditionary Force Headquarters under the command of a colonel, but it did not interfere in operational matters.

Because the Korean landscape was much like that of Greece, the mountainous terrain was less troublesome to Greek troops than those of many other nations; their ability to move quickly impressed command. The Greeks had a few problems with Americans, primarily based on language. They brought their own doctors with them as well as litter bearers. They held the welfare of the civilians as a high priority and of all the troops were perhaps the most protective.

The Greek Flight became involved immediately and carried out 2,916 missions that included medical evacuations, transportation of troops and prisoners, and supply drops. They were also involved in the evacuation of Marines from Hagaru-ri. According to their records they carried 70,568 passengers, 9,243 of them wounded, and logged 13,777 flight hours.

The ground contingency first saw action on 29 January 1951 at Hill 381 west of Inchon as Eighth Army moved toward the Han River, where they beat off an attack by an estimated 3,000 Chinese of the 334th Regiment. They took part in the March to the Yalu. Later they were involved at Hill 489 north of Gonjiam-ri and took part in the defense of Hongje-dong near Seoul.

On 4 August 1951 the Greeks were involved in the defense against Chinese attacks on Churadong and in October of 1951 they took part in the battle of Scotch Hill. In May 1952 they were attached to the 15th Infantry Regiment, U.S. 3rd Division, after which they were called upon to join a unit to put down the prisoner riots at Koje-do. They participated in the battle of Nori Hill on September 28, 1952, and fought at Cheolwon and Yujeong-ri. At the battle of Outpost Harry, they fought it out with the Chinese for eight days, during which a reported 88,000 rounds were fired on the hill by the Chinese, but the Greeks and their American counterparts held on. They were involved in the defense of Hill 492 on 25 July 1953 just two days before armistice was signed.

Politically a strong ally of the United States, they nevertheless had some difficulty with the direction of the war policy. Never particularly fond of General Douglas MacArthur, the Greek government expressed strong support of the decision to remove him from command when it was announced.

The casualties among the Greeks of the Hellenic personnel included the death of twelve Air Force officers and non-commissioned officers as well as the loss of two C-47 transport planes. Among the Greek Battalion, 183 were killed in action and 610 officers and men were wounded. At the end of the war three Greek prisoners of war were repatriated. A memorial to the 186 men who lost their lives during the Korean War was built at Gyeonggi Province in 1974. The 13th Flight was awarded the U.S. Presidential Unit Citation for its participation in the evacuation of Marines at Hagaru-ri in December 1950. The Greek Expeditionary Force received a Presidential Unit Citation for its capture of Scotch Hill in February of 1952 and for the defense of Outpost Harry. Individual Greeks received six U.S. Distinguished Service Crosses, 12 Silver Stars, and 110 Bronze Stars, and 19 members of the 13th Flight were awarded U.S. Air Force Air medals. The Greeks awarded their troops the United Nations Service Medal. From their own people the battalion was awarded the Commanders Cross of the Cross of Valor in 1954.

The Greek contingent supplied all its initial equipment but counted on the U.S. to provide all supply and logistic services, including transportation. Supplying the Greeks was a little more difficult than most. The Greeks eliminated all sweet potatoes, canned corn, pineapples, peanut butter, dehydrated pea soup and salad dressing and added 500 pounds of bread, 42 pounds of rice, 33 pounds of dehydrated potatoes, 63 gallons of olive oil,[25] 42 pounds of macaroni, and 86 pounds of lard. The Greeks, like the Turks, seem to have wider feet than most Americans and sometimes had to slit the side of their boots to get them on.

The only American made movie made that pays tribute to other nations fighting in the Korean War was *The Glory Brigade* (1953) that depicted an American assigned to a Greek battalion during the early days of the war.

Luxembourg

The Duchy of Luxembourg is a landlocked country in Western Europe. It considers the Treaty of London (1835) to be the date of its independence. Nevertheless the nation was not granted autonomy until 1867 by King William I of Netherlands. Nearly ninety percent of the population is Roman Catholic. The nation was occupied by Germany during both world wars and suffered a great deal during this time. The population in 1950 was estimated at about 296,000. Luxembourg is a representative democracy within a constitutional monarchy. The commander in chief of the military was the grand duke (duchess) who was the only general in the army.

Luxembourg was internationally conscious and had recognized the Republic of Korea in 1949 and appeared anxious to show support for it. It had been a member of the United Nations since 1945. The small unit incorporated its troops with the Belgian United Nations Command, also known as the Belgium Volunteer Corps. The sending of troops was authorized by the Grand Duchess Charlotte, who served as the ruling monarch from 1919 to 1964.

Even though Luxembourg has had compulsory military service since 1944 and served with distinction as the artillery group of the 1st Belgian Liberation Brigade (also called the Piron Brigade), during World War II, the army was still very small. At the time of the outbreak of war in Korea, the Luxembourg military had no navy (the nation is landlocked) nor air force, and the army was integrated into the *Force Publique,* which included the military and the police. The Luxembourg contingency served as the 1st Platoon, A Company, of the Belgo-Luxemburgish Battalion, from November 1950 to January 1953. It formed at Camp Bevero in October of 1950, arrived in Korea on 31 January 1951 and was attached to the United States 3rd Infantry Division. During the war two different sections were sent, the first under Lieutenant Jos Wagerner and the second under Lieutenant Ruby Lutty.

The unit sailed in October of 1950 on the AP957 *Kamina*, a converted German naval submarine tender, and arrived in November. The unit remained in Korea until late 1953 when it returned home. It was disbanded in 1955.

The contingent from Luxembourg originally arrived with British-type equipment but this was gradually replaced by the Americans. At first the U.S. only supplied petroleum products but gradually that expanded to cover most things. When it came to accepting U.S. rations the troops from Luxembourg asked for an additional 500 pounds of bread and 300 pounds of potatoes to be added to the regular 1000 man ration.

The Luxembourg detachment fought in nearly every engagement in which the Belgium forces were involved. They are remember primarily for three engagements. In August of 1951 they took part in the battle of Imjin River. On 6 September 1951, following action against Chinese forces, the Luxembourg detachment (along with the Belgian United Nations Command) received the United States Presidential Unit Citation for exceptional execution of its mission and for remarkable heroism in its actions against the Communist forces on the Imjin River near Hantangang, Korea. At the battle the small detachment was credited with inflicting thirty-fold casualties compared to its own. The citation read in part: "The Belgian battalion with the Luxembourg detachment launched furious counter-attacks with bayonet. The enemy, surprised by the tenacity of these attacks became disorganized and withdrew in disorder. Finally, the Belgian-Luxembourg battalion withdrew by order of higher authority, evacuated its wounded, and was resupplied and requested to be put back in the line."[26]

They were also recognized for their efforts at Haktang-ni during the Battles of Broken Arrow in October 1951. The Belgium and Luxembourg force was posted on the far ridge to prevent Chinese setting up artillery, and held the position 9–13 October 1951 against a persistent Chinese force. Decimated by casualties and rotations, the small detachment was vastly understrength but held through several artillery barges and frontal attacks. Finally, on the 13th, on orders from 3rd U.S. Division, they pulled back and regrouped on Hill 362. A second Unit Citation was issued following the battle of Haktang-ni.

The unit was also involved in the defense of Chatkol, at the eastern section of the Boomerang. In the center of this defensive line the village of

Chatkol served as a communication and transportation center and was the goal of the Chinese offensive. Three outposts along the line — Alice, Barbara, and Carol — were named after the corresponding companies of the Belgian unit that operated there. This Chinese offensive lasted for more than fifty-five days.[27]

Always in the heart of the battle, the little Luxembourg contingent suffered the death of two of its members — Sergeant R. Mores and Corporal R. Stutz — and the wounding of seventeen additional. No members of the contingency were taken prisoner nor were any reported missing in action.

On 1 March 1952, South Korean President Syngman Rhee added the Republic of Korea Presidential Unit Citation to those already received. The citation included this comment: "The extraordinary heroism shown by the members of these units during that period greatly honors their country and themselves." The government of the Grand Duchy, in 1993, bestowed the gilt class Military Merit Cross, instituted in 1951 by the Grand Duchess Charlotte, on those surviving members of the Korean Volunteer Corps. The Republic of Korea issued a stamp in honor of the Luxembourg Volunteers in 1951. The people of South Korean have erected a memorial to the brave men of the Luxembourg command at Tongduchon, Kyonggi Province. Several members of the original units were on hand for the 60th Anniversary Celebrations held in the Republic of Korea.

This was the smallest contingency of troops sent to Korea. While the United Nations Command continually faced the question of its multi-language command, there was some increased difficulty with this contingent. The written language in Luxembourg is primarily German with some French being used for cultural communications, but in the main they speak a language called Letzebuergesch; which while based on German, is vastly different. Given the lack of Americans speaking Letzebuergesch, most commands were given through the Belgian forces. Most nations did not acknowledge, or at least comment on the smaller contingent, that was mostly associated with Belgium. One American's only comment was, "They seem to me to be short."[28]

Netherlands

The Netherlands had claimed its neutrality at the beginning of both World War I and World War II, but the Germans nevertheless invaded in May 1940 and occupied the country during the Second World War. Queen Wilhelmina was forced to set up a government in exile in London. After the war the government was reorganized and the queen returned to power. In the years following, the Empire of the Netherlands worked with its colonies to set up their independence. As a signatory power of the North Atlantic Treaty Organization and the Western European Defensive Alliance, the Netherlands responded to the UN request for help. Before the war the Netherlands had been a member of the United Nations Commission for the Unification and Rehabilitation of Korea (UNCURK).

At the time of the call for assistance the Netherlands was not in a good position to offer aid. The conscripts who had been called up for service in Indonesia had been released, and, at the same time the army was trying to raise a force for its contribution to NATO.

Nevertheless, with this in mind and despite the difficulties at home, the government set about raising a volunteer force. In time they would eventually contribute the *Netherlande Detachement Verenigde Natie* (Netherlands Detachment United Nations) and a destroyer. In order to raise the necessary troops they advertised in Dutch papers calling for volunteers and accepted only trained personnel. In doing so they created an especially diverse group, including ex–Resistance or Free Dutch Forces as well as a former Nazi or two. The group was identified as the Van Heutsz Regiment, honoring a Dutch East Indies general from the 19th century. They remained in Korea until October 1954. A total of 158 officers and 3,192 other ranks fought in Korea. The Dutchmen who served in the NDVN consisted of two from the Netherlands' Antilles, 73 from Netherlands' New Guinea, and 115 from Suriname. The Dutch first arrived in Korea on 24 October 1950 with the bulk of their units following in December of that year. Because the battalion was always below its allotted number, it was also assigned a significant number of KATUSA[29] soldiers who fought along with them.

The Dutch ship HrMs *Evertsen*, then in Indonesia, headed to Korea. From July 1950 until January 1954 the Netherlands Navy was represented by a warship in Korean waters. Involved were the destroyers *Van Galen*, *Piet Hein* and the frigates *Johan Maurtis van Nassau*, *Dubois* and *Van Zijll*. At first they were attached to the Blockade and Escort Force divided between the east and west coasts. The *Evertsen* took part in the prolonged Siege of Wonsan. The HrMs *Piet Hein* became a member of the infamous "Train Buster Club" after destroying an enemy train by gunfire, though the ship had some early difficulties with the American procedures for airplane spotting. Each of the vessels received a Presidential Unit Citation.

The ground force contribution, the Van Heutsz Battalion called in response to the Royal Decree Number 27, dated 27 October 1950, was composed of members from all of the provinces. It arrived in Pusan, South Korea, on 23 November and was attached to the 8th Army's 38th Infantry Regiment, the "Rock of the Maine." The detachment consisted of two rifle companies, an auxiliary company and a staff company. In May 1951 a third rifle company was added. The Dutch contingency arrived from the fighting in Malaysia. Since the newly formed regiment did not have colors yet assigned, a Dutch flag was used as the battle-flag. During parades and formal functions the unit also flew the American and Korean battle streamers.[30]

They came to Korea aboard an old World War II liberty ship that left Rotterdam and stopped at several places adding soldiers who were heading to Korea from England, France and Germany. The Dutch rifle company and heavy weapons company that had come from Indonesia were first put to test by Korea's cold climate. Assigned to the U.S. Second Infantry Division, they were often seen, by command at least, as having a sense of independence that made them difficult to deal with. It was a criticism leveled at a good number of the "other nations," but it was also useful in those occasions when initiative and discretion were needed.

During the first months they were occupied in anti-guerrilla duty and in protecting the flanks of the Second Division. They were then assigned to replace the U.S. Marines at their position along the 38th parallel. When the Chinese attacked in January 1951 the battalion was called in to fill the gap this had created, and entered Hoegsong to re-establish the line from Osan to Samchok. In this role they engaged in numerous skirmishes as they patrolled the Hoegsong perimeter, moving to block infiltration and suffering from a series of furious Chinese attacks. They were shaken when Chinese troopers, dressed as ROK and saying they had come for ammunition, shot and killed Lieutenant Colonel M.P.A. den Ouden, their commanding officer, and four of his officers.

On May 1951 the Dutch Battalion was ordered to protect the flank of the ROK 5th and 7th Division near Hangye-ri and No Name Line, where they stood their ground in the face of a series of Chinese assaults, but responding too slowly in one case, they lost Hill 1051 where two company commanders and several other officers were killed. From September to October 1951 the battalion took part in the capture of Heartbreak Ridge. In 1952, while fighting with the 38th Infantry Regiment, they took part in the battles for Star Hill, Silver Star Hill, Sagimak, and Chungmoksil. They were pulled off line in April of 1952 and joined a Greek detachment, a Canadian Regiment, and elements of the 187th Airborne to assist in quelling the prison riots that had gotten out of hand at Koje-do.[31]

Old Baldy, the name given to Hill 266, became the center point for a series of attacks that began on June 26, 1952, and lasted ten months. During the time in which the Netherlands detachment was involved the hill changed hands six different times.

Later they participated in the elongated battles for the Iron Triangle, north of Kimwha, which was held by the People's Volunteer Army's 15th

Corps. In a battle that started on 14 October 1952 and lasted for forty-two days, the UN attempted to take the hilly wooded area but failed. The Netherlands detachment was involved in all three of the major efforts. After the truce the troops were moved to Tokyo for a rest and then sailed home.

The Netherlands furnished a small part of their initial equipment using British type materials, but these were later replaced by American equipment. After that all commodities were supplied by the U.S. They did, however, provide their original transportation to Korea. For every 1000 rations the Dutch received an additional 500 pounds of bread and 30 pounds of dehydrated potatoes.

A total of 1,360 men of the Netherlands Navy served in Korean waters; of these, two men lost their lives.[32] Among the Dutch detachment, which during the war employed 3,972 men 123 men lost their lives while 645 men were wounded in action, three were listed as missing and one died in a prisoner of war camp. Twenty KATUSA soldiers were also killed while fighting with the Dutch detachment. At the end of the war three Netherland prisoners of war were repatriated.

A memorial in honor of Netherlands troops who fought in the Korean War was built in 1975 at Ucheon-ri. The citation reads: "Valiant fighters who acted in the spirit of the Prince of Orange and were filled with loyalty, 768 of them fell or were wounded in the struggle against the red invaders. To their determined fight this monument is dedicated." There is a small monument at Salemal highway where a number of Dutch military are buried where they fell. All military personnel who served in Korea were awarded the Cross for Justice with clasp "Korea," the UN Service Medal with clasp "Korea," and the Army personnel, the Korean War Medal. Individuals received three Military Order of William (two posthumously), five Bronze Lion, nineteen Cross of Merit, 120 received American issued awards, and 43 ROK awards. The NDVN was awarded the Presidential Unit Citation four different times. In memory of the KATUSA soldiers who died while assigned to the Netherlands Battalion, a plaque was placed at Oranje Barracks near Arnhem, where the Netherlands commemorates their service. The three destroyers and the frigate *Johan Maurits van Nassau* were awarded the President Unit Citation of the Republic of Korea.

In October of 1950, while there was still some hope among nations that the war would end at the 38th parallel and a united Korea would follow, the UN established the UN Commission for the Unification and Rehabilitation of Korea. The Chinese intervention made this a moot point, but the commission continued its efforts, among other things, to restrain the dictatorial actions of Syngman Rhee. The Netherlands served as a member of this commission.

New Zealand

During World War II New Zealand had placed itself beside Great Britain and contributed troops and supplies to the war effort. A strong ally, it was under pressure from the expanding Japanese excursions and was increasingly aware of their interest is Asia. Like Australia, with which it is often associated, New Zealand had a strong geographic interest in what was happening on the Korean Peninsula, but claimed to have little to no strategic or economic involvement. In 1950 it had joined the Colomau Plan for the economic support of South East Asia,[33] and initiated compulsory military training. It also had some larger international interests as the small nation was trying to gain a commitment from the United States to provide military security. On 24 July 1950 Premier Sidney Holland informed the British prime minister that his government was responding to the request for aid.

Originally New Zealand had contemplated joining forces with Australia, but the powers behind the British Commonwealth could not agree fast enough, and so New Zealand unilaterally decided to send its own units. The tie to Great Britain was perhaps stronger with New Zealand than with other Commonwealth nations, and it did not require that her troops serve only under its own commander. This speeded up the availability and accessibility

New Zealanders prepare to push a deuce-and-a-half stuck near Old Baldy.

of its contribution. A cartoon in the *Auckland Star* at the time of the December embarkation of New Zealand's soldiers shows one young man carrying a sign, "Wh'ere Britain goes we go."[34]

Earlier, on 29 June, the government had authorized sending two frigates to be deployed with the UN forces. They sailed for Japan in July. Beginning 1 August 1950 the HMNZS *Pukaki* and HMNZS *Tutira* joined with the UN Blockading and Escort Force, took part in patrolling missions near Wonsan and then served as a screening force during the Inchon invasion. During 1951 and 1952 the frigates *Tutira*, *Pukaki*, and *Hawea* patrolled the coastline. They joined with the ROK Marines and the U.S. Navy to bombard guerrilla insurgents on the islands in the Han estuary. On 24 April they shelled in front of Canadian troops, dispersing a Chinese advance. During the course of the war the Royal Navy of New Zealand provided six frigates which during the war performed shore raids and inland bombardments. The ships served intermittently until 1959.

After some prolonged debate the government of New Zealand decided it would also provide a ground force for service with the United Nations in Korea. In the process of putting the troops together they stressed the recruitment of men with European or Maori descent.[35] The deployment followed the New Zealand Army Act of 1950 that received a Royal Assent and created the New Zealand Army. The debate centered on Chief of Staff Major General K. L. Steward's concern that the force would not be of sufficient size to be self-sufficient in a distant war. Nevertheless, the action was taken. Known as Kayforce, it provided 1,044 men and consisted primarily of the 16th New Zealand Field Regiment and the 10th New Zealand Transport Company.

Within nine days of when the government of New Zealand decided to send the Kayforce to Korea, it had nearly 6,000 volunteers. The first ground unit arrived in Pusan on 10 December 1950 and was attached to the 27th Commonwealth Brigade. It went in to action 29 January 1951. In July 1951 the Kayforce was integrated into the Commonwealth Division.

During the first week in February 1951 the troops provided fire support for the U.S. 24th Division during its advance to Chuam-ni. Shortly after they joined with Australian forces in the Battle of Kapyong Valley, 24 April 1951, where wave after wave of Chinese troops sought to breech the defenses. For their part in the effort the New Zealanders were awarded the Korean Presidential Unit Citation. They also fought in Operation Commando along the Imjin River.

In April 1951, they supported the 6th ROK Division at the UN line above Seoul when the Fifth Chinese Offensive began. They ran into trouble moving their equipment through the rugged terrain and were unable to provide the support intended, and then the ROK defense broke and the New

Zealanders were forced to retreat to Kapyong, bringing their guns with them. They played a significant role when reinforced by the 213th Field Artillery Battalion, and they fought at Kapyong and Maryang San in support of Allied troops. In May they helped the 24th defeat a Chinese advance, and then advanced to the Kansas line.

In July of 1951 the U.S. suggested a joint Australian–New Zealand force be formed, but the arrangements could not be made and they later merged into the 1st Commonwealth Division. The New Zealanders were not all that comfortable with the British, however, complaining that they were taken for granted. While maintaining their original contribution throughout the war, when General MacArthur asked them in late 1952 to send more troops they declined. They believed that based on their country's population they had sent their share. They rotated their troops individually after one year of service but maintained about the same level of troops at all times. New Zealand troops remained in Korea until 1954.

During the course of the war 3,794 New Zealanders served in Korea. The only casualty in the Royal New Zealand Navy was a sailor who was killed during a shore raid. Among the ground forces there were 33 members killed and 79 wounded, and one was taken prisoner. Following the armistice the single prisoner was repatriated. In September 1989 the ROK dedicated the Mokdong-ri monument to commemorate the contribution of the New Zealand warriors who served in Korea. A monument also stands at Yeonong-ri in honor of Canadian and New Zealand troops who fought in the Hongcheon Area Battle.

With concerns over the Korean outbreak and aware of its own security, New Zealand entered into the Southeast Asia Treaty Organization (SEATO) in 1954. As a side effect of its involvement, New Zealand's wool industry and textile production expanded greatly and sparked an economic boom.

Philippines

America suffered some of its greatest defeats during World War II in the Philippine Islands, and most Americans maintained strong attachments to this nation where so much had happened. Later, General MacArthur managed to lead a liberation army back on to the islands in 1945 and the nation, which had long struggles for independence, was granted independence in 1946. But the comeback was hard and the Philippine government was near bankruptcy when war broke out in Korea. At the time it was appealing for more American aid to avoid a financial crisis. The destruction caused by World War II and the long Japanese occupation, as well as the fight against Communist guerrillas in the highlands had taken a toll. The country had few resources with which to aid the cause. While a member of the United Nations since 1945, it may well have been this latter insurgency at home that was the overriding factor in the decision to send troops to fight in Korea.

After the war the Philippines had little influence in the area but their interest in Korea had been marked by several diplomatic initiations prior to 1950. Its leaders had served as members of the Commission on Korea, the Additional Measures Committee and the Commission on Unification and Rehabilitation of Korea. It was one of the first nations to recognize the Republic of Korea, doing so on 22 August 1948, only a few days after Rhee's announcement. When war broke out the Philippines, given its situation, briefly considered neutrality as the wisest course, and then changed its mind and supported the United States and the United Nations. The General Military Council, as well as the opposition Nationalist Party, resisted the deployment of the Filipino Army outside the homeland and so a volunteer force was considered. At first the government sent only goods to support the troops in Korea, but then on 10 August, the Philippine House approved a proposal to "give every possible assistance." President Elpidio Quirino was afraid that a Communist victory in Korea would support the Hukbalahaps against which he was fighting. It was a fairly dramatic move for the nation and the military continued to buck it. But Quirino took the obligation seriously. In his deployment of troops President Quirino spoke to the soldiers: "Poor as we are, this country is making a great sacrifice in sending you there, but every peso invested in you is a sound investment for the perpetuation of our liberty and freedom."[36]

The Philippines Expeditionary Force to Korea (PEFTOK) consisted of five 1,500 man battalion combat teams which composed a regimental combat team. Arrivals were provisioned from mutual security money allotted to Manila, with equipment provided on a repay arrangement though the U.S. 8th army. The battalions consisted of three rifle companies and an artillery unit. They were deployed with a motorized reconnaissance company armed with light M24 Chaffee tanks. While in Korea the Philippine forces fought with the U.S. 3rd Infantry Division and the 25th, the 45th and the 1st Cavalry Divisions. The 10th Battalion Combat Team was under the command of Lieutenant Colonel Mariano Azurin. The 10th BCT was the first Philippine unit into Korea. The members spent the first weeks conducting combat training in Miryang.

The Philippine detachment received its first combat mission in October 1950 when it moved against troops at Waegwan. With the Chinese intervention General Walton Walker was moving his troops back carefully and needed more troops. He committed the Philippine battalion that had just arrived, hoping to slow the retreat. But, realizing it was unwise to fight at that point, he began to withdraw all along the peninsula.

The Philippine detachment took part in General Matthew Ridgeway's Operation Killer during the UN offensive of February 21. It was attached to the 25th U.S. Infantry division and was assigned to wipe out the Communists hiding in the hills. The men succeeded in this mission and in the protection of supplies lines feeding much needed resources into Seoul. Later a battalion of North Korean soldiers ambushed the 10th BCT near Muidon, but the Filipinos were able to counterattack and maintain the line.

In April 1951 while holding the vantage points over the Imjin River, a Chinese offensive cut off the Gloster Regiment on Hill 235. The Filipinos were assigned to help fill the gaps and seek a rescue of the surrounded regiment. However, they arrived too late and General Brodie decided that given the circumstances they were inadequately trained to bring off so difficult a mission like this in the dark and over country that had not been reconnoitered.

During the fighting the Philippine force recorded 92 men killed in action and 356 wounded. At the end of the war 41 Philippine prisoners of war were repatriated during Operation Big Switch.

The South Korean government has erected a memorial at Gajeong-dong, Seo-gu, and Inchon, built in September 1975 in tribute to the 112 Philippine soldiers who gave their lives in defense of freedom in Korea. A second memorial was built at Yeoncheon-eup to commemorate the Philippine involvement in the battle of Uyi-dong-ri. As late as March 2011 the Republic of Korea sponsored a rally at the Filipino monument at Yeoncheon in memory of those from their land who had served.

Troops sent from the Philippines received all their equipment, supplies, and service from the United States and well as the original transportation to Korea. When it came to rations they requested that the quartermaster supply an additional 1000 pounds of rice to the usual 1000 man ration. The cost of supplying the Philippines was estimated at 47.2 million dollars.

In many respects the Philippine detachment was not well treated by the UN. In the first place they had been promised Sherman tanks from the U.S. but never received them. In the second place they had not received the promised cold weather gear that was necessary and many of the Filipinos, who had never even seen snow, suffered greatly. The arguments led to Colonel Azurin being relieved of command. His replacement, Lieutenant Colonel Dionisio Ojeda, would go on to become a legendary hero of the Philippine military. The Filipinos were assigned to the 65th Puerto Rico Regiment on the mistaken belief that they spoke Spanish (they speak Tagalog).

When word was received that General MacArthur had been released, the Philippine government was critical of the decision and invited the general, who was still considered a hero in the islands, to stop at the Philippines on his way home. Cooler heads prevailed.

Republic of (South) Korea

This was their war and despite the arguments over it being a civil war it was, nevertheless, an invasion of their homeland and demanded a response. While events moved quickly there were few who believed that the South Koreans would be able to defend the nation against the forces that came swelling over the border. The Korean Military Assistance Group (KMAG) had either been unable or unwilling to prepare the army of South Korea to meet such a challenge, and earlier decisions at the time of the original withdrawal of occupation troops had denied them weapons and tanks. The DPRK forces, armed with Russian tanks and artillery, were moving at a rapid pace. The situation was desperate as Rhee called out to the UN to come to his aid.

The reasons behind the outbreak of war in Korea are many and complicated; they are a subject of discussion and disagreement among many excellent scholars. Many see it as a civil war that got out of hand when other nations began to be involved. Some still consider it a probe by the Russians to see how the U.S. and its allies would react. Even the question of who was responsible for the initial strikes is open to question, despite pretty strong evidence it was North Korea that made the first move. But the area had been unsettled for a long time, with both sides violating the 38th parallel and mounting vast political campaigns for the reunification of the nation. The outbreak of war should not have been a surprise and it has not yet been well explained why so little preparation was made to deal with it.

Whatever the questions when the hostilities began — it was their war. They were involved from the first moment to the last day of the armistice. During the war the Republic of Korea fielded the largest contingency of troops, provided troops for a significant number of battles, and suffered the largest number of United Nations casualties. Hundreds of thousands of civilians were killed or displaced. Both North Korea and South Korea were devastated by the war that seemed to offer proof to the old Swahili saying, "When the elephants fight it is the grass that suffers."

The ROK Army had been formulated after the withdrawal of occupation troops. Between June 1948 and May 1949 the 1st, 2nd, 3rd, 5th, 6th and 7th Infantry Divisions[37] were established from what had been the Constabulary Brigades. The 8th ROK and Capital Divisions were organized in 1949. By June 1950 the ROKA consisted of 98,000 troops established in eight divisions. In July 1950, after considerable reorganization following the outbreak of war, the ROK was composed of the I ROK Corps, II ROK Corps and the ROKA Troops and Reserve. They were, however, primarily deficient in artillery, antitank, antiaircraft, and armor capabilities, and supplies of equipment and munitions were inadequate. Communications and transportation were primitive. The training was in the earliest of stages and morale questionable. By law President Syngman Rhee was the commander-in-chief while the deputy commander was Major General Chae Byong Duk.

The ROK I Corps had maintained its sector throughout most of the war. It was responsible for anchoring the extreme left flank of the Eighth Army front on the east coast, with the U.S. X Corps operating on its left flank. The ROK II Corps fought in the central zone of the U.N. front during the advance into North Korea, flanked by the I and III ROK Corps. The II Corps was inactivated in January 1951 after the battering and inactivation of three of its divisions. The corps was reconstituted in April 1952 and committed to the front east of the center, fighting between U.S. IX and X corps, and remained there until the cease fire. The ROK emerged from the war as the fourth largest army in the world.

The Republic of Korea Air Force (ROKAF) was formally established on 1 October 1949 with L-4 Liaison aircraft and about 1000 men. When war broke out they were placed under the command of Far East Air Force. They were used primarily in reconnaissance and spotting missions, and the efforts to build the Korean Air Force stressed pilot training and ground support. At the end of the war its force consisted of several dozen L-1, L-2, L-4, L-16 and 78 F-51D planes, as well as a C-47 transport plane. Despite the preparation and considerable effort to increase training, the ROK Air Force did not play a significant role in the fighting during the war.

On 15 August 1947 what had been the Chosun Coast Guard was renamed the Republic of Korea Navy (ROKN). At the time its ships consisted of eighteen minesweepers, some Japanese ships used as patrol boats, a landing ship and an oiler. The small navy purchased, through subscription of ROK officers and men, a submarine chaser (*Bakd Du San*). Three additional submarine chasers (*Kum Kang San, Sam Kak San, Chi Ri San*) were en route from Hawaii when the war broke out. The Navy had about 5,800 men under the command of rear Admiral Sohn Won Il. They were first assigned to U.S. Task Group 96.7, but in September were reassigned to the UN Blockading and Escort Force (95). During the war more vessels were added, some transferred from the U.S. Navy, but the force never became very large.

Later the ROKN was primarily involved in coastal patrols and in securing and supplying the garrisons of off shore islands. Nevertheless, while considered primarily inactive, the ROKN did successfully conduct one of the few naval engagements of the war. On 25 June 1950, ROK Patrol Craft 701 spotted an armed North Korean transport eighteen miles off the coast of Pusan, and heading to cut off ROK troops at Pusan. The small craft engaged and sank the transport with a loss of 600 men, thus preventing the attack.

The Korean Marine Corps (KMC) was a small force established from volunteers taken from the Navy. Advised by U.S. Marines and organized along American lines, it was a component of the ROK Navy. At the beginning of the war it consisted of two battalions, about 1,200 men. The 1st KMC Regiment and the 5th Independent KMC Battalion were organized at the Pusan Perimeter in 1950. The two units together served as the Fourth Regiment to the 1st Marine Division and fought throughout the war as assigned. A second KMC regiment and artillery battalion was raised toward the end of 1952 and served with the Western Island Command and Eastern Island Command to provide protection for the United Nations–controlled islands off both coasts.

The armed forces were supported by members of the Korean National Police. The police force was originally established by the Japanese during occupation and then reorganized by the U.S. military government in 1945. Augmented with U.S. occupation forces, the police officers were located in each county, and there were several stations and substations. Para-military in organization, several of the KNP combat battalions were formed up during the war to provide counter-guerrilla security duties behind the lines.

In addition to the regular troops, South Korea also provided individuals who were embedded into existing United Nations outfits as replacements. Called KATUSA (Korean Augmented to United States Army), they were primarily civilians pulled off the streets, uniformed and equipped, and sent in to beef up the head count in United Nations units. They were first initiated in the U.S. 7th Infantry Division, where as many as three out of ten men in the units were KATUSA. The KATUSA troops were either well received and adopted by the host units or, unfortunately, were badly mistreated. There was also some concern about their loyalty, and historian Max Hastings suggests they were primarily untrustworthy.

Despite the spectacular cross country capabilities of the American three-quarter ton truck and the jeep, they were no match for the terrain troops had to contend with in Korea. The final leg of most every journey was conducted by Korean carriers who, using the A frame back pack, were expected to transport 50 pounds of supplies a distance of ten miles. Long distance hauls, of which there were many, were covered by the creation of a shuttle system made up of a series of six-mile hauls between relay points. In nearly every war it has been necessary to shift troops away from battle. These assignments have most always been done on an ad hoc basis with few plans. Without the civilian worker in Korea it would have been necessary to assign whole divisions of combat troops to operate the supply lines.

From the beginning the Civilian Transport Corps was involved in carrying supplies. This effort was organized in March 1951 as the CTC but was soon reorganized as the Korean Service Corps (KSC) on 14 July 1951 and expanded to include over 20 regiments that provided porters, laborers and

Korean Service Corps bearers head up to Outpost Kelly.

road repair, but mostly the movement of supplies and evacuation of the wounded. The force eventually expanded to more than 100,000 men and women who were known by the American troops as "mules" and "yo-bos" and the British as "Chiggies." They served under military control and discipline for periods of six months, but often volunteered to remain in service. At one time there was consideration given to the fact that they could be armed with old Japanese weapons and added to the fighting force when necessary, but this never occurred.

Fighting alone at first, the Republic of Korea was soon joined by a U.S. task force, then occupation troops brought over from Japan, and finally by many member nations of the United Nations. For them the war has never really been over and the Republic of Korea did not sign the cease fire. They remain at war, and ever ready for the fighting to break out, even today. The ROKA was involved from the firing of the first bullet to the most recent of outbreaks along the DMZ.

The relationship between the ROK leadership and the UNC had been shaky at best. When word came down about the firing of General MacArthur there was considerable concern. The president and the general had difficulties but had generally gotten along. Rhee felt that his loss would mean that there

Republic of Korea troops move up to the front line.

was far less a chance that Korea could be unified, and his support became more irrational.

The true number involved and the costs of battle for the ROK fighting force will probably never be known. In addition to those in the official armed forces, thousands served in partisan and guerrilla units, and some in unidentified independent bands. The casualty rates among the ROK were the highest United Nations losses of the war. The number killed in action ranges from 137,899 to 227,800. The wounded are numbered between 450,472 and 717,500. The records also list from 24,495 to 43,500 as missing in action and

8,343 as prisoners of war. There is no adequate count of the hundreds of thousands of civilians who were killed during the war.

Not even the most optimistic of military planners had any hope that the Republic of Korea would be able to pay its own way. Any extended costs would, in fact, have proven to have serious consequences on the economic situation in this devastatingly poor country. The military contemplated that the cost of equipping a Korean division would be between 40 and 42 million dollars, while maintaining the division in combat would, depending on the intensity of the fighting, amount to between 85 to 110 million. This was less than the cost of the American division, but it needs to be kept in mind that this was in addition to the provisioning of the U.S troops. At the end of the war it was estimated that the cost of supplying the ROK amounted to something over three billion dollars.

There was at the time, as there is now, a great deal of criticism of the fighting capacity of the ROK Army. While there are certainly some grounds for the concern, there is some evidence that it became an easy generalization often applied but not always warranted. The *Times* of London, 25 October 1950, gave an unflattering report of the behavior of ROK troops in North Korea,[38] and this was picked up and became the theme of many media reports. Colonel Paul Freeman of the U.S. 32nd Infantry was bitter about his experience, but saw some reason for the poor performance. "It was pitiful. But it wasn't their fault. They lacked the training, the motivation, and the equipment to do the job. Whenever their units were on our flanks, we found that they were liable to vanish without notice."[39]

But, what could have been expected? These men and women had been occupied for nearly fifty years and unlike many of their North Korean neighbors had not been involved in fighting a prolonged civil war in China. They had little to none of the traditions of a modern army and, up to that point, few resources for arms and supplies. Much of the loyalty of the individuals still rested along regional lines and few were sure who the national government was. Internal strife had been rampant since the rise of Rhee and the harshness of his regime had done little to encourage a sense of national loyalty. That they were able to provide what resistance they did against North Korea is a subject for more consideration.

By 1951, however, the ROK army was beginning to show some signs of the training effort that Eighth Army had put into effect. The units were more cohesive and there had been an improvement in officer selection and training as well, and the individual was becoming more acquainted with the modern weapons.

Nevertheless, the American reaction to them, as well as the reaction of troops from other nations, was based on the belief that they were often an unstable entity. At several times during the war the UNC had considered that the best response to troop shortages was to expand the size of the ROK Army. But as this was considered, and the U.S. believed that an expanded South Korean force would release the U.S. from the necessity of raising more troops, there was always the shadow of the belief that they were not good fighting material and this consideration was delayed. General James A. Van Fleet, when in command of Eighth Army, argued that until they had demonstrated competent leadership and a will to make a stand, the U.S. should not be arming and equipping additional ROK forces.[40]

The South Koreans have not forgotten the war or the nations that fought in it. Libraries, museums and memorials dot the Korean nation and celebrations are conducted in memory of battles and sites. A monument has been raised for nearly every nation that sent troops to fight. They even raised a statue of General Douglas MacArthur near the site of the Inchon landing. As late as October 2012 they were conducting honorary ceremonies in the United States and other nations to continue the recognition of those who came to their aid. The Korean government helps sponsor veterans revisit programs for those who fought and wish to return to see modern South Korea.

Thailand

Since 1932 when the military, backed by the civilian population, overthrew the monarchy and instituted a constitutional government, political affairs in Thailand were dominated by the military. The nation had been involved with the Korean question early on and had participated in the ongoing government as a member of the United Nations Commission for the Unification and Rehabilitation of Korea (UNCURK).

Leader Phibun Songhram was concerned about the security of the nation and was worried about the many Communist uprisings in the region which he felt were threatening his nation. He believed that a contribution to the cause in Korea would encourage the U.S. Congress into giving further consideration to his nation's requests for financial and military aid. As a member of the UN since 1946, Thailand responded to the call for help by originally announcing that it would send a full regimental combat team (about the size of a British brigade).

In time the Thai government deployed the 21st Royal Thailand Regiment that consisted of 3 infantry battalions, or a total of about 2,100 men. In Korea they were affiliated with several units, including the 187th Airborne Regimental Combat Team, the U.S. 1st Cavalry, 2nd Infantry Division, 3rd Infantry division and the 29th British Commonwealth Brigade. At its peak strength 3,600

Thai soldiers were deployed. The advanced elements of the Thai unit arrived in Korea in August of 1950 and some troops remained in Korea in defensive and occupational positions until June of 1972.

The government of Thailand also contributed four frigates to the cause in Korea as well as a cargo transport. One of the frigates, the *Prasae*, was lost when it went aground during a snowstorm and could not be recovered. It was destroyed by UN forces to keep it from falling into enemy hands. The others were the HTMS *Bangprakong*, *Bangpako*, and *Tachin*. These were former U.S. patrol gunboats that had been purchased by Thailand. The destroyed *Prasae* was replaced by the USS *Gallup*, thus there were actually five ships involved. A total of 2,485 sailors served during the war. The frigates and gunboats were assigned to Task Force 95, and provided escort and blocking service in the Yellow Sea off Korea's west coast.

Deployed to Korea as well was a cargo and transport flight, the Douglas C-47 Skytrain. It arrived on 24 June 1951 and was attached to the U.S. 21st Troop Carrier Squadron (Medium) and flew missions in Korea, moving men and equipment back and forth from Japan to Korea.

Thailand's involvement was not without controversy. At first Thailand had announced that it would send a full regimental combat team and a large headquarters staff. When they arrived the headquarters was as expected, but the troops consisted of no more than a battalion; some 300 men strong. The headquarters was well out of proportion. The large staff included judge advocates, medical staff officer (without a hospital), a director of finance, adjutant-generals and a quartermaster section, a Red Cross and welfare staff. They were commanded by a major general. In time the unit was sent to the rear to train reinforcements. The residual battalion, however, proved to be composed of good soldiers who fought bravely.[41]

On New Year's Day the British 27th Brigade was fighting hard along the Uijeongbu road. But the brigade was spread out over territory that should have been held by a division, and thus the line consisted of numerous gaps. In an effort to support the defense, a battalion of Thai infantry was attached to the brigade to hold the line. The Thais made the effort but suffering unduly from the cold, they were eventually withdrawn and sent into positions in the rear.

Other than the fact that they provided their own transportation to Korea and their summer uniforms, the U.S. provided all supplies and services. In addition to the normal 1000 man rations provided the American troops, they asked for an additional 800 pounds of bread, a 10 percent increase in salt, and a 10 percent increase in canned meat; in return they were willing to delete half of the potatoes usually offered and 25 percent of the peanut butter. The Thai troops were uncomfortable with the immersion heaters provided to clean their mess gear and preferred to wash their utensils in the closest stream. Their troops generally had smaller feet and required special replacements.

In the course of the fighting 6,500 Royal Thai forces were involved and had a loss of 129 killed in action, 1,139 wounded and 5 missing.[42] Thailand was the last country other than the U.S. to withdraw its military presence in 1972.

They were generally regarded as good fighters and well respected for their toughness, but some reports state that the Thais were numbed by the cold despite the fact they were heavily clothed in U.S. issue, and sometimes had to be relieved.

Turkey

Of all the foreign troops that fought in the Korean War the Turks are perhaps the best remembered by other ranks who fought there. They were often identified as the standard of toughness. At the beginning of World War II Turkey took a neutral stance but increasing pressure from the Soviet Union eventually led the small nation to declare war on the Axis Powers in 1945. Following the war the leadership of the Democratic Party was committed to the advances of economic reform and national growth. With a boom in agriculture investments and new trade agreements, the country of some twenty million enjoyed an economic and population expansion. During this time Turkey received considerable economic aid from the United States.

By 1950, more pressure from the Soviet Union, primarily regarding the control of the Turkish Straits, meant that Turkey was looking for allies. It did not consider itself to be Asian, and in fact protested the Western press using that alignment. Almost in desperation Turkish President Bayar went looking for security and turned to NATO, which it would join in 1952.

At the time the Korean War broke out Turkey was anxious to show its allegiance to that cause as well. Spurred on by a fear of the Soviet Union and the expansion of Communism, the Turks felt it was necessary to send a message to the Western powers, and immediately supported the UN decision. They were facing hostiles from Afghanistan at their borders, and wanted to encourage a defense treaty with the United States. On 25 July the president agreed to send troops to support Korea in an effort to maximize its cooperation with the West.

Nevertheless, the decision was controversial, and the prime minister was highly criticized for committing troops without parliament's permission. There was as well some discontent among those Turkish citizens who believed the action to be in support of what many considered the expansion of imperialist powers. Some of the resentment carried over to the battlefield, where the Turks felt the Americans did not provide them with enough intelligence, often leaving them out of the loop.

The advanced party of the Turkish Brigade (Turkish Armed Forces Command) arrived in Pusan on 12 October 1950. The main body numbering 5,190 troops arrived on the 17th. They served in Korea all during the war until the cease fire agreement. The Turkish force was composed of a full brigade headquarters and a regimental combat team. The troops were a mixture of volunteers and conscripts, many from the Anatolian peasantry, which tended to add to the language problem. Before leaving Turkey, the commander, Brigadier General Tahzin Yazici, who had commanded a division at Gallipoli in World War I, was given a flag signed in their own blood by the students of Galata High School in Istanbul.[43] Colonel Celal Dora was the assistant commander.

The Turks also brought a headquarters unit when they arrived, but unlike many of the other contingents they took their headquarters into the field with them. After its arrival the brigade bivouacked near Taegu, where it underwent training and received U.S. weapons and equipment. The Turkish Brigade was one of the larger participants in the U.N. Command and one of the most involved in the fighting.

On their arrival at Pusan on 12 October the Turkish Brigade was fully equipped except for weapons. When arriving at Taegu the Turks settled down to receive advanced training and to receive additional supplies. They were attached first to the U.S. IX corps and then to the U.S. 25th Infantry division. At first the brigade was used primarily for the defense of the supply lines as the U.N. advanced into North Korea. On the 20th of November they were transferred to the reserves of IX Corps where on the 26th at Tokchon they entered their first combat mission assigned to guard the flanks of the 2nd Infantry Division. Their commander, General Yazici, apparently misunderstood his orders and believed he was to withdraw and he did so, leaving the flank open. This would lead to some concern by U.S. commanders that the Turks could not be relied on.

They were employed again at Wawan, where they came up against an onslaught of Communist forces. On orders they moved into the hills near Kunu-ri to limit the expansion of Chinese forces in the area, where they were again ambushed, a good many of their vehicles destroyed, and the Turks suffered heavy casualties. Nearly half of the Turkish force had been destroyed but they had retained their weapons and ammunition and were still able to fight. Under orders they drew back to an area near Chongchon River as the Chinese kept pushing on the UN forces. By the first of December the Turks reached Pyongyang, complaining that the allies had failed to support them.

Elements of the Turkish brigade left Pyongyang to support the 25th Infantry on Kangwha-do Island and delayed the enemy advance across the Han River. After suffering several significant attacks, the Turks were evacuated to Kaesong to recuperate and were attached to the 2nd Infantry Division. There was considerable unrest there as the language problem grew to major proportions; some U.S. officers complained that the Turks were unruly, while the Turks were complaining that they were not being adequately supplied. It took a great deal of effort on both parts to resolve the issues, but it was done and after two weeks in which to reorganize they were moved to Sosa-ri.

In January 1951 they became part of the battle force sent to retake Seoul. Following a long artillery bombardment the Turks moved ahead with bayonets fixed to overrun the Chinese and regained some of the respect they had lost through miscommunication. After the battle at Seoul they dug in near the Han River with the orders to guard Kimpo Airfield. The following month they moved forward to Hill 431, where they launched a series of attacks against the Chinese in yet more bayonet charges. Despite the courage and aggressiveness they suffered major losses in April 1951 while defending Seoul.

After once more regrouping they were put into service in campaigns that moved north to the Iron Triangle, and then were assigned to defend several of the forward outposts, primarily Nevada, Berlin and East Berlin some eleven miles northeast of Panmunjom. There they held the line until the last of May, when they were ordered to withdraw. Between the dates of November 1950 and July 1953 the Turkish brigade participated in the battles of the Kunu-ri diversion, the Kumyangjangni-Imjin attacks where it gained a considerable reputation, the Chorwon-Seoul diversion, the Taegyewonni defense, the Barhar-Kumhwa attacks, and the Wegas defensive battle.

Unfortunately language barriers led to continual misunderstandings and left the Turks with a deep distrust of the Americans. They suggested that in the future they would like to be assigned to fight alongside allies who would still be in their positions in the morning and willing to fight.[44] Despite these moments of irritation the Turks were considered by most as some of the best fighters, most likely to hold ground under difficult situations.

The Turks paid a high price for their involvement in Korea. A total of 14,936 served during the war. They report that 717 were killed in action, 2,246 wounded, 168 missing in action and 766 taken prisoner. The Turks were considered tenacious prisoners and none of the prisoners either died or accepted Communism while imprisoned. Many historians considered the Turks to be the standard against which prisoner of war behavior was considered best. The Turks did not collaborate and when one of their numbers was considered to be cooperating they killed him themselves. When the war ended 243 prisoners of war were repatriated.

In honor of the Turkish Brigade which fought so gallantly at the battles of Geumyangjang-ri, Jangsungcheon, and Nevada, the Ministry of Defense in the Republic of Korea built a monument at Dongbak-ri, Sung-myeon, Yongin, and Gyeonggi Province on 6 September 1974. In recognition of their service General Douglas MacArthur said the following: "In these concerned days, the heroism shown by the Turks has given hope to the American nation. It has inculcated them with courage. The American public fully appreciates the value of the services rendered by the Turkish Brigade."[45] In fact the Turks, known also as the Anatolian Lions, had captured the hearts of the American people. *Time* magazine praised "the Turkish Brigade for its many courageous battles and for creating a favorable effect on the whole UN force."[46] Later an American radio station in December 1950 relayed thanks to the "Turkish Brigade's heroes for giving hope to a demoralized American nation."[47]

While the Turks were authorized to wear the United Nations Service Medal, they either refused to wear it, or wore it on a background of a dark red ribbon. The reason; the colors of the metal are the national colors of their bitter historical rival Greece. The Turks do not give out medals for valor. They were, however, as amenable as any soldier to a pretty face. One young man remembered seeing the American actress Debbie Reynolds at a USO show near Seoul where "the majority of the show consisted of her taking off a pair of ermine cuffs."[48]

The Turks were some of the strongest defenders of the United Nations policy and were not inclined to waver in that support. When the rapid retreat before the advancing Chinese Volunteers had dampened much of the confidence in the U.S. military powers, the Turks remained steadfastly supportive of the American policy. They also seemed to trust the American artillery. Corporal Wayne Funmaker, manning a fire control bunker for 7th DivArty, told his buddy back home, "When the Turks want fire, they want it right at their doorsteps, and that is where we give it to them."[49] When hearing the announcement that General MacArthur had been recalled, the Turks, even then, expressed strong support for the decision. The Turkish contingent had become so well received, and the support of the nation in international matters so acceptable, that on 25 April 1951 the Pentagon announced that Turkey was now ranked equally with Western Europe in the priority system for receiving weapons and ammunition.[50]

Though the Turks were generally popular with the UN Command, the command would report having some problems with them. They were primarily criticized for not always following orders, but much of this had come more from language problems rather than obstinacy. They were well known for being able to improvise when supplies were lacking. Perhaps more than any other country the Turkish Brigade was recognized for its hard fighting and heroic involvement. General Walton Walker reported, "The heroic soldiers of a heroic nation, you have saved the Eighth Army and the Tenth Army Corps from encirclement and the 2nd Division from destruction."[51] U.S. Senator Claude Pepper announced, "There is no one left who doesn't know that the Turks, our glorious allies, are hard warriors and they have accomplished a great deal at the front."[52] It was generally believed that the Turks were good on offense but not as good on defense. The Turks' use of the bayonet led General Matthew Ridgway to order all infantry units to fix bayonets.

More than any others of the allied nations fighting in Korea, the Turks seem to have come out with the best reputation. Lieutenant General G. G. Martin of Great Britain wrote, "While the Turks were for a long time fighting against the enemy and dying, the British and Americans were withdrawing. The Turks, who were out of ammunition, affixed their bayonets and attacked the enemy and there ensured a terrible hand to hand combat. The Turks succeeded in withdrawing by continuous combat and by carrying their injured comrades on their backs. They paraded at Pyongyang with their heads held high."[53]

Turkey provided its initial equipment but all resupply and logistic services, including transportation, were provided directly by the United States. Since they did not eat pork and American rations were heavy on pork,[54] their rations were altered in order to provide additions to what was in the American rations for 1000 men. On agreement they received an additional 23 gallons of vegetable oil, 3 pounds of dehydrated onion, and 23 pounds of beans, an extra two pounds of bread a day per man that was baked with un-bleached flour, and they favored a very thick and sweet coffee. From what was offered they rejected 50 pounds of American coffee and all sweet potatoes, canned corn, pickles and mustard. A special effort was made and a processing firm in Japan began making separate diets for the Turkish soldiers. Nevertheless, they were always happy to receive the weekly supply of ice cream. At the end of the war the bill sent to Turkey for supplies was $62,259.00

There were some other complaints, among them the medical staff claimed they were often infested with parasites that made medical attention difficult. And, for religious reasons as well a privacy, the Turks often bathed with their clothes on. They maintained a strict morality and were often disillusioned at the Western sexual behavior.

The Turks contributed a good deal to the successes of the UN troops, of that there is little doubt. General Ridgway reported on their success after the Battle of Taegyewonni, "I had heard of the fame of the Turkish soldiers before I came to Korea. The truth is I had not really believed what I had heard. But I now understand that in fact you are the best and most trustworthy soldiers of the world."[55] But there were other problems. One had to do with the long term hatred between the Turks and the Australian and New Zealanders, against whom they had fought in World War I. As it turned out there were few, if any, conflicts between these nations, but the possibility remained a concern. Few of the Turks spoke English and there was a lack of translators available, and the few provided were not fluent. Another problem was with supply. The Turks, to a man, seemed to have much larger feet than Americans and the supply of boots became a problem.

While Turkey emerged from the Korean War with an enhanced reputation in the West, it did increase their difficulties with the Eastern bloc.

Union of South Africa

The Union of South Africa was one of the more prosperous and advanced countries on the continent. It was the historical predecessor to the present-day Republic of South Africa and came into being on 31 May 1910 with the unification of Cape, Natal, Transvaal, and the Orange Free State. After having fought the Italians in East Africa during World War II, South Africa had been a founding member of the United Nations and was supportive of the fact the UN was taking action but, despite the fact that they were reverently anti–Communist, they were reluctant to send troops.

The 1950s were the beginning of years of turmoil as the Transvaal Indian Congress began its decade of defiance with the passage, in July 1950, of the Population Registration Act. The act required all individuals to be registered in accordance with racial characteristics, beginning a long period of apartheid. The nation, one of four of the 54 nations in Africa that was independent, was the home for more than 13.5 million persons. They were fiercely nationalistic but not unwilling to be involved internationally. The Nationalist government came to power in 1948. Prime Minister Dr. D. F. Malan, who had stood against South African involvement in World War II, nevertheless felt that it was necessary for South Africa to join the fight against the aggression of Communism. Just a year after the Union of South Africa had responded to the call for help in dealing with the Berlin Blockade, the nation responded again, this time in Korea.

The road to involvement was not completely easy, for the Union government felt that Korea might not be an isolated incident and the possibility of other acts of aggression could not be ruled out. It was, therefore, reluctant to weaken its own position by sending forces to Korea. The justification it gave included commitments for the defense of its continent in case of a larger war, the strategic position of South Africa in case of war, and the inadequacy of forces and equipment. South Africa was assured by the United States that if it needed help then help would be provided, "not as a token for propaganda effects but actually to help with the fighting."[56]

There were other factors. The government of South Africa was appealing to the UN for aid in settling claims against it by a former German colony. Inside the nation there was considerable political pressure against sending troops to fight outside the continent. There were also suspicions about any foreign power and concern over any kind of foreign alliance that might commit the country to further action. But at the same time, the government wanted to establish relations with the Western powers as security against the growth of Communism. It was a balancing act that had to be solved.

An additional problem is that the Union of South Africa was not in good favor in London. It was in the process of applying the rigid policies of apartheid that affronted the British sense of fair play. Nevertheless, while openly announcing it had no political or economic interest whatsoever in Korea, the South African government agreed on 29 July that rather than send a military unit, it would call for a volunteer force to serve as attachments to the three armed services of Great Britain. However, much to the relief of an embarrassed Great Britain, South Africa changed its mind and decided on 4 August to send instead the trained aircrew and technical manpower needed to maintain a fighter squadron that would be placed under U.S. command.

The unit that was offered to the UN was the South African Air Force's (SAAF) 2 Squadron known as Cheetahs. The squadron consisted of 49 officer and 157 other ranks, all of whom were volunteers. They were assigned to the U.S 18th Fighter Bomber Wing and flew F-51 Mustang fighters purchased from the United States. In 1953 the squadron was re-equipped with F-86F Sabres. The members of the unit, all white, were volunteers and veterans of the Italian campaign. They had to be volunteers since the government believed that conscription would cause dissent between the Boers and the British.

On 26 September 1950, the squadron left for Johnson Base in Tokyo prior to moving on to Korea. In Korea it joined with the UN air efforts at K-9 (outside Pusan). The first flight of four F-51 D Mustangs departed for Korea on 16 November and their first sortie was flown on the 19th. The squadron was primarily assigned to ground attack and interdiction missions. At first located at K-24 (Pyongyang East Air Field), they were moved to K-13 (Suwon Airbase), then to K-10 (Chinhae Airbase) and finally to Osan (K-55). In January 1953 the squadron was converted to F-86F Sabre jets and on 11 March 1953 they flew their first sortie with the new jets. During their time in Korea the South African Air Force flew 12,067 sorties, during which they lost 74 out of 97 Mustang planes and 4 out of 22 Sabre jets.

They primarily flew strafing and escort missions, taking out trains, tunnels, bridges, and transportation and communication hubs. Because their original Mustangs were slow they concentrated on ground support. In April of 1951 the squadron joined with the Australian and Canadian pilots, and even granted the British permission to assign the targets. The U.S. wanted to form a Commonwealth Wing in which to consolidate the Commonwealth forces, but South Africa refused, saying they preferred to work with the Americans, so joined them. Then in July 1952 it took part in Operation Pressure Pump, a 24 hour blitz on the city of Pyongyang.

All in all the South African squadron was a significant addition to the fact that the UN could take, and then keep, air superiority. Unfortunately most of its achievements are lost in the records that were maintained primarily by the larger commands. The South African volunteers were considered professional and likeable. One Marine pilot said "half of them [are] square-headed blond Dutchmen with heavy accents and funny first names, the rest [have] proper English types named Nigel or Geoff. Good soldiers,"[57] and described a British flight mechanic as "good blokes."

Casualties consisted of 34 pilots and two other ranks with 20 killed in action and 16 wounded in action. Eight of their pilots became prisoners of war. At the close of the war eight South African prisoners of war were repatriated. During their service, members of the unit were awarded a total of 797 medals, including 2 Silver Stars, 3 Legions of Merit, 55 Distinguished Flying Crosses, and 40 Bronze Stars. The Republic of South Africa Monument is located at Yongyidong, Pyeongtaek-si, in Gyeonggi Province. It was dedicated on 3 October 1974 in honor of the South Africans who fought for freedom.

The bill for goods and services supplied by the United States was 278,902.00 dollars.

During the war the atmosphere in the government was changing. In October South Africa withdrew from the wartime conferences and refused to sign the United Nations resolution that, in March 1954, warned China against any further aggression. It did not take part in the prisoner exchange agreement or attend the postwar conference in 1954

United Kingdom

In 1950 Great Britain was in a tough spot with pressures and obligations weighing heavily on its resources. It had been severely wounded as a nation during both World War I and World War II and was dealing with the decomposition of the British Empire. At the same time it was fighting Communists in Malaya and Kenya. And while maintaining a deep and long-time friendship with the United States, it had substantially different views of the Far East. It was much more comfortable with Communist China and had recognized the nation early after the civil war, and had established significant trade relations. These were an easy fit. The U.K. did not understand what leaders saw as an American obsession with Chiang Kai Shek and the idea that Taiwan was the real China. What they wanted was an increase in America's contribution both to their own recovery and to the strengthening of NATO. There was some consideration given to trying to avoid becoming involved in the problems of Korea; neutrality seemed a positive but distant hope.

However, the U.K. reversed this decision on 25 July as the Foreign Office raised the even more pressing question of affronting the United States and the growing fear of an expanding Cold War. There was a profound difference of opinion, however, about what was happening in South Korea. The British did not believe that the North Korean invasion was being acted out on the orders of Moscow, and while they certainly identified the Soviet Union as a threat, they did not consider Communism in all its nationalist implications as evil. Britain was friendlier toward China, and in August 1950 it voted to allow the People's Republic of China to be recognized in the United Nations. Like France, however, Great Britain saw involvement in the Korean War as a means to gain American support for its colonial policies. Thus every step it took was taken with considerable concern over its effect on relations with both the U.S. and China. While America's closest allies, it was nevertheless aware that it needed to avoid provoking the Chinese into acting either in Hong Kong or Malaya. Nor did it want to increase the Chinese Communist dependence on the Soviet Union, and citing that as a reason, voted against the United States' proposal to blockade the Chinese mainland as advocated by the UN in May 1951. As the war progressed, leaders blamed much of the problem with China on the belligerence of General MacArthur, and exerted what influence they had to counteract him.

And yet they were there when the United States needed them, offering immediate help. Almost without hesitation they offered the UN command of the warships that were already in the area. Their communications offering naval vessels in support of the war, however, contained the important clause, "It is important that no British forces should participate in operations related to Formosa."[58]

While all this was going on the United Kingdom had responded almost immediately to the United Nations' call for military support. On 28 June a message arrived from Admiral Sir Patrick Brind, commander in chief, Far East Station, Hong Kong: "I shall be very glad to know of any operations in which my ships could help" and reported that Admiral Andrewes' carrier the HMS *Triumph*, and the HMS *Belfast*, HMS *Jamaica* and two destroyer HMS *Cossack* and HMS *Consort*, plus three frigates were available. In a cable to the

A Scots piper plays before a mission call.

leading British delegation in Washington the minister of defense explained: "We consider such demonstrations of solidarity are more important than the actual strength of the forces deployed, and we hope other members of the United Nations will quickly follow suit."[59]

The British also made available the hospital ship HMS *Maine*. For some time it was the only hospital ship in Korea. Formerly an Italian cruise ship, taken in the war, it had been in Kobe, Japan, and when the war broke out it was quickly sent to Korea. Small and out of date, it nevertheless served two tours until February 1952, when it was replaced with newer and larger ships.

Well-armed and trained British commandos were rushed from Hong Kong to make an immediate appearance. However, despite what may have appeared as an instantaneous reaction, the decision had not been reached easily. The Labour Party was divided by the fact that the conditions in Korea did not pose an immediate threat to Britain's interest. With all their colonial concerns Korea appeared to be low on their list of priorities. There was also concern that their actions not affront the Chinese government, for there was the legitimate concern about what the Chinese reaction might be. The British colony at Hong Kong was intensely vulnerable. The British government had gained some favor when it recognized the People's Republic of China in January 1950 and was not anxious to lose it. As well, the British had extended themselves by their commitment to defending the government in Malays against Communist insurgency. They had also promised the French aid in their war in Indochina. With these concerns in mind the Cabinet, on 6 July 1950, decided against sending further military forces to Korea.

While the Americans perceived Communism as a unified ideology and identified it as evil, Great Britain was more focused on the Soviet Union as the primary threat. It was more inclined to recognize that Communism came in a variety of forms. The Labour Party did not put the People's Republic of China in the same category as the Soviet Union, nor did it see China as anything like the threat imposed by the Soviet Union. It was aware, as well, that it had over reached its resources in promises of aid to other governments. On 6 July the cabinet decided against sending further military forces but then, suffering from a bad case of reality, it reversed itself on 25 July as American pressure increased.

There was something else that was not well understood by Americans. On 13 May 1953 the new president, Dwight Eisenhower, admitted to the members of the National Security Council that he was having some serious troubles with America's allies in Europe. Pointing out the difficulty with the United Kingdom, he said that the relations between the nations were at their lowest point since World War II.[60] What Eisenhower should have understood, considering his long and intimate association with the European nations, was that what Britain and many of the European nations feared the most was the outbreak of another world war and that they saw the policies of the United States in the Korean conflict as moving the world precariously in that direction.

One of the unanswered questions that remain to be given serious consideration about the war is the role that President Eisenhower played in it. Certainly his experience with Korea had been limited and his promise to go to Korea to see for himself was little other than a three day trip visiting various commands. He had been against the withdrawal of troops from Korea in 1949 and yet as a member of the Joint Chiefs of Staff he had advised the president that there was little strategic advantage in maintaining a military force in Korea. It is doubtful that he had any clearly constructed policy toward Korea.[61]

In meetings between Great Britain and the Truman administration it was made very clear that while the British would never desert the cause, and would support the United States as much as possible, they were not happy with the unrealistic and dangerous polices being considered in relation to Communist China. When the Chinese mounted their offensive in Korea it caused severe criticism in Great Britain and they reverted to recalling that they had not been in favor of crossing the 38th parallel or the push to the Yalu, and believed that the world was now suffering the consequences of those acts.

Nevertheless, the British continued to send naval vessels. To participate in the naval war the British provided four Glory class aircraft carriers, the *Triumph*, *Theseus*, *Glory* and *Ocean*, which served in rotation during the Korean War. From these carriers the British flew Fairey Fireflies, Seafires or Sea Furies, and operated in conjunction with U.S. Navy light or escort carriers. Their primary mission was with the West Coast Blocking Force. Ten different squadrons saw duty. In addition to the carriers the British supplied six light cruisers, nine destroyers, seven frigates, eight sloops, and more than twenty-eight oilers and miscellaneous support vessels and were involved in almost every naval action of the war.

The HMS *Jamaica* was the first UN nation's ship to be attacked and strafed by enemy aircraft. During the fight it suffered three casualties; later it sighted and sank floating mines 25 miles north of the Changsangot area. Joining up with the HMS *Black Swan*, it met and sank four North Korean gunboats. During the evacuation of retreating troops at Chinnampo the HMS *Kenya*, *Belfast*, *Jamaica*, *Cossack*, *Consort*, *Swan Black*, and *Alacrity* were protected by planes from the HMS *Theseus*. These were the first ships into Chinnampo on 10 November, and the water was declared open on the 20th.

Prior to the invasion of Inchon, Eugene Clark's survey team was delivered ashore from the HMS *Charity*.[62] On 12 October 1952 it was the same *Charity* that radioed, "Have succeeded in stopping train, but need assistance as I am almost out of star shells."[63] The *Charity* and its sister ship the *Crusader* were a part of the "Trainbusters Club" of Task Force 95, which consisted of ships that had destroyed trains on the rails by firing inshore.

The Royal Air Force did not maintain fighter squadrons in Korea; its entire air support effort came from the planes on their carriers. It did contribute two squadrons of flying boats, an Air Observation Flight and a Light Liaison Flight. The 88th and 209th Squadrons flew the Short Sunderland flying boats that operated primarily in the Tsushima straits and enforced the UN blockade. The 1903 Independent Air Observation Post flight, using the Auster Air Observation Post 6 aircraft, provided observation for royal Artillery personnel. The 1913 Light Liaison Flight operated in support of the 1st Commonwealth Division and flew Auster Air Observation Post 6 and U.S. L-19A Bird Dog aircraft.

On 29 August 1950 the first ground force, the 27th Brigade, arrived in Korea and joined the defense of the Pusan Perimeter. Joined by a 3rd Battalion and the Royal Australian Regiment, the Brigunitde was renamed the 27th Commonwealth Brigade. The British Royal Marines were active in the Korean War, having taken over the role of the commando in 1946. The first Royal Marines to participate in the Korean War were the 13 Far East Station Marines located in Singapore, who were assigned to the Eighth Army Raider Company in July 1950. For the first year they conducted a significant number of coastal raids until disbanded in April 1951, when they joined the 41 Independent Commando Royal Marines. The 41st was already in Korea, having arrived in October 1950. It served with the 1st Marine Division, after which they conducted coastal raids and occupied small islands in support of U.S. Navy operations. It was disbanded in February 1952 as the need for its special services had lessened.

The first British troops traveling from the homeland, the 1st Middlesex Regiment and the Argyll and Sutherland Highlanders, arrived on 29 August 1950. The last British trooper left Korea in July 1957. During the war, the troops entered the Naktong bridgehead and advanced with 8th Army to the Yalu. The British brigade and then the Commonwealth Division were engaged in most of the significant battles in Korea. They were involved in the retreat from Chosin, and participated in Operation Killer and the road back. In late April they were targeted by the Chinese, and the Glostershire Regiment found itself isolated and facing overwhelming odds. This battle for Hill 235 occurred on 22–25 April when the 1st Battalion Gloucestershire Regiment, the "Glorious Gloucestershire," was assigned to Hill 235, a vantage point that overlooked the Imjin River. After supporting the withdrawal of the Belgian infantry from the far side of the river, they were attacked by a massive Chinese offensive. No sooner had the Belgians crossed the river than they were ambushed at close range. Holding the line was essential to allowing the Belgians to escape. An estimated 750 men who were totally surrounded and with no chance for replacements withstood seven successive assaults until, nearly annihilated, they determined to withdraw. Afterwards, Ernest Moscrop remembered the battle and summed it up simply, "It was worth it." When the battle was over more than 600 had been killed or captured, with 58 managing to get back to UN lines. In July 1, 1951, the British formed into the 1st British Commonwealth Division, after which it remained online primarily on the Samichon.

During the course of the war somewhere between 68,000 and 90,000 Britons served in Korea, depending on when you count the end date. Of these 1,078 were killed in action, 2,612 were wounded and 1,102 were taken prisoner or missing. Eighty-two prisoners have not been returned. At the end of the war 977 prisoners of war were repatriated.

With the exception of a few vehicles, ammunition, gasoline and perishable food supplies, the British got most of their logistical support from their own sources. Even then the bill submitted to Great Britain amounted to 50.5 million dollars. On 15 July 1957, the Royal Sussex regiment lowered the Union Jack for the last time and the United Kingdom left.

English and Commonwealth troops are recognized at the Gapyengeup monument which the Republic of Korea erected in honor of the 27th Brigade's fight against Chinese forces. A second monument, the Sulmari Battle Monument, is located at Gapyengeup and is dedicated to the 1st Battalion Gloucestershire Regiment.

Of considerable significance to the troops, if not to the governments, was the fact that the Expeditionary Force Institute, a branch of the Navy, Army Air Force Institute (NAAFI) followed the British forces. The NAAFI operated wagons selling commodities like writing paper, toiletries, and confections, as well as hot tea, beer and spirits. This was particularly appealing to the Americans who were, at times, without liquor. The temperance movement had joined forces with evangelical women to lobby Congress to deny liquor to the fighting men,[64] and deprived them their spirits. NAAFI spirits quickly became a kind of currency between troops of the various nations.

One of the many unheralded British units that provided significant service in Korea was the 78th Motor Ambulance Convoy, Royal Army Service Corps. Its drivers were reservists who had, in civilian life, been long-haul drivers, and they were given the nearly impossible jobs of moving men and supplies across the rutted Korean roads. Because every unit borrowed them to maintain their own supplies, the group was nicknamed after their commander and called "Potter's Prostituted Pool."

United States of America

The United States' relations with Korea go back to the 1870s when efforts at opening trade led to the sinking of the USS *General Sherman* and the first Korean War.[65] Since then the U.S. had been involved in treaty relations over the years until, in 1945, its troops occupied the southern area of the peninsula, and remained there until they exited along with the Soviet Union in a pullout in 1948.

At the close of World War II the United States carried a new influence in Asia, primarily in Japan. The Truman administration believed in what was later named the "domino theory," and was committed to preserving a democratic government in Japan, which in time would unite with the Western nations. Truman's sometimes ill-defined "containment policy" promised aid to those who were fighting Communism. Both public opinion and the policies of the Truman administration viewed the Soviet attitude with some concern and witnessed the Soviet consumption of Poland, Bulgaria, and Romania as a sign of expansion desires. In this view the United States approached the attack in Korea as an attempt by the Soviet Union to expand its dominance and ideology over the rest of the world.

After the war the United States had occupied Korea, along with the Soviet Union, in accordance with the decisions made at Cairo. In fulfilling their agreement both the United States and Russia pulled out their forces, but left behind advisory groups. The United States had maintained the Korean Military Advisory Group (KMAG) to advise and strengthen their military. It authorized a unit of 180 officers and 290 enlisted men and operated with four or five Americans assigned to each of the Republic of Korea divisions. KMAG came directly under the Eighth Army and was identified as the 8668th Army Unit. It underwent several name changes and size designations but continued to operate as an advisory body during the war. This small unit was the only American presence when the war broke out. When the occupation troops were withdrawn, however, the United States left the ROKA primarily naked in terms of modern combat.

The Soviet Union also maintained an advisory group in Korea whose responsibility was to strengthen and train the DPRK Army. When they pulled out according to the agreement, however, they left behind their heavy equipment and weapons, including tanks.[66] These would later appear in the invasion force unleashed by North Korea.

In both Europe and the United States the members of the North Atlantic Treaty Organization feared that the opening of hostilities in Korea was but a diversion and that the real goal would be the opening of war somewhere in Europe. As a result, they demanded, and generally got, a significant share of what was available.

The entire breakdown of U.S. military involvement is vastly complicated and would require another work to define. But a brief summary will identify something of the size and complexity of American participation.[67]

An Army division at the 1948 standard, which was the case when war broke out, was about 18,804 troops. This included three fighting regiments of approximately 3,774, a division artillery (DivArty) at 3,669, and dozens of specialized units which include a tank battalion, engineering battalion, medical battalion, and signal, ordnance, quartermaster, headquarters, engineering and replacement companies. In addition they might have several other special operations units attached.

America's war in Korea was fought by the Eighth U.S. Army, which was composed of several Army divisions and, eventually the First Marine Division. Stationed in Japan with primarily occupational duties, when authorized by President Truman it established a forward headquarters in Taegu, South Korea, on 9 July 1950. Four days later Eighth Army assumed command of all U.S. forces in Korea. On the 17 July, the Eighth United States Army Korean (EUSAK) also took command of all Republic of Korea forces. It was commanded at the time by Lieutenant General Walton H. Walker, a tough officer who had been mentored by General George Patton. General MacArthur's Far East Command controlled the supporting units of the U.S. Army, the Air Force, and the Navy in the region. The initial formation of Eighth Army was composed of four Army divisions, the 1st Provisional Marine Brigade (later the First Marine Division), the British 27th Infantry Brigade, the 5th U.S. Regimental Combat Team, five divisions of the ROK Army, and the Pusan Logistical command.

A small specialized force called Task Force Smith was the first unit into Korea. The 2nd Infantry Division (Indian Head Division) was the first division. Thereafter the force was expanded by the 1st Provisional Marine Brigade, and then in order the 3rd Infantry Division (Marne Division), the 7th Infantry Division (Bayonet Division), the 24th Infantry Division (Victory Division), the 25th Infantry Division (Tropic Lightning Division), the 40th Infantry Division, National Guard (Grizzly Division), and the 45th Infantry Division (Thunderbird). Several independent infantry regiments also served: the 5th Regimental Combat Team, the 29th Infantry Regiment (The Two Niner), 65th Regimental Combat Team (Borinqueneers) from Puerto Rico, and the 187th Airborne Regimental Combat Team (Rakkasans).

As the war progressed, further troop accumulation and the rotation of troops, as well as some reorganization, led to the identification of three additional U.S. Corps and two ROK Corps, which included five Army infantry divisions, a Marine division, eleven ROK divisions and the Commonwealth Division. The Far East Command Liaison Group was formed in November 1950 to coordinate all services' intelligence collection activities.

The Miscellaneous Division, Attrition Section, was formed under Eighth Army G-3 Section to direct all partisan activities that were being conducted from the offshore islands. This unit also underwent numerous unit and identity changes, but basically operated these clandestine activities. It conducted a wide variety of operations, undercover raids, reconnaissance rescue, surveillance, and special operations both in North Korea and South Korea. It was also responsible for keeping the headquarters supplied with enemy prisoners when needed.

Far East Air Forces (FEAF) was stationed in Tokyo, Japan, and controlled all U.S. and UN Air Forces. It entered combat when it was ordered to provide protection for the evacuation of all U.S. personnel from Korea on 26 June, and thus was the first of the services to be involved. On the following day offensive air operations were authorized. The composition of the fighting force was basically as follows: the Fifth Air Force (Japan), the Thirteenth Air Force (Philippines), the Twentieth Air Force (Guam), FEAF Bomber Command (Japan), FEAF Combat Cargo Command (Japan), and Far East Air Logistics Force (Japan). Within these commands were bomber groups, fighter groups, fighter-bomber groups, tactical support wings, fighter-interceptor wings, tactical reconnaissance groups, tactical control groups, troop carrier wings, and military air transport services.

The naval presence was under the command of Naval Forces, Far East (NAF) headquartered in Yokohama, Japan. The principle force was Seventh Fleet (Task Force) 70. It provided a striking force, amphibious force, blockading and escort force, as well as specialized operational landing forces. During the course of the war it provided four battleships, thirty-six carriers, thirteen cruisers, a hundred and thirty destroyers, escorts, frigates, thirteen submarines, more than sixty minesweepers, and hundreds of auxiliary ships. The majority of naval air units operated from carriers but there were, as well, several stationed in Japan.

Not disregarding the significant contribution of other nations, it is nevertheless a fact that the largest contingency of foreign forces under the United Nations flag was provided by Americans. This contribution in terms of men, equipment, supplies, and costs is difficult to over-estimate. While an accounting of the involvement of American forces would be little other than a history of the war itself, and would a separate volume, it is necessary to point out that there were few points of action on land, on the sea, or in the air, where United States military personnel were not involved. The U.S. became involved almost immediately and has remained involved ever since. The first combat troops were on the ground as soon as MacArthur was authorized to protect American dependents trying to get out of Korea ahead of the advancing North Korean forces. And they remain today, more than sixty years later, still on defensive duty.

The cost of America's long and active participation in this war was high indeed. While the numbers keep changing as more and more information is located about those who were missing, the combat casualties are generally listed as 36,940 dead, 92,134 wounded, 3,839 missing in action, and 4,439 prisoners of war. The non-combat deaths are listed as 3830. At Operation Big Switch most of the prisoners returned with the exception of 21 who chose to remain with their Chinese captors. A little more than eight thousand prisoners and military men and women listed as missing in action still remain to be accounted for.

Since the war several monuments have been created by the people of South Korea to preserve the memory and honor those Americans who fought and died there. Some of the more significant include the Osan Battle Memorial built in October 1975 at Munsan-eup, Paju. Also at Munsan-eup is a moment to the 2nd Infantry Division. At Deokyang-gu, Goyang, a joint ROK–U.S. Marine Corps monument was built in 1958 to commemorate the recapturing of Seoul. At Jon-myeon, Paju, a monument has been erected in honor of the

U.S. Marine Corps. In Washington, D.C., in West Potomac Park just south of the reflecting pool stands America's memorial to this war. Authorized in 1986, it was dedicated on 27 July 1995 by South Korean President Kim Young San and U.S. President William Clinton. The inscription reads, "Our nation honors her sons and daughters who answered the call to defend a country they never knew and a people they never met."

The South Koreans have not forgotten the American veterans and have over the years gone to considerable trouble and expense to remind them that the people of the Republic of Korea are still and forever in their debt. For the 60th anniversary Korea sent the Little Angels children's folk ballet to tour the United States. This group has been entertaining veterans all over the world since they were organized in 1962. Dr. Bo Hi Pak, the director, saw this as their most important performance "because it will be perhaps the final 'thank you' we can make to our precious Korean War veterans in the twilight of their lives." He also went on to comment that he wanted these Americans to be astonished "with the contrast to the ragged children they remember begging in the gutter in 1953."[68]

Hundreds of volumes have been written about why the United States entered the war, and nearly as many about how America fought the Korean War. As World War II ended there was a stampede for demobilization with little regard to the postwar tensions that remained behind after the victory. Both the secretary of war and the secretary of the Navy had voiced their disagreement to this idea as early as October 1945, but the demobilization pushed ahead with little real consideration as to how unprepared it left the country. The United States entered the war in Korea armed only by drawing on World War II equipment still in the Far East and America. Supply stocks that were being maintained were made up almost totally of World War II supplies. There had been virtually no new procurement of military items since the war ended. Looking back, it appears that the decision to enter the war on the peninsula with ground troops was made somewhat hastily and without much serious analysis of the logistics involved. Questions about logistics asked at that time appear to have been answered more on the basis of faith than fact. There had been no preplanning, no model to follow, other than what was left over from World War II — an entirely different war.

When considering the logistic problem in the Far East, it is necessary to remember that it had a serious competitor in Europe, even during the Korean War, when it came to the procurement of goods and services. The situation was reminiscent of the same conflict between Europe and the Pacific during World War II.

While the validity of American involvement continues to be analyzed, there has been a general tendency to be hard on the U.S. military, claiming that it was ill prepared to fight the war, blaming it in part on the fact that since then end of World War II the systematic dismantling of U.S. forces had left every service understrength and poorly equipped. Some claimed that the Americans were soft and should have provided a better performance against this "band of poorly trained peasants," comparing their performance with those of the veterans of World War II. The poor performance of American troops is identified as one of the many factors after the war that has contributed to the long memory loss concerning the U.S. participation in this tragic event.

5

Nations That Provided
Medical Units

My God, maybe there is a real war going on.
— Soldier seeing his first casualty

As was the case in just about every area considered, the medical facilities available to UN troops were found wanting when they were called to war in July 1950. Medical personnel, mainly doctors and nurses, had gone back into civilian life after the war and the equipment level was just about where it had been on V-J Day. What little medical help was available began with those medics assigned to the KMAG units but they were quickly overwhelmed. The medics that entered Korea with Task Force Smith tried to provide aid to the retreating forces, but as the North Koreans advanced so rapidly it sometimes became necessary to leave casualties behind. With considerable effort the front line aid stations and the much heralded MASH units were available by the time the fighting was closing in on the Pusan Perimeter. In the early stages because of lack of facilities, many casualties were sent to Japan, often by small planes or even open boats. A quickly assembled group of physicians and nurses took part in the Inchon Landing, and as replacements and supplies began to come in from Japan and the U.S., the aid, evacuation, and treatment system grew quickly into a highly efficient program. Some part of this, of course, was the gift of other nations.

Physicians and nurses, as well as ambulatory units, have accompanied men and women into battle almost since the earliest days of warfare. By the time the Korean War broke out the medical departments of most armies were well advanced in care and treatment of the wounded. In Korea the treatment of those injured was remarkable and, especially with the establishment of an

131

air evacuation system — pushed forward by the development and use of the helicopter — proved highly effective and resulted in a much smaller casualty count than might have been experienced.

Several nations contributed medical teams, hospital units, or medical personnel to the United Nations effort. The number of nations acknowledged in this activity depends on whether it is appropriate to include Japan. While it was not considered a participant, it was nevertheless the source of considerable medical attention in behalf of the United Nations. The same is true when questioning whether West Germany's contribution meets whatever criteria we have established. I have chosen to discuss Japan's contribution under that nation's role as a silent partner, and West Germany in this section.[1]

The efforts to provide medical aid to men and women wounded in battle was a great crusade and considerable effort and expense were involved in providing the very best care. New and experimental methods of surgery were developed, highly pragmatic handling of blood plasma saved many lives, and the proximity of specialized machines allowed for the treatment of injury close to the trauma, thus making recovery possible. New and unusual methods for evacuating front line casualties in hilly and sometimes violent terrain were significant in the saving of so many lives, as was the well-developed and first rate well-equipped mobile hospitals that drew close to the front lines.

Without diminishing its humanitarian value, however, the purpose of military medicine in the field is to return the soldier to combat. Because of the essential nature of medical facilities and how often wounded soldiers were returned to battle (80 percent in some areas), it is hard to distinguish between those that are distinctly military and those medical. This would be the case with the Indian medical team that actually dropped with the 187th Airborne and thus provided direct military support. But in the minds of many politicians, and certainly in the best interests of some United Nations members, it was better to be seen in support of humanitarian efforts than the war efforts. During the war this was the case, with several nations depending on their national interpretation.

Denmark

Denmark was neutral during World War I but in the Second World War was invaded and occupied by German forces. It suffered greatly during that war and as it fought to reaffirm its national identity after being liberated, it was well aware of the tension growing between the major powers. Having been a charter member of the UN, Denmark was anxious to support it, but

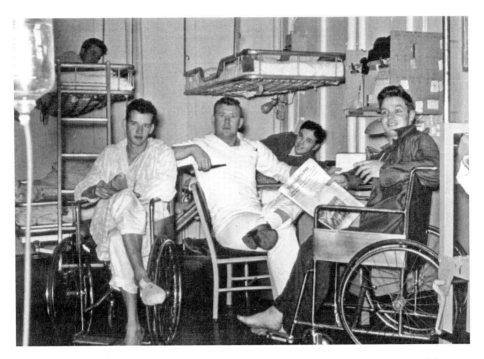

Three Americans and one British wounded (with pipe) on the Danish hospital ship *Jutlandia*.

had to do so in terms of the political realities Denmark faced. Concerned about security, it joined NATO in 1949. While the nation was not interested in aggravating its own positions, it was nevertheless sympathetic with the United Nations cause. The solution was to avoid military involvement and provide humanitarian service. To do this it immediately arranged to supply medical assistance through what it had determined were to be civilian means. The civilian status of the hospital ship *Jutlandia* was strongly emphasized. According to international regulations a red cross was painted on the side of the ship and the activities were organized and maintained by the Danish Red Cross. It is true, however, that the government paid the costs involved in preparing and maintaining the ship throughout the war.

When the war first broke out the HMS *Maine*, a 7,500 ton vessel under the control of the Queen Alexandra's Royal Naval Nursing Service that had been in Hong Kong, became the only hospital ship. It was the first to serve the wounded American and British casualties in the early days of the war. It was replaced by the *Jutlandia*.

The *Jutlandia* was built by the East Asiatic Company in 1934 as a cargo-passenger ship. Registered at 8,456 gross tons, the ship was 425 feet in length with a beam of 61 feet. This particular ship was one of three that operated under this name. Upon completion it worked the coastal trade carrying cargo until the beginning of World War II. It was essentially mothballed during the German occupation to avoid use by the enemy. On one occasion it was attacked and damaged in an allied air raid on 3 May 1945 but survived. After the war it re-entered commercial service between Europe and the East Coast of the United States. When the Korean War broke out the Danish government had the ship totally refitted, turning the *Jutlandia* into a modern hospital ship with four operating theaters and an announced 356 bed capacity.

After considerable preparation, and flying under three flags — the Danish national flag, the Red Cross and UN flag — it departed on 23 January 1951 and arrived at Pusan, South Korea, on 7 March 1951 to begin its first tour. Its second tour ran from September 1951 to March 1952. During the first summer, and because it was not air conditioned, the hospital ship was primarily used to transport wounded to Europe. After resupplying in Rotterdam, it sailed back to Yokohama on 2 November 1952. It moved on quickly to be stationed near Inchon, where patients began arriving directly from the front line. It returned to Pusan on 13 November 1950. To the dismay of the crew, while it saw a never ending stream of patients, no wounded prisoners of war were allowed on board. It sailed for home again on 29 March 1952 with patients on board. After it third tour, it finally departed Inchon on 17 August 1953 after the ceasefire. The ship arrived home on 16 October 1953.

Captain Kai Hammerich was the senior officer onboard. He also had the rank of commander in the Dutch Navy and served as the contact person with the Red Cross. The senior medical officer, Dr. Mogens Winge, was second in command. Captain Christen Kondrup was the ship's skipper. Despite the fact all the participants were considered civilians, they all held military rank. The ship carried about a hundred medical personnel. It served first as a primary case hospital dealing with serious cases that came aboard, and second, it was to provide evacuation transportation for the wounded. Most surgery was carried out when the ship was at sea. The 360 bed facility with its staff of 200 accounted for an estimated 15,000 patients that were examined and treated. The ship was popular among the wounded and among the civilians that they also treated. A small children's department was created, which was apparently put to use. "The ever present problem of the little ones hanging around the front line," wrote Sergeant Jimmie Quackenbush, a medic with the 7th Division, "was solved recently by the arrival of a bunch of danes [sic] who took over. It was good to see someone doing something."[2]

A refurbishing, which added a helicopter landing pad as well as air conditioning and an update of the wards, made the *Jutlandia* far more serviceable.

The pad added to the speed with which casualties could be brought directly from the forward aid stations. The pad, which was the first on a hospital ship, soon became the model for other ships.

Even considering their close involvement with the fighting front, there were no casualties suffered by members of the staff or crew. There were, however, thirty-two marriages between members of the crew during this period, perhaps explained by the fact they spent 999 days together in the care of the wounded. Eventually the *Jutlandia* was joined by the hospital ships USS *Haven*, *Repose*, and *Consolation*.

The services of the Danish ship have been well recognized. During its medical tours it housed wounded from a dozen different nations as well as 6,000 Korean civilians. During this time only 29 patients died. The ship received the Korean Presidential Unit Citation. Denmark's medical assistance during the Korean War has also been acknowledged by the Republic of Korea at the Medical Treatment Support Group Monument built on 20 September 1976 at Dongsam-dong, Yeongdo-gu, and Busan. It commemorates the medical aid provided by Denmark, India, Italy, Norway, and Sweden. In December 1986 the song *Jutlandia* by Kim Larsen became a major hit in Denmark. On 15 June 1990 at the Langelinic, a promenade quay in Copenhagen, a memorial stone was placed in honor of Denmark's contribution to the United Nations during the Korean War.

The *Jutlandia* was involved in some interesting asides during its time in Korea. On its arrival one of the crew, 21-year-old Jytte Skov, was refused permission to enter Korea. The United Nations had established the unique requirement that no female under the age of 27 could serve in country. No explanation was found for this. Given the circumstances, she was finally given special permission to enter the country but "for her protection" she was assigned an official guardian to watch over her. The ship's officers were also somewhat independent in their reaction to rules and regulations. The Geneva Convention required that hospital vessels were to display an illuminated Red Cross. But the Danes soon learned by experience that the North Koreans often fired on such lighted ships. So the *Jutlandia* developed a lights on — lights off routine which they believed greatly reduced their risk.

The ship came close to establishing an even larger reputation. During the negotiations with the Communists about possible peace-talks, General Matthew Ridgway first suggested the *Jutlandia* as the location for the North Korean–United Nations talks to begin, but the Communists refused, preferring a more neutral ground. The vessel returned to normal shipping duties after the war. In the 1960 it served briefly as the royal yacht for the king of Thailand. It was finally decommissioned in 1965.

India

During the war Nehru was wary of the Soviets for what he considered their encouragement of reactionary responses, particularly in Asia. On the other side, his disagreement with the United States' position on India's dispute with Pakistan over Kashmir was heightened by his disappointed with America because it was not willing to bring consideration of the admittance of PRC into the UN as an item for discussion during the Korean negotiation talks.

There was little reason that India could not have sent a token force to fight in Korea without unduly weakening its own defenses, but Nehru decided that he would not because of his delicate diplomatic situation. Even his offer of an ambulance company was made on condition that the offer did not acknowledge any obligation for financial reimbursement for logistic support furnished by the United States. The Department of Defense took the hard line on this and refused the offer. However, the State and Treasury Departments agreed to the conditions if India would be open to later discussions as to whether any obligation existed. Seeing this as an issue with potential for

Indian 60th (Parachute) Mobile Field Ambulance dropping with the 187th RCT.

future involvement, the comptroller, W. J. McNeil, issued this warning: "A primary consideration is the precedent which is being set for all future United Nations 'police actions,' and it would appear undesirable to establish any general principle that the United States military supplies and equipment would be donated without any obligation on the part of the recipients."[3] This point of view prevailed in this discussion and it was not until the president made a special exception in this case that the ambulance company was accepted. To accommodate this need the Indians requested and received poultry or other fresh meats in lieu of beef. In every 1000 rations they also received an additional 350 pounds of bread, 159 pounds of rice, 37 gallons of vegetable oil, 245 pounds of macaroni, 100 pounds of canned cheese, 43 number ten cans of tomatoes and 6 number 10 cans of tomato paste. They removed from the rations of canned carrots, canned corn, jam, jelly, uncooked cereal, dehydrated cranberries, pickles, pineapples, dehydrated pea soup, sweet potatoes, dehydrated onions and dehydrated apples.

So, beyond all the rhetoric and posturing among the non-aligned nations, the government of India offered the 60th Parachute Field Ambulance Platoon which, despite its name, was by all accounts a mobile army surgical hospital (MASH). The field ambulance had seen service in the Burma theater during World War II and had an excellent reputation. It was a significant addition to the UN Command. The total contribution would consist of about 300 personnel at any one time. The Indian government expressed the wish early in the war that its field ambulance should serve under Commonwealth command, and despite the objections of the British director of Army Medical Services, that was arranged.

When the unit first arrived the UN was in retreat and moving so quickly that the train load of needed supplies was nearly lost to the enemy. The cars had been left without an engine to pull them. Nevertheless the troops rallied around until they located an engine that managed to pull them away, preserving the equipment. The Parachute Field Ambulance was quickly involved with 8th Army's withdrawal from North Korea.[4] The contingency was divided into two groups; one that moved with the troops into the battle zone as a mobile first-encounter unit and one that remained in Taegu as a field hospital. The mobile unit was assigned as the medical evacuation team for the 27th British Commonwealth Brigade (later redesigned the 28) and supported the unit throughout the war. Members of the medical platoon also jumped with the U.S. 187th Regimental Combat Team at Munsan-ni on 22 March 1951 in one of the two parachute jumps of the war. At the operation site the team administered to over a hundred patients who had been injured in the drop. The 60th also took part in Operation Commando in October 1951 and followed the advance of the 28th Commonwealth Brigade during the rest of the war.

The medical team was admired by all the UN forces in Korea for their availability, medical expertise, and surgical and nursing skills, and their warm hospitality and courtesy to visitors. At each visit people enjoyed at least a mug of superbly made tea and, if lucky, some of their legendary curries. The nearly 1000 bed facility, staffed by three hundred and forty five, treated an estimated 20,000 cases.

The Indian medical team came under artillery fire on several occasions and one ambulance was blown up by a mine, but casualties are rarely mentioned in the reports. Though not considered when accounting for Korean War casualties, the number given by the Indian government is four killed and 23 wounded while operating in Korea. At one point the Australian battalion presented Indian Commander Lieutenant Colonel A.G. Rangaraj with an inscribed silver tray in appreciation for the medical service their units received. The United Nations Command cited the unit for meritorious conduct. Members of the unit received from their own government these medals for distinguished service, all getting the Chungmo and the Distinguished Service Medal, Two MahaVir Chakras, six Vir Chakras, one bar, and twenty-five Mention-in-Dispatches.

After the war the 60th Parachute platoon joined the Indian section of the Neutral Nations Repatriation Commission Custodian Force on August 1953 to oversee the controversial procedure by which prisoners of war would be repatriated. The commission consisted of two Soviet satellite nations, Poland and Czechoslovakia, two nations friendly to the United States, Sweden and Switzerland, and was chaired by non-aligned General K. S. Thimayya.

Italy

Italy had fought with the Allies during World War I, but after Benito Mussolini's rise to power in 1922 and he attacked the neighboring country of Ethiopia in 1935, Italy moved further and further into Germany's camp, joining it in World War II in 1940. In 1943 Italy surrendered to United States and British troops, though the battle continued as German troops tried to maintain the territory. Following the war Italy went through a period of ease and high prosperity called La Dolce Vita (the sweet life). When the call went out for aid to South Korea, Italy was not a member of the United Nations. It did not attain membership until 1955. Behind the scenes, however, it was still recovering from years of Fascist rule and the defeat at the hands of the Allies, and did not believe it was in a position to send troops to the cause. Italy did respond to a request by the International Red Cross to provide medical assistance.

The Italian medical unit that was organized was the *Croce Russia Italiansa Osdedale 68*. The original force consisted of seven doctors, six nurses, a chaplain, and 50 non-commissioned ranks and sixty-seven administrative personnel. Once they arrived in Korea they were assigned as the medical unit for the British Commonwealth Brigade. In order to provide the service requested they built and operated their own hospital unit.

Their fifty bed field hospital was established in Yongdongpo, South Korea, with surgery, medicine, pediatrics, ophthalmology, dentistry and other departments. After a year of servicing the wounded the hospital facilities burned down, most probably through actions by Communist partisans, but no patients were lost. By February 1953 personnel had reconstructed a building with room for of one hundred forty five beds. The hospital operated on a 24 hour basis and during the first eight months, with a staff of 131, treated an estimated 17,000 military personal and an untold number of civilians.

The Italian medical unit operated near the line but there are no recorded casualties among the medical staff or personnel. On 2 June 1989 the Korean government placed a plaque at the Usin Elementary School not far from Seoul in commemoration of the Italian medical team and hospital that was located in that spot. This unit was one of the medical groups honored by the Medical Treatment Support Group Monument built on 20 September 1976 at Dongsam-dong, Yeongdo-gu, Busan. It commemorates the medical aid provided by Denmark, India, Italy, Norway, and Sweden.

While the Italian personnel were considered friendly and efficient, supplying the Italian personnel was complicated somewhat by their dietary demands. They preferred fewer potatoes, more rice, a great deal of cheese and tomato sauce, as well as a fairly steady supply of macaroni. Like the troops from most nations they took well to the UN weekly allotment of ice cream.

Norway

Norway, which borders both the North Sea and the North Atlantic, is approximately 355,000 square miles in size. It is about the size of the American state of New Mexico. It lies to the west of Sweden. In 1950 it had an estimated population of 3.5 million. While a good portion of the nation is within the Arctic Circle, the weather is far more temperate than might be expected. As a result of the Napoleonic Wars in 1814 the area now identified as Norway was separated from Denmark and combined with Sweden. In 1904 Norway gained its independence. The new nation offered the kingship to Danish Prince Carl, who took the name Haarkin VII. He ruled Norway under a hereditary constitutional monarchy until his death in 1957.

During World War I, Norway was a non-belligerent nation and made an effort to claim that status in World War II. However, the Germans had other plans. Great Britain and France sent an expeditionary force to its aid, but by June 1941 they were forced out and the Germans invaded and occupied the country. Norway established a government in exile in London. After the war several members of the puppet Norwegian government under Vidkun Quisling[5] were prosecuted. Following the war, and seeking collective security, Norway joined the NATO alliance and became a founding member of the United Nations.

The fact that Norwegian Trygve Halvdan Lie was secretary general of the UN at the time of the outbreak of the Korean War put certain pressures on Norway to participate. However, there seemed to be good support from the people of Norway when, in early February 1951, its parliament authorized sending the 1st (Norwegian) Army Surgical Hospital, generally known as NORMASH. It was nearly a year, however, when on 2 March 1951, the Norwegian government passed the resolution needed to provide the funds for a medical surgical unit.

It was finally decided that the fastest and easiest way for accomplishing its purpose was to purchase a MASH unit from the United States and then staff it themselves. For the first year the mobile unit was maintained and administered by the Norwegian Red Cross and then, in late 1951, was transferred to the Norwegian Ministry of Defense, and the staff had to exchange their uniforms and rank.

The initial contingency included 83 men and women consisting mostly of army reserve volunteers who had been equipped with materials purchased from American stock. They operated with the United Nations under the organizational structure of Eighth Army's I Corps. Eventually the unit involved grew until it consisted of 653 personnel. During the war Norway rotated seven crews (634 men and women) in and out of Korea.

The Norwegian detachment first arrived in June 1951. NORMASH opened for business at Uijeongbu about four miles north of Seoul and later near Tongduchon some forty miles north of Seoul. The surgical united remained in Korea until November of 1954. While in Korea it operated about 14 miles from the front. The 60 bed facility was expanded so that it could take up to 200 patients at a time and the staff increased. It had four operating rooms that functioned twenty-four hours a day. Operating as an emergency care facility, it usually held patients for less than three days before evacuating them to a hospital or hospital ship. Over the course of the war the staff performed more than nine thousand surgeries and treated ninety thousand patients. Twenty-seven percent of all the casualties served by the Norwegian detachment came from the Commonwealth Division. Cases came from a vari-

Three Norwegian medical staff cooking up lunch from C rations.

ety of countries, and included numerous Korean civilians as well as 172 Chinese and North Korean prisoners of war.

When in October 1954 the unit was ordered to return to Norway, the medical equipment was returned to the U.S. Army. Official reports of the unit's activities indicate that there were two casualties suffered during the war; nurse Anne Christinsen, who was shot in 1952, and lab technician Brit Reiskether, but there is no information beyond that.

The United States completely supplied Norway with the initial equipment necessary and supplied rations and transportation throughout the war. Norway was one of only three nations that accepted American rations and supplies with nothing added and nothing taken away. On 18 September 1951 the government worked it out that the Norwegians would reimburse the U.S. each quarter on receiving a financial statement, and that the costs of deployment would be settled after the troops had returned to Norway.

NORMASH received two Korean and one United States Presidential Unit Citations and 18 other citations from the government of South Korea as well as the Norwegian Korea Service Medal. In 1972 a memorial was raised in Korea by the Korea-Norway Friendship Association that also maintains the NORMAS Welfare House on the site. Because of this aid, relations have remained very strong between the two nations. Norwegian soldier Hendricus

Adrianus Cornelis van Doremalen, on his second tour, remembered that his outfit had adopted a little girl that they named Koia.[6] Nurse Kan Roll, who served with the NORMASH, returned to Korea in 2008 for a special celebration hosted by South Korea in honor of the medical team, as the ROK continued to honor those who served.

An example of the unit's determination is shown by its pastor, Padre Lorentz Pedersen, who volunteered for Korean service and then paid for a substitute pastor to care for his flock while he was gone. The NORMASH unit was generally appreciated not only for its excellent care, but unlike the Queen Alexander Nursing Sisters which prohibited nurses in the field, they maintained a full complement of nurses. The influence remained, as shortly after the war the hospital area was converted into the Korean National Medical Center.

Sweden

When the United Nations' appeal went out Sweden was involved in a transition of government. King Gustaf, who had been the nation's leader since 1907, had passed away and was being replaced by his son. The nation, with a population of about 351,000, was experiencing uneasy relations with the Soviet Union. After the war it had joined the UN and was a strong supporter of its decision concerning the invasion of Korea. The Swedish economy was growing in strength and the government was increasingly stabilized. The influence of the Communist party was dwindling; in the September 1950 election it lost nearly two-thirds of its delegates. Relations with the Soviet Union were growing tense as the two nations argued over fishing rights and the Russians confiscated some Swedish fishing vessels. Nevertheless, Sweden was one of the first nations to recognize the People's Republic of China and had made considerable efforts to establish normal relations with it. There was no hesitation, however, as the Swedish government responded almost immediately and provided the first of the medical teams that arrived in Korea to aid the United Nations' cause.

The Swedish unit left Stockholm in August and arrived at Pusan on 23 September 1950. It remained in Korea until April of 1957. Personnel set up their two hundred bed hospital in Pusan and began accepting patients in October 1950. It was significant that eight of the ten doctors assigned the hospital unit were surgeons and that while it was equipped as a four hundred bed evacuation facility, it managed to function more or less like a rear area MASH unit with expanded holding facilities. The facility grew to some 450 beds with a staff of 160 treating an estimated 900 military patients and thousands of civilians. Between 25 September 1950 and the end of the first year, the unit had handled 3,190 patients, most of them American soldiers and North Korean prisoners of war. According to the Swedish government, no casualties resulted from Sweden's participation in the war.

The long and dedicated service of the Swedish medical unit is recognized by the South Koreans at the Medical Treatment Support Group Monument built on 20 September 1976 and located at Dongsam-dong, Yeongdo-gu, and Busan. It commemorates the medical aid provided by the nations of Denmark, India, Italy, Norway, and Sweden. Sweden and the Republic of Korea have continued to be close since the war. As late as June 2010, President Lee Myung-bak publically thanked Sweden when he said, "The Korean people will never forget the valiant medical personnel who courageously supported the fight for freedom in the republic."[7]

The United States provided complete initial equipment, supplies and resupply, as well as transportation for the Swedish unit. Sweden was one of only three nations that accepted American rations and supplies with nothing added and nothing taken away.

When the time came for a commission to supervise the armistice agreement, the Soviet Union suggested as neutral nations Poland, Bulgaria and Czechoslovakia. The UN selection would have included Sweden, Switzerland and maybe India. When it was finally decided that prisoners would be turned over to a Neutral Nations Repatriation Commission, Sweden was included along with India, Poland, Czechoslovakia, and Switzerland. Sweden continued to hold that responsibility for many years.

West Germany

Including West Germany in our list of participants is a toss-up and depends on how inclusive you wish to be. Although West Germany did not become a member of the United Nations until 1973, and its contribution to the war effort came late, it is still important to acknowledge this divided nation's interest in being involved. What was to be called West Germany was just emerging from the destruction of World War II and struggling to establish itself both as a national identity and as an ally of the Western nations, thus they made this effort to be engaged.

The aid sent by West Germany was a German Red Cross Hospital (*Deutschen Rotkreuz Lazarett*) unit that went to Pusan, South Korea, just after the signing of the cease-fire. The hospital unit remained there for some time. As far as can be determined there were no losses to West German medical personnel that resulted from their time of service there. The German Red

Cross is surprisingly reluctant, or unable, to supply information about this effort, but the indication is that the unit arrived shortly after the cease fire and well within what is considered the "combat period" (June 1950 to January 1954) of the war.[8]

6

Nations That
Provided Commodities

It is fatal to enter any war without the will to win.
— General MacArthur

The Korean War not only took a lot of lives, it cost a lot of money, and ate up vast amounts of commodities and supplies. The United Nations went to considerable effort to encourage its members to participate in the Korean crisis not only because it needed military and logistic support, and the political affirmation, but because of needed resources. If fighting men were not available for deployment, then at least member nations could help with the expenses and the materials needed for the war. And, as hoped, several members who did not send troops were still willing to be a part of the United Nations efforts. These contributions, often in kind, were well received.

One rich area of support came from Latin America. Early in the war some consideration had been given to the creation of a Latin American battalion made up of small numbers of troops from several countries, but it was eventually considered too impractical and dropped.[1] But many of them gave commodities. Several Asian nations were also involved. Recently there has been talk out of South Korea that it was supported by the contribution of materials from the governments of Austria, Haiti, Myanmar, and Vietnam.[2] So far no further documentation of this support has come forth.

The costs of the Korean War were, at least in theory, to be paid for by the member nations who participated. But the financial cost of the Korean War, like so much else about the war, has never been adequately explained. It is far easier, for example, to find out the cost of the French and Indian War than it is to locate the expenses of the Korean War. So, while no adequate

145

accounting has been provided, and probably will not be because of the variance of what is to be include in the accounting, it is estimated that the direct costs of the Korean War was 390 billion dollars, the indirect costs 216 billion and the related costs 70 billion, which with the inclusion of veterans benefits provides a figure estimated at 1.5 trillion dollars.[3] To compensate for this somewhat Truman raised taxes an additional four percent of the gross domestic product, keeping in mind that most of the expanded taxes of World War II had never been ended. And, that during this period the American military was expanded both in Korea and elsewhere. Some of that cost was offset by nations who were willing to support the war, just not participate in it.

Argentina

Argentina was a founding member of the United Nations and when the test came in the form of requests, it decided to support the UN decision to take action in Korea. Its practical involvement was limited by strong political and social pressure from a significant number of isolationists, as well as by the opposition of the highly independent labor unions and a small but vocal Communist minority. The military had ousted the constitutional government in 1943 and Juan Domingo Peron came to power and established a new government in 1949. When called on for aid, Foreign Minister Hipolito Jesus Paz felt the need to reply, "In accordance with our desire to comply with our obligations as a member of the United Nations, we are waiting for unified command to enter into direct communication."

In the long run, however, Argentina did not feel it was in a position to provide military aid. In the first place it had experienced declining relations with the United States for the past decade and was in no mood to support it. In the second place while Argentina had a reasonably large army, it was concerned with the deteriorating situation in its own part of the world and did not want to weaken its own position. But, in good faith, and as a token effort, it did make available significant amounts of canned goods and frozen meat to supply United Nations troops. The allocation and distribution of these commodities were handled by the army.

Brazil

The United States was the first nation to open a consulate in Brazil in 1808. Relations with the United States since then have been friendly but not always strong. They improved during World War II as the Brazilian government sided with the Allies, sending into combat the Brazilian Expeditionary Force.[4] During the presidency of Eurico Gaspar Dutra (1946–1951), Brazil's foreign policy was aligned with the United States. In 1947 he outlawed the Brazilian Communist Party and severed relations with the Soviet Union. After this time relations with the U.S. cooled and by the time the Korean War broke out there was considerable effort waged (led by the returned Brazilian Communist Party) to prevent Brazil from sending troops to fight in Korea.

With all this pressure at home and in order to avoid any entanglement, the government of Brazil offered money in support of the United Nations cause.[5] At one point it suggested an interest in sending troops, but only in return for significant military and economic aid; it actually sent a list of supplies it required.

Chile

The rather unique shape of Chile makes it easily recognizable and earned it the name from the Aymara word meaning "land where the earth ends." This long and narrow strip of land in southwest South America won its independence in 1810 from Spain. Its formidable natural barriers that separated it from the rest of the continent gave it both a political and military advantage. A unitary republic run by a democratic presidential system, it has always been congenial with the United States but never particularly close. During the early phases of World War II, Chile's president, Juan Antonio Rios was pro–Nazi and kept his country out of the war. However, by 1944 he had changed his mind and led Chile to join with the Allies. The nation joined the UN in September 1950 and when called upon by UN Resolution, Chile announced it would cooperate with the action taken in Korea.

It was a member of the United Nations Commission for the Unification and Rehabilitation of Korean (UNCURK) and had some immediate knowledge of the Korean situation. However, when called upon to supply troops, Chile claimed that popular opinion was not ready to support the commitment of troops out of the country. Chile fulfilled what it considered its obligation by "ensuring regular and adequate supplies of copper, saltpeter, and other strategic materials to countries responsible for operations."[6]

Cuba

Cuba in the late 1940s was witnessing a slowdown of the rapidly expanding economy of the previous decade, and was experiencing political and social unrest. With one of the highest literacy rates among Latin American countries, it had a progressive media and entertainment industry. Cuba was the first Latin American country to begin television broadcasting. But it was also suffering from corruption in government and social disparity. By 1952 the political unrest boiled over in the return of the dictatorship.

In 1950, however, the ties with the United States (which had overseen its independence in 1902), were still strong enough that the government of Cuba voted with the United States on the 27 June 1951 UN Resolution. In addition, it offered to send a rifle company to serve with the military forces operating in Korea. This offer of troops was initially accepted. However, the unit was never trained nor was it deployed. Nevertheless, Cuba did make good on its agreement to provide large amounts of sugar, alcohol and blood, which were delivered when needed.

Denmark

The political situation for the nation of Demark and its willingness to participate in the United Nations activities in Korea are considered in Chapter 5. Strongly supportive, however, in addition to the medical treatment team Denmark provided, the nation also made available significant amounts of much needed commodities. Among these were medical instruments, 500 tons of sugar, oil, and vaccines for numerous diseases.

Ecuador

A representative democracy, this small country straddles the equator, borders on the Pacific and is adjacent to Peru and Colombia. It gained its independence from Spain in 1839. On 5 July 1941 it entered a war with Peru over some contested land but it was settled on 29 January 1942 primarily in an effort to maintain a strong front against the Axis in World War II.

The American born president Galo Plaza had come to power in 1948 and was working hard to establish a democratic nation. He maintained good relations with the United States and supported the United Nations. He was, nevertheless, facing considerable troubles at home. During 1949 and 1950 the nation suffered an unprecedented series of floods and earthquakes that further hit their struggling economy

The country was, however, interested in participating in the UN effort in Korea and provided medical supplies as well significant amounts of rice. The nation also offered the use of the Galapagos Islands, where Darwin had done much of his work, for military bases. During World War II the U.S. had built some sophisticated bases there and turned them over to Ecuador at the end of the war. While Ecuador was not directly involved in the war, it did benefit. The demands of the combat in Korea created a price war over bananas, which in turn provided an essential boost to the Ecuadorian economy.

Ethiopia

The political situation for the nation of Ethiopia and that country's willingness to participate in the United Nations activities in Korea are considered in Chapter 4. But in addition to troops, it was willing to offer extended support. As a member of the UN since 1945, Ethiopia offered 40,250 American dollars for the purchase of medical supplies.[7] The actual delivery of the promised dollars has never been clearly verified.

Iceland

Iceland is a Nordic European island country located at the convergence of the North Atlantic and Artic Oceans. During the heat of World War II the United States had taken on the responsibility for the military defense of Iceland, but when the war ended so did this responsibility. Iceland became an independent republic on 17 June 1944 despite the fact it was still occupied. Following the end of World War II American troops withdrew. However, when the Korean War broke out NATO began to have some concerns about the safety of Iceland. With Iceland's agreement, on 5 May 1951, a formal relationship was reached whereby the United States once again took over the defense of the nation. A military base was established there in 1951.

This nation felt a considerable debt to the United States and to the United Nations, of which it had been a member since 1946. Leaders believed it was in their national interest to support the effort in Korea. When Iceland joined NATO it has done so with the stipulation that Iceland would never participate in an aggressive war against any other nation and the government of Iceland felt that this limited its involvement. Nevertheless, it allowed the stationing of 3,000 U.S. troops at Keflavik. Iceland was the only NATO nation without a standing Army, Navy, or Air Force.

In response to stated needs, Iceland also provided the United Nations with more than 125 tons of cod liver oil that was used to treat burns, as a base for paint colors, and as the medium through which a number of medicines were administered.

Iran

During World War II Iran was occupied by troops from both Germany and Great Britain. At the end of the war, in 1945, it joined with other nations as a charter member of the United Nations. Following the war there were increased tensions developing in the region, primarily between Iran and Great Britain over the nationalization of oil companies. This eventually led to an attitude change as Iran's displeasure over American support of the British increased the gap between them. This led to the CIA supported coup on 19 August 1953 against Mohammad Mosaddegh the prime minister. President Truman had tried to play a calming hand on events in Iran but when he assumed the presidency Dwight Eisenhower was afraid that Mosaddegh would unite with the Soviet Union and he authorized the step. In 1950 the U.S. was aware of the push of Iranian nationalism and the fact that the Soviet Union was looking to expand its influence.

During the debates over UN involvement, and in support of American based resolutions, Iran wavered in its loyalties, often working with the non-aligned nations. It came out in support of Truman's 30 November speech suggesting the possible use of the atomic bomb. Its stability, however, was limited as far as the Western nations were concerned. By the time of the Chinese offensive, the government of Iran had already completed a trading treaty with the Soviet Union and had outlawed the continuation of the broadcast of the Voice of America and the British Broadcasting System. It lost considerable confidence in the United States when the PRC moved so quickly south after the intervention.

In light of this tension, the state nevertheless felt some commitment to the UN and provided a variety of food stuffs and some medical supplies.

Somewhat ironically, Iran's Nasrollah Entezam was the president of the General Assembly when the U.S. sponsored a resolution that called on the body's president to constitute a group of three persons who, besides Entezam, were to determine the basis on which a satisfactory agreement could be reached in Korea.

Israel

Following years under the supervision of Great Britain, Israel proclaimed independence on 14 May 1948. It was immediately recognized by the United States and by the UN. However, the proclamation would quickly lead to mass migrations and eventually war with its Arab neighbors.

The Israeli government had hardly been in existence for two years, and only a member of the UN since 1949, when the United Nations called on its members to support the military actions in Korea. Having just arrived at an armistice in the Arab-Israeli War (1949), it remained under immediate threat from its neighbors and was fighting for national identity and economic security. The tiny population and the hostile nations that surrounded Israel meant that it needed to maintain its own military for its own defense. The nation was not really in a position to provide military support of any kind. Despite its own precarious position, Israel was concerned with its role in relation to the United Nations, recognizing how vulnerable it was and how much it might need UN support.

Prime Minister David Ben-Gurion called a meeting to discuss Israel's involvement and urged that a defense force be sent in support of South Korea. However, in a heated debate among the leadership it was determined that they could not afford to send troops, but that it was necessary to support the UN decision. In departing from its cautious course and backing the U.S position, Israel was voicing its support for the idea of collective security. Thus, once Israel departed from its policy of neutrality, it went on to make a statement on the validity of the UN standing up to this act of aggression. During the course of the war Israel provided contributions of medical aid and $100,000 in food supplies.

More than 4,000 Jewish men and women served in Korea during the war. In 2010 Korean officials, aware of this large number, went to Israel to express thanks and to acknowledge the help they had received from the fledgling State of Israel.

Lebanon

Located in the East Mediterranean, Lebanon is bordered by Syria and Israel. After World War I France was given a mandate over the northern portions of the Ottoman Empire (Syria) and finally in 1943 France granted it independence. Its troops were gone in 1946. It operates under a unique form of government called confessionalism that involves power sharing among several religious communities. In 1948 it sided with its Arabian neighbors against Israel. It was, however, willing to contribute to the UN action and provided 50,000 dollars, a considerable sum in terms of 1950 dollars.

While there are no memorials to the Lebanese reflecting help during the Korean War, the Republic of Korea had not forgotten. Remembering the gift to their cause in the 1950s the Republic of Korea provided peacekeeping forces in Lebanon in 2007, commenting at the time that it was a gift that had gone unreturned too long.

Liberia

Liberia was originally founded by freed slaves that came primarily from the United States. In 1819 the United States appropriated 100,000 dollars to help in establishing the state. Located in West Africa, it borders Sierra Leone. This small English speaking nation gained its independence on 26 July 1847 from the American Colonization Society. In 1862 American president Abraham Lincoln officially recognized the state of Liberia. In 1914 it declared neutrality in World War II but became a member of the League of Nations in 1919. In 1944 it joined the Allies in the war against the Axis powers and 1951 signed a mutual defense treaty with the United States.

In 1950 Liberia was in a state of civil stability and was undergoing a strong period of economic growth. It had good relations with the United States and had been a member of the United Nations since November of 1945, and was interested in taking a more active part in international affairs. Under the long-term leadership of President William Tubman, who served from 1944 to 1972, the nation was anxious to participate. Leaders suggested they might be able to provide a battalion to join the fight, but the United States managed to avoid any formal offer. The Liberian government was in no position to offer fighting men to the UNC as their small armed forces, though trained by the U.S., were not well-enough armed or equipped to join the fight. But, though the nation was poor, it provided 10,000 American dollars' worth of much needed cerate rubber.

The capital of Liberia is Monrovia and was named in 1824 after the American President James Monroe. Monroe had been prominent in the sending of freed slaves to Liberia.[8]

Mexico

The largest Spanish speaking country in the world, it had a population, in 1950, of about twenty-five million. The Mexican government, a member of the UN since 1945, acknowledged receipt of the request on 29 June 1950 and then responded more fully on 8 July 1950, "Mexico is prepared to cooperate, within the limits of its resources, to restore international peace and security."[9] However, it finally decided that public opinion within the nation did not allow any commitment of troops to fight in a foreign country. The nation of Mexico did, however, arrange to provide significant quantities of beans for the war effort.

Mexican President Luis Padilla Nervo, in an attempt to end the negotiations that had been deadlocked, submitted a new call for reconsideration of the prisoner of war issue. He was not alone. A combination of Latin American nations, plus some nations from the Arab-Asian Coalition, and backed by some of the smaller NATO countries, came close to forming a majority to seek a compromise in Korea. The proposal was lost in the move towards accepting the Menon plan.

Nicaragua

Nicaragua had been a supporter of the Allies during World War II and was a charter member of the United Nations, joining in June 1945. In its 5 July 1950 communication with the secretary-general, it suggested it was "prepared when deemed advisable to cooperate by contributing personnel since the Nicaraguan people obviously wish to collaborate in defense of democracy and the principles of world rule of law which the United Nations represents."[10] As a result the government of Nicaragua, though not willing to send troops, made an offer to provide rice, assorted food stuffs, and alcohol.

Perhaps the greatest effect of the Korean War on the nation of Nicaragua was the tremendous increase in the need for cotton that led this nation to become a significant exporter.

Norway

A brief background of the Norwegian people and the political situation in which this nation indicated its willingness to participate in the United Nations activities in Korea are considered in Chapter 5. In addition to their contribution of a medical unit, the country also offered the use of a 9,000 ton cargo ship that was in San Francisco at the time.

As it was, Norway was rather unexpectedly involved in the Korean War right from the beginning. When war broke out one of the few ships available to aid in the evacuation was the Norwegian fertilizer ship *Reinholt*, which was quickly unloaded at Inchon and boarded with dependents. Although the fertilizer ship had only 12 berths, and was in less than sanitary condition, on the night of 26 June 1950 it managed to take 682 evacuees, mostly women and children, safely to Japan.

Pakistan

In return for its help during World War II, the British government had promised India (which then included Pakistan) some measure of self-government. Finally, in 1947, the nation of Pakistan was formed and it was separated politically from the larger state of India. It considered itself a self-governing dominion of the British Commonwealth, and yet its economic and cultural ties were often with Communist China. In 1947 it fought a war with India over the disputed Kashmir region. After UN involvement the dispute was temporarily settled along the Line of Control. In 1950 it was one of the first nations to recognize the People's Republic of China. With the death of its first head of state, Muhammad Ali Jinnah, and the assassination in 1951 of its first prime minister, Liaquat Ali Khan, the nation was in political turmoil. Later, with the passing of its new constitution in 1956, Pakistan became an Islamic republic.

When the question of Korea came before the United Nations in 1950, Pakistan sided with the United Nations, and its leaders expressed an interest in contributing two divisions. The United States very much wanted them to be involved. But the government of Pakistan wanted something in return. It wanted U.S. support for its claims on Kashmir and Poshtunistan. It also wanted a military commitment for the defense of Pakistan. But the U.S., as much as it wanted to maintain bases in Pakistan, did not want to further antagonize India and Afghanistan, believing that it might well lead to war in South Asia. Thus while this nation was not willing to commit troops to the conflict, it did contribute 5,000 tons of wheat to the United Nations cause.

Some early analysis of the Korean War period suggests that the government of Pakistan also provided some material aid to the North Koreans, but further investigation reveals no evidence that this is true. Since 1950, the government of Pakistan has been the largest contributor to United Nations peace-keeping efforts, with troops stationed in difficult areas all over the world. Since 1971 Pakistan has increasingly become a trading partner with North Korea.

Panama

In 1950 the Congress of the United States passed the Thompson Act, which created the Panama Canal Company. This provided for the area to be administered by the governor of the Canal Zone, appointed by the U.S. president, and the use of revenues for the maintenance of the canal. The military also maintained bases in the Canal Zone. The Panama Canal was widely used for the transportation of troops and supplies during the Korean War. While the Panama government's offer of military bases and a volunteer force was deferred,[11] the United Nations did accept its offer of merchant vessels to be used in the transportation of men and supplies, and the free use of its highways for troop movement.

An American destroyer passes through the Panama Canal on the way to Korea.

Paraguay

A land-locked nation in South America composed of something over 150,000 square miles, Paraguay recorded its population in 1950 as 1,270,000. Having achieved its independence from Spain in 1811, it was identified as a Constitutional Republic. For half a century, however, the nation suffered from considerable political instability, having 31 presidents between 1904 and 1954, most of them removed from office by coup. Following the Paraguayan Civil War (1947) there was a series of unstable governments until 1954, when Alfredo Stroessner came to power and ruled for the next 35 years. In 1950 Paraguay was growing in economic strength, as it was exporting vast amounts of cotton, vegetable oil, meat, corn, rice and tobacco, primarily to other South American countries.

During World War II Paraguay reflected a strong pro–German position that caused the United States to pour considerable amounts of money into the nation to wean it away from this position. While Paraguay did not declare war on the Axis, it did sever diplomatic relations in 1942. Despite instability at home Paraguay was involved in the international scene, joining with other nations in 1947 to support the United Nations when that body called for national elections in Korea. It supported the Temporary UN Commission established in 1947 to encourage the reunification of Korea. It also voted in favor of all of the UN proposals for the unification of Korea. When the crisis developed it joined with others to support the call for military intervention.

In response to the UN request for help, Paraguay, on 24 July 1950, offered to provide military assistance to the UN Command, but this was not integrated primarily because at the time Paraguay did not have a trained and equipped force available. Later it promised $10,000 for the purchase of medical and sanitary supplies for troops in Korea, and in April 1951 delivered on the promise. In 1953 the government was instrumental in the collection of nearly ninety million dollars as a contribution to the UN.

Never really free of its pro–German feelings, Paraguay accepted a significant number of Nazis following World War II, providing them with permanent homes, including Dr. Josef Mengele, who was protected despite several international efforts to put him on trial.

Peru

Peru is the third largest state in South America. It received its independence from Spain on 28 July 1821. Always in dispute with Ecuador over borders, it fought a war in 1941 that ended in a treaty. In 1950 newly elected President Manuel A. Odria, seeking recognition, supported the United Nations efforts in Korea. But, while a member of the UN since 1945, Peru was only minimally involved in the UN effort in Korea. The government of Peru was nevertheless concerned over the continuation of the war. In its reply to the secretary general on 30 June 1950, the government stated that Peru was "prepared to concert its action with that of the other members to furnish such assistance to the Republic of Korea as may be necessary to repel the armed attack and restore international peace and security."[12] During the war the nation of Peru committed itself to providing one million shoe soles for troops, some food stuffs, and medical supplies.

While the government of Peru was not taking a military role in Korea, it was actively interested in the political implications of the war. When the continuing impasse over repatriation produced a series of suspensions of the negotiation talks, Peru submitted a proposal on 3 November 1952 to the General Assembly that they hoped would break the negotiation deadlock resulting over the repatriation of prisoners of war. It called for a commission of five member nations, a UN appointee and one non-member representative to ensure prisoners repatriation and to provide a neutral zone for those who did not wish to be repatriated. The resolution, one of many coming in at that time, did not go very far, as the Soviet Union rejected it on 10 November as being unworkable.

Based on this early involvement, during the 21st century both political and economic ties between Peru and South Korea have expanded considerably.

Philippines

The political situation under which the Philippines operated and that nation's willingness to participate in the United Nations' aggressive actions in Korea is discussed in Chapter 4. In addition to the military forces that it would make available, the government acknowledged that its support would also include commodities. "To this end" the Philippines reported, "my government is also prepared to contribute, if called upon, such amounts of copra, coconut oil, soap, rice, and anti-cholera, typhoid, dysentery vaccine; also smallpox virus that may help facilitate the implementation of the program."[13]

Uruguay

In his reply to the United Nations call, E. Rodriguez Fabregat, Uruguay's permanent representative to the UN, announced his country "will resolutely support the measures adopted by this international organization in the defense of the supreme ideal of living together in peace and international security, and confirms its faith in the action of the United Nations."[14] Uruguay apparently had every intention of participating, but under pressure from the opposition Blanco Party, as well as its anti–American neighbor Argentina, it finally decided against it.

Despite these dissentions at home, the government of Uruguay provided small amounts of money and quantities of blood plasma. It also offered 2000 troops but they were not accepted.

Perhaps the most significant thing to remember is the degree to which the demand for wool for uniforms in the Korean War played a significant role in the capital expansion of Uruguay giving it a much needed economic boost.

Venezuela

The political instability of Venezuela increased with the assassination of President Carlos Delgado Chalbaud in November 1950. While a member of the UN since 1945, it was in no position to make a major contribution to the

UN action. On 4 July 1950, Venezuela wrote to the UN that "Venezuela, as a member state of the United Nations, is prepared to collaborate within the limits of its resources in the establishment of international peace and security."[15] In time the UN reported that Venezuela provided 100,000 dollars in medical supplies, blankets and blood.

7

Silent Partners

War does not determine who is right, only who is left.
— Bertrand Russell

There were nations on both sides of the conflict that are not generally listed as participants but who made significant contributions to the Korean War. Perhaps the most aggressive of these nations was the Soviet Union, which provided considerable political support and military aid — as well as an unaccounted number of military personnel — in support of the People's Republic of China.[1] There were several, in their positions both as Communist satellites and from their non-aligned status, that supported the North Koreans during the war: the People's Republic of Czechoslovak, the People's Republic of Hungary, and the People's Republic of Poland, the Romanian People's Republic, and the nation of Mongolia.

For those in the United Nations camp the involvement was perhaps less dramatic and generally volunteer. In the case of Japan the aid was both natural, considering its proximity to the conflict, and somewhat clandestine. Since their roles were generally conducted with little fanfare, and because some anonymity was advantageous, there is not a lot of information about them and in some cases their involvements is often minimalized. Nevertheless, the contribution was significant and their roles a necessary part of the history.

India

India's role in the Korean War is still pretty much an untold story. For the United States the position of this often critical nation was reflected in the role it played as the head of the non-aligned nations, but also as the intermediary in relations with Communist China. Both Korea and India celebrate their liberation after World War II on the same day. Both would soon witness the partition of their motherlands. India was concerned about the division of the Korean peninsula and as a member of the United Nations Commission on Korea pushed for that nation being granted independence as a united nation. India, because of this failure to unite, was reluctant to recognize South Korea as the national government of Korea.

For years India was considered the "brightest jewel in the British crown," but following World War II it was granted its independence. The British continued to have considerable say in Indian affairs while, at the same time, the U.S. was trying to expand its influence there. Caught between sides in the emerging Cold War, India decided to play it neutral. It was a new nation dealing with the vast domestic and international problems that were, in many respects, tied to and in disagreement with, the Western powers.

As a member of the Security Council it voted for the initial resolution on June 25, 1950, which acknowledged the invasion and called for the withdrawal of troops. But two days later the nation abstained from voting for the far stronger U.S. resolution asking for military assistance for South Korea. Again India declared its neutrality.[2] Nehru believed the fight that was developing in Korea was in reality a fight between the United States and the Soviet Union and wanted no part of it. The Indian army was small and poorly equipped and was overwhelmed by dangers within the country and waiting on its many borders.

The United States, on the other hand, believed that India had more at stake with the Western powers and that it would be to the advantage of all concerned if India would participate in the endeavor. The U.S. wanted India to send troops.

The Korean War was to be the first test of Prime Minister Jawaharlal Nehru's thesis of non-alignment that called for India to take a well-considered position on international matters without being unduly influenced by the larger powers. It had been involved earlier with events in Korea and had lent its support to the UN resolution calling for general elections in South Korea in 1948. In this case its leader followed the United Nations and supported the decision, believing that North Korea was indeed the aggressor and needed to be stopped. However, Nehru informed the secretary general, as well as the ambassadors of both the United States and the Soviet Union, that he believed that the People's Republic of China should be involved in the discussions. To accomplish this the PRC needed to be brought in to the United Nations. Citing his own problems, as well as the desire to remain outside the superpower disagreement, he further declined to send troops. Instead he followed the path of non-alignment that guided his nation into a series of efforts to restrict the scope of the war, and to push for a cease fire. This allowed the nation to play an important role in trying to work something out to avoid further bloodshed.

India was still upset with the UN failure to support it in its land disputes with Pakistan, and the government believed that the United States and other Western powers had identified themselves with Pakistan in this dispute. India had also been working hard to cultivate a working relationship with China and saw the UN actions as further isolating that nation and, at the same time, pushing it toward the Soviet Union.

The United States and Great Britain were not pleased with all of India's actions, and actually sneered at some of the peace proposals offered, believing them naïve and impractical. They were displeased at the lack of participation in the military force being established. The British *Economist* expressed something of this unhappiness when it wrote: "Nehru was as much an appeaser as Chamberlain, if anything more dangerous."[3] This theme, considered a sound argument for the nations to be involved in Korea, comes up over and over in the discussions with the non-aligned nations.

Both the United States and Great Britain, nevertheless, continued to rely on India's neutral status to maintain contact with the Chinese and the non-aligned nations. This communication was highly important. Despite their hostilities these nations had a great deal to talk about and used the good offices of the Indian government on several occasions. It was India's Girija S. Bajpai who, in September and early October 1950, relayed the information to the United Kingdom and the United States that Foreign Minister Zhou Enlai had warned if UN forces moved north of the parallel, Chinese troops would intervene. General Nieh Jung-Chen, the PCS chief of staff, told Sardar Panikkar that the "People's Republic of China did not intend to sit back with folded hands and let the Americans come to their borders."[4] The Indians were so concerned that the message be delivered that in order to be sure it was received, it was endorsed to Loy W. Henderson, the U.S. ambassador to India. Sometime later it was the government of India that conveyed President Eisenhower's warning that unless some negotiated settlement was reached within a short time the war in Korea would be escalated.

From the beginning India had been concerned, and expressed its displeasure, about General MacArthur crossing the 38th parallel. Bipan Chandra, well known Indian historian, claimed, "India voted against it [naming China the aggressor] because they believed that it was clearly MacArthur and not China who was the aggressor in North Korea."[5] However, India abstained from voting for the Soviet resolution, presented in November, asking that the U.S. cease its aggression against China. Then, it abstained from voting for the U.S. resolution that asked for China to withdraw from Korea. India was looking ahead to a time when it would be playing a dominant role in Asia and did not wish to be identified as siding with either of the great powers in this Cold War struggle.

The nation was also concerned both about the continuation of the war and the possibility that it might get out of hand, ending up in a larger conflict that would endanger them all. In late 1952 when the Panmunjom truce talks were stalled once again, it moved to get the nations back to the negotiations table. Nehru asked Indian ambassador to the UN V. Krishna Menon to initiate a compromise regarding prisoner repatriation that would break the deadlock. The Menon version called for the creation of a commission made up of four neutral powers to monitor prisoners that did not wish to return to their homelands. So, while both China and the Soviet Union rejected the idea, it was most likely the basis for the later proposal that was approved.

They did, however, offer some support to the UN by sending a medical team. This was not simply a stationary medical unit designed to receive the wounded, but rather a combat ready airborne unit capable of supporting battlefield action. Having been borrowed from the Commonwealth Division, this medical unit dropped with the American 187th Airborne Regimental Combat Team, an action many considered to be direct combat support.

As plans were being made to implement the cease fire agreement, India, because of its well established and hard-won neutrality, was chosen to provide the force the UN needed to enforce the provisions of the armistice agreement. At first the UNC wanted to involve Switzerland as the custodial nation but the Communists were not happy with this selection and pushed for India. The other four nations on the Neutral Nations Repatriation Commission were Switzerland, Sweden, Poland and Czechoslovakia. The UN agreed to India on the condition that it would provide all the troops and administrative personnel needed to carry out the program.

South Korean President Rhee opposed the selection of India, as he saw India's position as being less than neutral and historically unsupportive of the South Korean government. At first he would not allow Indian troops to cross over Korean territory to get to the armistice site. However, with additional security promises from the United States, Rhee agreed. What was to become the Custodian Force India was a divisional size organization whose job it was to guard the nearly 23,000 war prisoners waiting repatriation. This service was provided by the 190th Indian Infantry Brigade supported by the 60th Parachute Field Ambulance that was already in Korea. The brigade, commanded by Brigadier R. S. Paintal, consisted of the Rajputana Rifles, the Jat Regiment, the Dogra Regiment, and the Garwhal Rifles. The Repatriation Commission and Indian Custodial Force did not leave Korea until February 1954.

Over the years, however, South Korea has been more willing to acknowledge the role that India played, and how that role provided a positive effect on the outcome. In recognition of this, in November 2011, the Republic of South Korea sent its ambassadors of goodwill, the Little Angels children's folk ballet, to perform in Delhi as a tribute to the Indian contribution to the Korean War.

Japan

It is easy to forget that when war started in Korea, World War II was not officially over. There was still no peace treaty with Japan. Preceding the Korean problem, the U.S. State Department had been in favor of settling on an early peace treaty, but the Defense Department was delaying, suggesting there were still security issues to be addressed. General MacArthur on the other hand was anxious to have the questions of military bases and troop dispersal settled and opted for an early treaty. After the Korean War began the Joint Chiefs of Staff began to consider the danger created in Japan by the decline in occupational forces, and the fact that a strong Communist element was still at work in Japan. It became obvious that the situation in the occupied nation was critical and, as David W. Mabon suggested, "Instead of waiting for a peace treaty until Japan was pro–Western, it became desirable to begin negotiations of a treaty that would encourage Japan to be pro–Western."[6] For the time being, however, Japan was officially neutral. In the treaty that was finally signed on 8 September 1951, Japan renounced all territorial claims to Korea and recognized the independence of Korea.

But for all intents and purposes it had never been neutral. And, while some effort was made to play down its involvement in order to avoid criticism from the Soviet Union, its contributions to the war in Korea were hard to hide. Japan's participation was varied and widespread. Perhaps the greatest contribution was in the production of thousands of items needed by the military in Korea and providing thousands of civilians as employees for military bases. A special procurement system was worked out with the Department of Defense that allowed for local purchases without the complex procurement system set up by the Pentagon. In the course of the war more than 3.5 billion dollars was spent with independent Japanese contractors on items needed to supply and maintain troops in Korea.

Japan was also involved in some of the military action; perhaps the most significant was the mine sweep at Wonsan Harbor in October 1950. When General MacArthur planned for an amphibious landing at Wonsan, he was not prepared for fact that the North Koreans, using Soviet mines, had sewn the harbor. The mines were making it impossible for the Marines of X Corps to land as planned. It quickly became apparent that the ten American sweepers available were not enough to clear the harbor so that the UN ships, carrying the Marines, could enter. Admiral Turner Joy asked General MacArthur for permission to use Japanese sweepers. The situation was dangerous but soon necessity overcame the political objections and the general agreed. It was determined that the Japanese crews had to be volunteers and that they would receive double pay for their service.

As it was, the sweepers were used to great advantage supplementing the United Nations sweep, but when on 17 October one of the Japanese sweepers hit a mine and sank, command scrambled to cover it up in hope of avoiding a Chinese propaganda victory. Then, and later, MacArthur would defend their use by asserting they had been hired for humanitarian and not combat purposes, and so did not violate the accepted rules of warfare. Nevertheless, sweepers and landing ship tranports (LSTs) continued to be used for less humanitarian reasons.

Yet another influence that the Japanese exerted had to do with the availability of equipment. Since 1947 members of the Far East Command had been working on a plan called Operation Roll-up. In this effort reclaimed military equipment, weapons, and ammunition were being collected from the battlefields of World War II and refurnished. The plan functioned out of Japan where thousands of damaged military vehicles were put back into working condition. It was planned that the operation would be completed in June 1950 and was well on the way to making its goal when Korea was invaded. The equipment was needed immediately. Somewhere between 75 and 90 percent of the armament available for front line duty in Korea was derived from this program.[7]

The Japanese also provided a significant number of bases for the Army and Marines, port facilities for the Navy, and fields for the United Nations aircraft. The Air Force maintained nine bases alone in Japan. The U.S. Naval base at Yokosuka served as the primary ship repair and maintenance facility and was staffed primarily by Japanese workers. On a more immediate basis they also provided crews that manned significant numbers of merchant and transport ships including LST (QO), which took part in both invasion and evacuation activities. The U.S. Military Sea Transportation Service (MSTS) contracted Japanese ships through the Shipping Control Administration, Japan (SCAJAP).

Under direct control of the Commander of Naval Forces Far East, the Shipping Control Administration, Japan, provided direct logistic and military support. Japanese crewed ships, primarily old American LSTs, were the backbone of the armada required to move men, equipment and supplies to the

Korean front. Admiral C. Turner Joy estimated that nearly three-fourths of all the ships involved in the amphibious landings at Inchon, Wonsan, and the evacuation at Hungnam were from SACJAP. Thirty-eight Japanese owned and crewed LSTs were involved in the supply and defense of Pusan.

The willingness to expand Japan's economy is seen in both the military and political decisions to extend the Japanese markets beyond Korea and sell to other non–Communist nations in the Far East, including French Indochina, Thailand, Formosa, the Philippines, Malaya and Burma. Such action would not only beef up the Japanese economy but, the occupation government believed, would increase the assurance that Japan would emerge from the conflict as an ally in the Cold War.[8]

Often forgotten in the accounts of the action is the role of the indigenous supply of labor. Japanese laborers, dockworkers, road and railroad workers, even carrying parties were an essential part of the logistic program, but it was also highly significant that Japan released thousands of occupation troops for combat in Korea.

Because of its situation first as an occupied country and then in the first steps of forming its own government, Japan played a small role in the political maneuvering behind the Korean War. It did respond when news of Mac-Arthur's firing was announced. The Japanese people were shocked and in general the response was very supportive of the general. He had done a good job in Japan, serving as something of a co-emperor, and the people there were aware of the benign nature of his occupation of their country.

Unfortunately no one was keeping track of the casualties among the Japanese people involved in military action. Most accounting for casualties do not list Japan as being involved and the one or two who do cite the Japanese use the term "several" under killed in action and list one person taken prisoner.

If any one nation can be said to have benefited from this war it would need to be acknowledged that Japan gained the most. When the Korean War broke out the United States and Japan were still officially at war; Japan was an occupied nation. While the peace was signed in September 1951, it was not until 27 April 1952 that the peace terms were ratified. Up to that time Japan's role was questionable both from a political point of view as well as under international law. However, once the peace terms had been ratified, Japan was free to establish the National Police Reserve. Once established, this semi-military force was able to take over many of the duties that had been assigned to occupational troops and thus to free up more American soldiers for service in Korea.

There has not been proper recognition of this contribution, probably due to the harsh relationship that existed between the Korean and Japanese people at the time, and because of the controversy that arose over the involvement of Japanese personnel. As late as 2010 an official news article from the Democratic People's Republic of Korea blamed the Japanese for their involvement in the Korean War, claiming that they needed to be punished for their "very grave war crimes and unpardonable crimes against humanity."[9]

8

Acceptance Deferred

We thought that North Korea would back off when they saw American uniforms.
— Phil Day of Task Force Smith

There were nations, which in gestures of good faith and in keeping with their membership commitment to the United Nations, offered men, money, or supplies to the war effort. But, for a variety of reasons their offers were not accepted by the United Nations Command. In the diplomatic language of the time it was noted that "acceptance was deferred." The memo sent out in regards to these countries identifies each of the deferred contributions with the phrase "Criteria for military aid furnished [name of government] representative."[1] These refusals were issued by both the JCS and the State Department, and there appears to be some difference between contributions turned down by the Joint Chiefs of Staff on primarily military grounds and those that were refused by the Department of State for political reasons. However, it is not always the clear which was the case. In most incidents the refusal was due to deficiencies in the size or condition of the military structure, but in some cases the decline was more politically motivated, a belief that the presence of these nations might increase the delicate balance so far established. In several cases, not considered here but illustrated in the non-acceptance of Liberian forces, the U.S. talked the nation out of making a formal offer in order to avoid what were considered embarrassing circumstances. The following nations had their offers deferred.

Bolivia

In 1950 Bolivia was a country of 2.7 million and was about three times the size of the American state of Montana. During the period from the Chaco

War until the 1952 political ideologies emerging from the Bolivian Revolution convoluted its politics. The war, fought with Paraguay over control to the access to the Paraguay River, was deadly and cost more than 100,000 lives. Following the war, which was solved by international negotiations and which left Bolivia about where it had been at the beginning of the war, conflicting political parties clamored for control. As a result of the revolution and the administration of Victor Paz Estenssoro, sweeping land reforms were conducted. Despite internal conflict and economic instability, the nation of Bolivia, a charter member of the United Nations, expressed a willingness to be involved; it voiced an affirmation of support and agreed to meet the request with whatever means was at its disposal in order to fulfill the responsibilities imposed by Article 49 of the charter.

The Bolivian government, however, was not willing to commit a military unit, saying that it had none to offer. It did identify the services of thirty volunteer officers who were willing to serve under other commands. The offer was refused on the grounds that, because of the language and cultural problems, integrating them into other units would be too difficult. In this case the deferral was made by the Joint Chiefs of Staff, and it was reported that consolations, in September 1950, were underway with their representatives concerning the possibility of deployment. In the end Bolivia did not participate.

After the Korean War Bolivia was one of the few countries in which the United States did not work against the leftist government.

Brazil

Few remember that the South American nation of Brazil played a very active part during World War II, sending troops and providing bases for the American Army, Air Force and Navy. Following the war Brazil was one of the founding members of the United Nations. After rule by a military coup for several years democracy was restored with the election of General Eurico Gaspar Dutra in 1946. At the outbreak of the Korean War the Brazilian government was in the process of moving its capital out of Rio de Janeiro to the interior in an effort to support the economic development of the country. The government of Brazil was supportive of the United Nations effort in Korea, acknowledging the aggression against a member state, and was willing to contribute to a military force designed to carry out the UN resolutions. It responded to the United Nations call by agreeing to meet the request by whatever means were at its disposal; its hope was to fulfill the responsibilities imposed by Article 49 of the charter.

When it came to making a contribution, however, she dragged her feet.

According to the State Department "memo of conversation," the Brazilian government offered to provide military assistance, without providing any clear distinction as to what it would be or when it would be available. This offer was then deferred by the Joint Chiefs of Staff. The reasons were not given in the communication, but as late as October 1950 the United Nations' criteria for furnishing military aid were still being considered by the government of Brazil.[2]

Costa Rica

Explorer Christopher Columbus reached this land on this fourth voyage and named it Rich Coast. It separated from Spain in 1821 and became independent in 1838. In 1855 an American backed adventurer, William Walker, defeated Nicaragua and planned on attacking Costa Rica and building a canal, but the plan failed. In 1919 when considerable civil unrest developed, the U.S. Marines invaded the country to secure the safety of American interests, and when a democratic government was established in 1920, the U.S. recognized the nation. In 1940 Costa Rica joined the fight against the Axis powers. In 1949 a new constitution established the vote for women and those of African descent.

Costa Rica was a founding member of the United Nations in 1945 and in 1949 was operating under a new constitution. It was interested in fulfilling its commitment to the UN, so despite the fact there were no troops available, the nation of Costa Rica offered to put together a small force of volunteers to serve as a rifle company in some existing unit. The offer was apparently refused by the Joint Chiefs of Staff because the men being considered had little to no training or equipment available.

Much of this discussion with Costa Rica was symbolic anyway as, on 1 December 1948 Costa Rican President Jose Figueres Ferrer proclaimed Military Abolition Day. The 1949 the constitution of Costa Rica abolished its standing army and therefore, despite any willingness to help, there was no force available.

Denmark

Denmark was a strong supporter of the United Nations cause and an active participant in the events in Korea. When first called upon to aid the Korean cause, Denmark immediately made available the transport motor ship *Bella Dan*.[3] The offer was declined by the United Nations Command as being unnecessary. Then on 18 August 1950, the offer of the ship was withdrawn. After that the government of Denmark made arrangements for a hospital ship to be sent. The contribution of this medical unit is discussed in Chapter 5.

El Salvador

The smallest nation in Central America, El Salvador became an independent nation in 1839. In a general election held 26–29 March 1950, Oscar Osorto of the Revolutionary Party of Democratic Unification won the presidency. The nation, however, was politically and economically insecure. As a member nation of the UN since 1945, El Salvador supported the UN decision regarding Korea and provided a positive response to the call for military aid. However, having no ready contingents, El Salvador offered a small force of volunteers to participate in the United Nations command if the United States would train and equip it. The acceptance was deferred (indefinitely) because El Salvador could not field a reinforced (self-sufficient) battalion. Other nations sent smaller units but the primary question was the cost of training and equipping.

As mentioned before the Joint Chiefs of Staff had given brief consideration to the creation of a Latin American Battalion, and El Salvador had indicated a willingness to be involved. It was finally determined to be impractical.

Panama

America's relationship with Panama has been a stormy one though, in many respects, it has been successful for both nations. The outbreak of the Spanish American War convinced Theodore Roosevelt that a canal was necessary to protect American military interests. When consideration was being given to the U.S. taking over the French effort in Colombia, an American backed revolution was necessary to break off the small country of Panama. The newly created Republic of Panama ceded the zone to the U.S. in perpetuity. After considerable difficulty the canal was finished and the first transient, a cement boat, passed through in August 1914.[4]

The Republic of Panama was small with a population, in 1950, of only 892,502. The nation of Panama had been growing during a period of economic expansion under the leadership of President Arnulfo Arias (1949–1951). Panama was one of the 50 signatory states of the UN, a member since 1945, and committed to its mission. It was anxious to be of help, though it was not in a position to provide much in the way of military services. Like several

South American countries, the government of Panama felt an obligation to the UN and responded immediately and with some enthusiasm to the United Nations call for support.

The nation of Panama did not feel that it was large enough to offer a significant number of troops, but offered the use of local bases for training and a small volunteer force of troops that numbered forty-seven. The offer was refused by the Joint Chiefs of Staff because the Panamanian force did not have the necessary training and equipment. At this point the equipment and training facilities available to the UN were limited and the addition of foreign troops was restricted.

The Panama Canal, of course, played a highly significant if unofficial role in the movement of troops and supplies from one coast to the other. In 1950 Congress passed the Thompson Act which created the Panama Canal Company operated under a board appointed by the president. The final formal relationship with the United States dissolved in 2000 when Panama took over complete control of the canal.

Republic of China

During World War II the Nationalists and Communists of China, in a unique agreement, managed to stop fighting each other and concentrate on the defeat of the Japanese invader. During this struggle the United States had been highly supportive, evolving its long time tradition of "oil for the lamps of China" into military and economic aid. Before, and during this fight, China had been a part of the decision making process, taking part in most of the leaders' conferences during the war. On the other hand, even during the war, the Nationalist leader Generalissimo Chiang Kai-shek played the United States and the Soviet Union against one another in an effort to further his own cause. When World War II ended and the Japanese invader had been expelled, the Communists and Nationalists resumed their massive struggle. After a long and bloody civil war, and as the result of a series of missteps and military reversals, the Nationalist Chinese under Chiang were defeated.

It must be acknowledged that most probably General Chiang Kai-shek did not like nor trust Americans. Nevertheless as it became necessary for the general's followers to leave the mainland and set up the government of the Republic of China on the offshore island of Taiwan in 1949, an alliance was essential to its survival. Chiang consider his defeat a temporary setback and was planning an immediate return to the mainland. He anticipated American support. At the same time, of course, the newly created People's Republic of China was preparing for an invasion of the island he claimed.

In 1950 the Republic of China, as the nation was now identified, was a member of the United Nations and felt some commitment to doing its part concerning the outbreak in Korea. Chiang's concern might well have been heightened by the fact that the members of the UN were involved in an effort to oust him and replace their delegation with one from the PRC. His interest in Korea was something of a paradox, for historically Korean nationalism had been directed toward countering Chinese influence and there was no great love lost between the countries. Chiang's strong anti–Communist position and his effort to maintain his own national identity required a willingness to invest in the international effort.

After Chiang established the government on Taiwan he was elected president in March 1950. Despite the fact that the government was a constitutional democracy, Chiang maintained most of the power and operated under his "Temporary Provisions Effective During Phase of Communist Rebellion" with all the powers and intentions of a dictator. Under his leadership conflicts between the natives and the Nationalist refugees were slowly overcome and the process of social and economic development began. He built the ROC army to his highest proficiency, at least in size, and based much of his policy on plans for the retaking the mainland that he still considered their rightful home.

It was the United States that took the first action to involve both Nationalist and Communist China. Recognizing the tensions that remained, the Truman administration was afraid that the outbreak of war in Korea might lead to a confrontation between the Chinas. There was every reason to believe that the Communist Chinese would see the conflict in Korea as the perfect opportunity to launch a long anticipated attack on land they believed belonged to them. It was just as likely that the Nationalist Chinese would consider the situation and see in it an opportunity to begin a military return to the mainland. Neither scenario was acceptable to the United States.

Thus one of President Truman's first actions following news of the North Korean attack was to send the ships of the Seventh Fleet to enter the Straits of Formosa. Their job was to prevent any movement either direction that would further aggravate the situation. The implications of this decision were to be more far-reaching than the administration apparently foresaw. The Chinese on the mainland were furious, as it upset the Communist time-table for regaining its wayward people. On the other hand, it also freed up thousands of troops who might otherwise have been occupied in the south. Highly reputable Navy historian Edward Marolda suggests that the move led Communist China to assume the U.S. was mounting a broad offensive action against them.[5] The usually supportive General MacArthur, reporting on his visit to China and considering the possible use of Nationalist troops in Korea, reported back that the acceptance of troops "might so seriously jeopardize the defense of Formosa that it would in inadvisable."[6]

In an effort to clarify the situation, and much to the displeasure of the State Department,[7] at the end of July 1950 General MacArthur visited Chiang in Taipei. They discussed the possibility of some military cooperation in Korea and the level of security maintained on the island, but little came out of it other than a reinforcement of the American policy of support. "The enemy of my enemy is my friend" sort of thinking provided the Nationalists a shade of legitimacy, and promised the continuation of the massive amounts of U.S. aid Chiang received. Aware of Washington's nervousness over his visit, MacArthur replied to the Joint Chiefs, "Under no circumstances would he think of extending or exceeding his authority as theater commander and hoped that neither the President nor the Secretary of Defense had been misinformed by 'false or speculate reports from any source.'"[8] He may have temporarily put their minds to rest but the relationship appeared to go downhill after that.

Despite the intervention of the Seventh Fleet, the Nationalists were quick to respond to the UN call for aid. They were the first nation to offer ground troops. Four days after the conflict began General Chiang Kai-shek offered the Truman administration three highly trained (his estimation) infantry divisions — an estimated 33,000 highly-experienced combat troops, if the U.S. would equip and transport them to Korea. He also offered the use of a squadron composed of twenty C-47 cargo transport planes. At the time these men and planes would have been very helpful given the situation. But the offer was declined for what, at least in hindsight, were obvious political difficulties.[9]

There was a great deal involved in the decision. In the first place, despite Chiang's assumptions the Nationalist troops did not have a good record as fighting troops even when they were defending their own nations. Besides that, the equipment and weapons that they would need were in short supply and would impose an additional, and considerable, burden on the already greatly overtaxed logistic situation. Besides in the taking of such forces from Taiwan the nation would become even more vulnerable to Communist Chinese intervention should they still chose to act.[10]

When the offer was made it was given serious consideration by the administration, especially since General Douglas MacArthur had, despite his earlier warning, become a strong advocate for involving Nationalist China.[11] Truman, however, was afraid that the employment of Chiang's troops would further aggravate the gap growing between the U.S. and the People's Republic of China. Even at this stage there was concern about how the People's Republic of China would react to any further escalation. Once the decision was made

MacArthur continued to make several efforts to get Nationalist China involved, and it finally it became necessary for the Joint Chiefs of Staff to remind him that any offer of Nationalist troop involvement in Korea had to be handled by the State Department.[12]

But the question was never completely settled. As the crisis deepened the possibility that America could meet MacArthur's increasing demands for more troops was slim. Secretary of the Army Frank Pace pointed out that the National Guard units being called up would not be ready until March of the next year, and even individual replacements for units already involved and suffering high casualties were not available until the first of the year. Once again the general suggested the acceptance of Chinese Nationalist troops but the State Department was still afraid of the political consequences, as well as the fact it was fraught with the danger that the war would spread to Taiwan. However, later, on 26 July 1952, consideration was again given and the Joint Chiefs of Staff decided that if the need continued, Chinese Nationalist troops could be used. Once the Chinese had entered the war in November 1950 General MacArthur reaffirmed his position on the use of troops from the Republic of China. Not only was he facing a whole new war, but the facts behind the earlier non-acceptance — the fear that it would provide the Chinese an excuse to become involved — was now a reality. This, however, was not acted on.

Certainly the Republic of China played an interesting role in the UN involvement in the Korean War. The reason the Soviet delegate had given for not being at the UN when the decisions on Korea were being made and the UN resolutions passed was that they were boycotting the UN's continued support of the Republic of China as the representative of the Chinese people.[13]

Despite its willingness to be involved, and some later support given in clandestine activities in Korea,[14] the Republic of China was on the losing side of a battle with the People's Republic of China over national identity. Despite the United States' commitment to the Nationalist government, much of the world, particularly the British, could not see the reason why Communist China was not the official body to be represented in the United Nations. The move to seat the People's Republic of China was like a shadow following the negotiations both with Communist China, and many of the nations allied with the United States at the time believed it was impossible for it to maintain the charade that the ROC represented the vast majority of Chinese people. The ROC was eventually expelled by United Nations resolution 2758 in 1971 and its seat given to the Communists. In 1979 the United States severed diplomatic ties with it though it has maintained economic and cultural exchanges ever since.

Conclusion

The time has come when Uncle Sam must put up or shut up and my guess is that it will do neither.
— New Zealand ambassador Robert M. Scotten, to his own government

The war in Korea was, for many nations, a distraction, an unwanted focus on the smoldering tension that was rising between the superpowers. The major Western powers were anxious to keep the United States' attention on the situation in Europe, where they expected the Soviet Union to eventually act, maybe even unleashing another world war. Europe was feeling its way toward a united front and the eventual formation of a defensive pact defined as NATO, and they were in need of American aid. But many were equally concerned that they avoid falling too deeply under American dominance.[1] The invasion of South Korea and the world's instant focus on Asia would distract the nations from this issue, and at the same time, would require many nations to commit themselves in this larger struggle over world power. In the end most nations involved seemed to direct their efforts at keeping the Korean distraction as low key as possible and their own contributions as limited as could be accomplished. But, for many, there was no way to avoid being involved.

The outcomes of this watershed conflict are still being counted with more and more scholarly studies appearing that deal with some of the many significant questions still without answers. Now more than sixty years later the United States, at least, is still living with the repercussions. The people of the Republic of Korea live each day with hostile troops on its border and constant threats against its nation. The world has to deal with the isolated but belligerent nation of North Korea with its threat of nuclear armament. What kind of conclusion can be offered as so many of the questions remain? Perhaps a few significant points can be identified from this brief look.

In retrospect we can arguably make the case that President Truman made the correct decision in Korea; that at least for America it addressed the immediate fears and threats and matched the agenda of the time. Second guessing is the job of the historian and will continue as more and more information becomes available, but it does appear that the events in Korea, and the eventual outcome of the UN involvement there, could be called successful in the pragmatic terms of the Cold War then evolving. In the first place the invasion of the south was halted and the invading forces driven back. That, certainly, was a victory. Granted, it may not have provided the ideal results sought by the many allies, and for the Koreans failed to unite their country, and so in that sense the decision was not productive. In the sense that the war was an ideological conflict, there is considerable doubt if one side or the other made much headway on the stage of public opinion. Yet, I think the case can be made that the war was a far more successful effort for the un-aligned nations that emerged with a greater sense of identity.

So if there are no clear successes, what were the outcomes? One of the most important was what it did not do; it did not expand into World War III. That fact alone is at once remarkable and fairly simple to explain, while at the same time nearly miraculous to achieve. The answer is that the two primary leaders most involved in forming the direction and policies of the war — President Harry S Truman and Chairman Joseph Stalin — did not want it to happen. That may well be too simplistic but there are numerous examples where careful efforts were made by both parties to keep events under control. From the restraints on the use of naval power on the part of the Soviets, to the agreement, calculated or otherwise, not to disclose to their own people that U.S. and Soviet pilots were flying combat missions against each other, the war was kept in check by avoiding key events that might have triggered an expansion. Consider the difference and potential outcome if the Pacific sea lanes through which much of the war was supported had been harassed by Soviet submarines. While an amazing amount of troops and materials traveled to Japan and Korea by air, the ocean routes were essential, and any interference to their free passage would have altered the war considerably.

The American control on the temptation to bomb Manchurian targets in order to avoid what was sometimes called "safe sanctuary" suggests an awareness of the expansion potential. Stalin, apparently aware of and worried about the possibility of a wider American involvement, made the same kinds of decisions. When, for example, Kim Il Sung was preparing his attack, Stalin gave in to the requests to use Soviet ships for the transportation of troops; however, he was not willing to allow Soviet crews to man these ships because "it may give the adversary a pretext for interference by the

USA."[2] The wrong move by either world leader might well have led to a disastrous expansion of the war, a war neither nation wanted nor was ready to fight.

As for the United Nations' involvement and its situation after the end of the war, it is arguably true as some historians maintain that the response of the member nations to the United Nations' call for action saved the UN from extinction as a significant international organization. It is also the case that at the end of the war the UN was not showing signs of having been saved. In the first place the body had not solved the question in Korea but only delayed it, and it still maintained the position that prevented the largest population of people on earth from being represented. And while the passage of the June resolutions, as well as the maintenance of a hard line while fighting the war, demonstrated the extent to which the United Nations was an extension of U.S. policy, it was also proving to be the body through which smaller less committed nations were able to band together to resist American ambitions. It was as well the body in which non-aligned nations discovered the use of their influence. Despite the suggestions from the Soviet Union that the UN was playing into American hands, the UN did not rubber stamp what America put on the agenda. Several nations played highly significant roles that were way out of proportion given their size and limited influence on the international stage. Among these certainly were Canada, India, Australia, France, Sweden, Switzerland, Great Britain and even Mexico and Peru. Thus it is difficult to judge the events in Korea in relation to the success of the United Nations, and while those events cannot be said to have saved the body, one has to wonder what would have happened, once the U.S. raised the question, if it had not responded.

In looking at the participants and attempting to evaluate the events, the cause grows even more difficult. Among other things claimed by some historians and political scientists is that the United States' involvement in the Korean War, and the stand taken against Communist expansion, would eventually lead to the decline, and eventually the dissolution, of the Soviet Union; that the Berlin Wall first started to crumble when the UN took aggressive action. This may be exaggerated, but the war certainly changed the position of the Soviet Union. It did have the effect of pushing the People's Republic of China and the Soviet Union closer together for the duration of the situation, as the PRC proved to be highly dependent on Soviet aid. But it is also true that events during the war sowed the seeds that would later add to the growing split between them. There is no doubt that the war increased the tension between the superpowers and in doing so gave each of those nations an increased leadership role in their own spheres of influence. But it also had the opposite effect in that the cementing of such hard ideological positions made many of the non-aligned nations all that more determined to avoid making a commitment to either side.

It is necessary as well to understand that the war would eventually lead to a more distinct identity for North Korea and, in that fact, the emergence of yet another form of Communism to be considered. Certainly one of the more significant and unexpected outcomes of the Korean War was that it provided the nation of North Korea with an unanticipated degree of independence within the Soviet bloc. In the years that followed after the Korean War, Kim Il Sung, showing highly nationalistic intentions, purged his government of many of the pro–Soviet and pro–Chinese zealots who had taken up leadership positions and adopted a remarkably autonomous course of action that is still pursued today.

The war also seems to have contributed to the survival of the anti–Soviet Communist government that ruled Yugoslavia, and allowed that state to maintain despite the Soviet expansion into the Balkans. While no friend of Yugoslavian leadership, Kim Il Sung would take on many of the characteristics of this other Communist nation, learning perhaps how to manage and maintain an even and productive balance between Communism and Nationalism.

In recognizing the unity that existed among the PRC, the Soviet Union, and North Korea, the question arises if there was so much dependency on Stalin, was it his death in March 1953 that finally brought an end to the war? There is not a lot said about this, but we need to keep in mind that the efforts at negotiation had taken a larger step — the opening discussion of an exchange of sick and wounded prisoners of war in Operation Little Switch — prior to his death.

For the United States it is important that, at least on the domestic side, the Korean War did not appear to be very costly for the Americans. That is, it did not cost enough to be taken too seriously. It was the Truman administration's policy to deal with the material requirements necessary to fight the war, by carrying out a form of creeping mobilization; that is, that the industrialization of the Korean War was to be partial, not total. This expansion would be accomplished with the least possible disturbance to the domestic economy as attainable. Americans were only five years away from the restrictions imposed on them by military industrial production in World War II and were really not in the mood for more. Apparently acknowledging this, and the fact that the Cold War tensions would be around for a long time, there was a concern that the rush to production might allow for an overproduction. In this case it would, by its very nature, carry with it the potential of built-in obsolescence. On the other hand, Secretary of the Army Pace did not want the administration to lose sight of the fact that material production needed to take precedence over personnel mobilization, believing that the military was constantly being limited and determined by the nation's ability to supply it.

Certainly the United States emerged from the Korean War with a belief in maintaining a highly competent and available military and the creation of a comprehensive military expenditure program that persists to this day. And while the war and the extended Cold War pushed both the Communist and anti–Communists camps into huge expenditures, it was the United States in which this policy was such a change of direction.

The war also provided the U.S. with the much needed excuse to retain U.S. military personnel and bases in Japan. This base of operations was essential to its influence in Asia. The downside of that is that it also helped focus American thought on Asia, which in time led to a series of questionable commitments. As an essential part of America's growing preoccupation with containing Communism in Asia, its eyes were on Indochina and along the "Great Crescent" that encompassed the East and Southeast Asia. If nothing else, the situation in Korea should have warranted close consideration as a military rehearsal for the later disaster that, in time, was played out with America's involvement and defeat in Vietnam.

At the end of the war the United States made one last effort in hope that any reemergence of the Korean War could be avoided. In the "greater sanction" statement they addressed this fear of a renewed aggression in the Far East, and it was signed on 27 July by nations that had troops involved in the war. However, it got little attention and did little to avoid friction in the area. From the member nations' reactions, it seemed clear that those who had participated in this long, costly war were not about to enter such venture again without sober consideration.[3]

The United States and the NATO nations emerged from the Korean War both better off and more essentially integrated and militarily and economically more secure. The security treaties worked out with New Zealand and Australia were directly related to concern that had to be met before making a peace settlement with Japan. It is very likely the case that the American success in Japan's economic and political development had the effect of preventing the Soviet Union and China from including Japan in their hopes for a Pacific security arrangement.

So what about the other nations? While working on this volume several colleagues, and more than one national representative, asked what it was that provided such an interest in what must certainly be considered the backwaters of history. Really, they would ask, what sort of difference did these other nations make? Weren't they just tokens? It was not enough to suggest that, if nothing else, it could be identified as a loophole in the history of a highly important war, and needed to be filled. And certainly it is hardly fair to the men and women who gave their lives to suggest that they were merely tokens. Nevertheless, such a question is difficult to answer, perhaps because in part their attitude may be justified.

There is no available standard against which to make an evaluation of their individual national contributions. It was an alliance much unlike that of World War II, and has hardly been repeated in the same manner since. In participating these nations certainly fulfilled the political obligations they had made when signing on to the UN. They gave credibility to the United Nations by virtue of their participation, and together provided the authority needed for the United Nations Command. The validity of their military contribution may be less obvious. Other than the Commonwealth nations and the Republic of Korea, no unit that participated in the war would have been able, by itself, to make much of a difference. But attached as they were to other commands, they filled in significant gaps that might otherwise been unfulfilled.

In looking through the literature of the war, it is evident that many of these nations did not consider their involvement all that essential, nor do they believe that it altered their national history to any large extent. Some nations find it hard to locate information about their involvement. There are a surprisingly few books and articles on the contribution or behavior of most of these nations, though most nations have provided some form of a history of their involvement. France was the only nation that did not. The Commonwealth nations, on the other hand, have provided a great deal. Many of the nations have monuments honoring their troop participation and some maintain associations and special days in order to remember them, even though in many cases these have been long in coming. Greece, Canada, the United Kingdom as well as the Republic of Korea, for example, still have an active Korean War Association. Some others have not gone to a lot of effort to remember; their veterans need to go to South Korea to find a monument to their service. Occasionally you find a nation that believes that since the administration of troops in Korea was conducted by the United States, that whatever records were kept would be in those archives. And yet there is very little at all in these records about "other nation" contributions.

For Americans it is easy to identify units and in that identity remember something of their service and the memories and traditions that the unit represents. For many, like the Belgium, their service was in association with other units, and in reporting were more inclined to mention their own rather than the activities of their affiliates. We know that both the United States and the individual nations identified heroes and honored both individuals and units, which among other things reflects on their value to the units attached. And yet, when pushed, we must take seriously that if you mean moral and social support, they may well have made a considerable difference as colleagues, representative of a larger involvement, fellow suffers, and the acknowledgment that the cause, however ill-defined it might have been for the front-line day by day combatant, was an event of international significance.[4]

If, however, you mean strictly military value — the pragmatic value of additional men at arms — the suspicion is that they did not make all that much difference. In the larger arena of a military campaign, specifically, on a one-to-one basis, their contributions can be judged on how they served in their individual assignments and contributed to whatever campaign or defense to which they were assigned. Whether they were guarding supplies and communications, rounding up guerrillas, or filling some gap on the line, they freed up other troops to participate in larger and more well-known events. Taken collectively these "other nations" provided the United Nations Command with eleven infantry battalions that fought in-country and provided significant tactical capabilities that otherwise would have been lacking. On the Yellow Sea and Sea of Japan the allied nations provided aircraft carriers, dozens of destroyers and frigates that augmented the Blockading and Escort Force (TF-95). They provided military and transport aircraft that flew thousands of missions, and fighters that were used for interdiction and ground support. They provided medical teams that dealt with the needs of thousands of wounded with excellence and kindness.

In the political arena the allies made some considerable contributions beyond showing up. Among these roles they served as counter-weights to America's tendency to escalate. This was particularly true of Canada and Great Britain, but was also true of several of the Asian nations. This influence was also felt as the U.S. realized that in order to maintain its policies at the armistice table they had to explore every potential and angle if they were to keep individual nations willing to support their resolutions, and as well to continue to contribute more troops to Korea.

What did participation do for the other countries? In some obvious cases it created friendships that are maintained to this day. Some gained treaties of mutual defense and thus some advance hope for national security. Others maintained a new credibility with the United States that paid off in the continuation of massive amounts of economic aid. In Europe it helped several nations gain membership in NATO and, in the long run, the war was most certainly partially responsible for the massive amounts of military aid the U.S. provided. In some respect NATO was little more than a political organization prior to the Korean War but the war, and the fear it expanded, had managed to galvanize many of the members and increase military aid.

So what sort of fighters did we place on the field of battle? Unlike many other interpreters of the events, I believe that the United States Army, considering its situation in June 1950, managed to fight a pretty good war. Limited in size, training, and equipment, it fought a long prolonged war at heavy costs. American soldiers did not win the victory some assumed was theirs to win, but they did manage to bring the armies of the Democratic People's Republic of Korea and the People's Republic of China to a stalemate.

Generally it is assumed that at the beginning of the war the morale of the American soldier was poor. Many were retreads and were angry. They could not understand why they were being called back to fight another war, particularly one that no one could explain to them. Marguerite Higgins did not do the nation any favor when she reported, "I saw young Americans turn and bolt in battle, or throw down their arms cursing their government for what they thought was embroilment in a helpless cause."[5] Her words carried a great deal of weight and few remembered the other side of the story which she told equally as well. The frustration shared by a good many is found in the words of a combat fatigued young lieutenant, "Are you telling them [your readers] that we have nothing to fight with and that it is an utterly useless war?"[6]

Yes, there were cases of retreat, of bug-outs, of cowardliness and even a few cases of desertion, but just as surely there is extended evidence of remarkable courage, dedication, and commitment. Given the military's twin roles of boredom and terror they performed adequately; they stayed the course. One is reminded of Edwin Rommel's assessment, "American troops know less but learn faster than any fighting man he had opposed." After the successful breakout at Pusan and the march to the Yalu River, morale seemed to go up only to drop again with the intervention of the Chinese and the long retreat. As the years dragged on morale leveled off and many accepted the interminable talk and change of position, seeking only an end.

There was a lot of criticism when it was over. More than was deserved. The nation, embarrassed by its failure to fully define a policy or implement a mission, took it out on the returning troops. One response offered by those who were seeking to explain the behavior of some American prisoner of war compared these servicemen to those of other nations. When the forces were close together there was considerable mingling between troops of the various nations. But when captured, prisoners tended to hang together by nationality. It is true there was not a single successful escape by UN prisoners. What is often lacking in that analysis is that there were in fact numerous attempts to escape, but they had not been successful. The Turks and the British soldiers have been looked at as a standard against which to consider the conduct and survival among the prisoners of war. These nationals were far more capable of dealing with captivity than Americans. The Turks were given the highest credit and the British acknowledged as suffering less "give-upitis" than Americans.[7]

The U.S. Navy served through the entire war, from the first submarine patrols to the last carrier strikes against North Korean targets. It was a war fought at a distance with few sea battles, with the Navy engaged in rather continuous intervention, shelling, bombardment, and blockade action, some so long and isolated that the commander of the ships at Wonsan considered himself the "mayor of Wonsan." Planes provided much of the ground support and escort service required and destroyers and cruisers were involved in amphibious landings and evacuation. Other than for a few days at Wonsan it can be said that the Navy had control of the sea.

The Marine investment was considerably smaller than the Army, but Marines fought well, as was their tradition. Used in amphibious landings and at point in smaller campaigns, they operated, in the main, as infantry. Cut off at Chosin, the Marines underwent a remarkable retreat under heavy enemy fire and yet were able to evacuate their units to fight again.[8] Often joined by the ROK Marines, they held a series of line positions during the stalemate period of the war. Generally well respected by the other services, the relations between the Army and Marines were not always good. Some army officers voiced their concern at the Marine tendency to find a head long answer to everything, barging forward while tactics might have been a better tool, while the Marines found the army sluggish and discouraged, and often lacking in professional skills. The disagreement pushed its way to the level of high command with internal disagreements between General Shepherd and General O. P. Smith, as well as with higher command.

The Air Force often claims to have won the war,[9] and while many a foot soldier would deny that, the newest of the Armed Services made a highly significant contribution. Not only did they conduct bombing raids on essential targets and engage in combat with the Soviet MiGs, they also flew escort missions and provided essential ground support. They were also responsible for much of the movement of troops and supplies in and out of Korea. After a while it became obvious that there was little left to bomb, and they were criticized by the allies, particularly the Asian nations, with vast overkill.

Certainly some consideration must be given to the fact that the Air Force appears obsessed with massive bombing attacks. And while the discussion within the military continues, there seems less and less justification for it. Serious studies conducted at the end of world War II argued effectively that strategic bombing of the type carried out in World War II — the massive attacks on cities, manufacturing areas, transportation hubs and communication lines — were not only ineffective but, in some cases, were a detriment to victory. There is considerable doubt how much the bombing destroyed North Korea's potential to wage war, nor can it be shown that it stopped the movement of supplies, a good portion of which were moved by hand and at night.

Between the constant bombing and the naval blockade the North Koreans were not only still able to continue moving supplies, but the individual soldiers appear to have gotten better at getting along with so much less than the UN that, by comparison, supply was not the biggest problem they faced. The ability of the North Koreans to rebuild bridges, reconnect railways, clear out tunnels, and repair communications continued to astound American bomber crews who discovered targets, bombed only a few days before, up and running when they appeared again. However, it must be acknowledged that with a few exceptions the Air Force took command of the sky and held it throughout the war.

Even the small Coast Guard[10] played an important role, holding sea and air rescue missions and marking navigational posts and communications areas. Theirs may not have been the most dangerous of the assignments but they had to be the most boring, as they often spent months maintaining station. The Merchant Marines, as always the unsung heroes of any war, plied their trade and kept the military supplied with all its needs.

Not to be ignored in this was the vitally essential role of the quartermaster. Overall, their service in the Korean War must be acknowledged as successful, but by a long shot not perfect. The failure, for example, to supply troops with cold weather garments before the arrival of the extreme cold in 1950 and 1951, and perhaps the question of ammunition distribution, could be seen as limitations on their perfection. The ammunition question haunts the logistic memory of the war. For weeks on end the stocks of significant artillery and mortar often fell below authorized levels. The answers given did not solve the problem, but they are indicative of the source of the difficulty. In part the shortage was caused by the unexpectedly high rate of artillery fire used by the combined units.[11] There were also few production lines for ammunition still in operation in the States and the lead time for start-up was often as much as 18 months.[12] Perhaps as significant was the fact that the Department of Defense had misinterpreted the war and expected an early termination, thus not providing the budget necessary for expanded production.[13]

Their job was made more difficult by the fact that in supplying foreign troops many of the requests they had for supplies and equipment originated out of immediate and felt needs. That meant, of course, that the U.S. had no warning or chance to prepare what was needed. The scramble for local sources increased the difficulties and the costs of such service. Finding a silver lining in the complexities of such supply, however, Secretary of Defense George C. Marshall observed, "The precedents which are now being established should become landmarks for future collective military action under the United Nations."[14]

Even for those nations taking on responsibility for their own replacement, and some of their own supplies, it became necessary to judge how this would be worked out. This included a vast number of questions, not the least of which had to do with how many of their offices spoke English. It was also necessary to have an accurate assessment of their training as well as when the contingents would be ready for embarkation and how they would be transported to Korea. It was necessary as well to understand what sort of communications systems they used and how well they adapted to those used by the Americans. The amount of supplies that the home country could provide had to be estimated and transportation provided. Even such smaller questions such as whether they could accommodate the U.S. 80 octane gasoline became essential.

In search of conformity it became obvious that this could only be achieved if something positive was organized. In response Eighth Army opened the UN Reception Center at Taegu. There processing and training were conducted for incoming troops and a familiarization course on American and British equipment was provided. It was also determined that units that were not already using American or British weapons and equipment should be re-equipped as quickly as possible in order to simplify the question of ammunition.

It remains, however, that the general tendency is to be critical of the American performance. The official histories set the stage by suggesting weaknesses. The American historian T. R. Fehrenbach, who some feel was the first to capture the mood of the war, suggests that "most Americans, privately, would admit that U.N. troops were better than they were."[15] One of the reasons given for the Army's inability to perform as wanted was that the selective draft[16] was not picking the best people and that once in training they were not being subjected to the harsh but effective methods that had proven so vital during World War II. The British, who had seen the U.S. operate in Europe, generally held a high opinion of the Army but thought their performance in Korea suffered in comparison to the U.S. Marines. The British official histories, while providing a masterful account of the war, are nevertheless somewhat critical of the U.S. high command.

According to the research done by Korean War historian Michael Hickey,[17] the Chinese identified which of the United Nations troops were the most likely to stand and fight. Their conclusions provided this order of priority. First the U.S. Marines, the 187th U.S. Regimental Combat Team, the Turks, French, Dutch, Belgian and Commonwealth contingents. The U.S. troops, as reported in documents captured in1951, were "too heavily equipped for hill fighting and are affected by terrain and weather conditions. Afraid of being cut off in the rear, once encircled they retreat in disorder."[18]

There is another side to the story, and it is interesting to look at a comment made by Xo Yan, a researcher at the Academy of National Defense in the People's Republic of China, who said in 2003 in an article entitled "Korean War: In View of Cost Effectiveness" that "the Chinese People's volunteers fought the war in a more marvelous way and produced in regard to fighting skills and war art, therefore they have every reason to [have] won reverence of modern military men."[19] In line with this is a statement suggesting that the Chinese were aware of the need for a victory. Chinese historian Ni Lexiong wrote in the *Asian Times* that for the Chinese, the war in Korea meant that for the first time in well over a hundred years, it was free from the fear of foreign invasion. After years of humiliation at the hands of the West, beginning with the Opium Wars and the Unequal Treaties[20] and the disastrous Sino-Japanese War, the nation had forced the West to a stalemate and an armistice. He goes on to discuss other outcomes but returns to this theme, expressing its importance.[21]

The "other nations" have received mixed reports. The troops of the Republic of Korea have been given bad press. Most of the American official histories report that they were poorly trained as individuals and not reliable as units. After action reports and letters of recognition, however, suggest that the contribution was significant. Some have played down this contribution. British historian Max Hastings reports on the feeling that the "relatively small numbers of troops of other Western nations which are represented are adventurous mercenaries who are as content to serve as part of an international fighting brigade in Korea as elsewhere."[22] This may well be overstated and fails to consider where they came from and how they were selected. Most that went to Korea were professional and the term "mercenaries" fails to consider the nations from which they came, or the national considerations that sent them. From the six foot Imperial Guardsmen of Emperor, to the bayonet wielding Turks, from the wild Algerians of the French battalion to the knife swinging warriors of Thailand, many of those involved had been recalled from combat for their service in Korea.

Unfortunately, even their commander was less than enthusiastic. The commander in chief, from his isolated position in Japan, as well as a series of Eighth Army commanders, showed mixed responses to the presence, and use of, the troops arriving from "other nations." Despite the fact that he continually called on these nations for more troops, and even identified the nations from which he wanted help, we know from his own words he did not really believe they played a very important part. At one point, when things seemed to be going well for him, General Douglas MacArthur said that the withdrawal of the other countries offering troops "would have no material effect upon the tactical situation." He may have been right to some degree, but I think the war would have had a different outcome without them.

When General Matthew Ridgway took command from MacArthur, he voiced his frustration at the logistical problems they created. He wrote, "Catering to all the particular preferences, in food, in clothing, in religious observances — gave our service and supply forces a thousand petty headaches. The Dutch wanted milk where the French wanted wine. The Moslems wanted no pork and the Hindus no beef. The Orientals wanted more rice and the European more bread. Shoes had to be extra wide to fit the Turks. They had to be extra narrow and short to fit the men from Thailand and the Philippines ... only the Canadians and Scandinavians adjusted easily to United States rations and clothes."[23] He also made it clear that he did not want anymore soldiers from Thailand or the Philippines, nor did he anticipate that a continued flow of troops from more nations could meet his needs for more manpower. Yet, he is on record on several occasions, going out of his way to congratulate various units when they fought well, and made several public announcements about how much he appreciated and relied on them. He sometimes seemed to go overboard when it came to the Turkish contingent.

The war, of course, solved little to nothing of the Korean question and left the nation divided and in a state of tension that would far outlive the Cold War. The demands for reunification still haunt most of the world's relationship with the Koreas. When the delegates met in Geneva on 26 April 1954 with a hopeful goal of reuniting Korea, it was in vain. The governments involved were no more interested in solving the problem than they had been during the fighting. The Soviet Union rejected any such idea, holding on to the end its unshakable position that the war in Korea had been a civil war and thus the United Nations had no authority to be involved. Nothing could be accomplished and the sixteen members were left with no more to do but reaffirm their declaration of 27 July 1953. The document that ended the war also perpetuated the division of the nation. The significant points are recorded here.

(1) There shall be a demilitarized zone to serve as a buffer to prevent the occasion of incidents that might lead to a resumption of hostilities.
(2) The Han River Estuary waters shall be open to civil shipping, and it shall have unrestricted access to the land under military control of that side.
(3) Neither side shall engage in hostile acts within, from, or against the Demilitarized Zone.
(4) No one, military or civilian, shall be permitted to cross the Military Demarcation Line unless specifically authorized to do so by the Commander into whose area the entry is being sought.[24]

The UN force was without a doubt shaped in many ways by the decision of disinterested member nations to preserve the integrity of the United Nations

Charter and support its principles of international morality. About 40,000 non–U.S. non–ROK troops were sent to Korea and served. It should not be forgotten that these troops demonstrated valor and tenacity in key circumstances that made their roles significant out of all proportion to their small numbers involved. True, their presence occasionally seemed to be a burden more than a blessing to their American partners.

There is yet one other idea to be considered: what if the war had not occurred? Some have argued that without the invasion and the war that followed, the world might have avoided the arms race that followed and with it the ever increasing tensions. Consider as well that the absence of such a war might well have limited North Korean independence, and thus its isolation, and perhaps some form of political reunification might have occurred.

Among the scholarly community there remains much discussion over why Chairman Mao was willing to become involved. Work by Chen and others have discussed this. If he had not chosen to do so, what would have been the outcome? Admittedly, there was much to be gained for China if it successfully defeated American forces, but without the conflict surely the question of PRC acceptance in the UN, and with it the recognition he desired, would have been worked out.

In the United States the end of the war was greeted with calm detachment. None of the excitement that had first greeted President Truman's announcement remained. For those with loved ones involved in the war, it was a chance to get them home again, but there was little of the public response that many remembered following World War II. Some small communities extended the effort to greet the members of their community who had served and were returning, but these were limited. Most men and women returned as they had left, as isolated individuals and thus no unit greetings as are now being practiced. The feeling was somehow dampened by the knowledge that twenty-one had refused to come back. For most it was simply a matter of landing, getting a new set of clothes, mustering out and going home. Few of them joined veterans associations; few held unit reunions, in the main they forgot, at least publically, what had happened. The word that describes the Korean veteran best is probably *silent*, for they too have chosen not to say much about it or their experiences there.

Fewer than 120 war movies about Korea have appeared and the movie fans still prefer World War II and Vietnam for their action adventures. Some novels have appeared as well as some poetry, but it pales in comparison to the literary output following other wars. The academic scholars have come alive since the late 1989 and some excellent histories are available, but if you follow sales you will discover the reading public seems to prefer romanticized portrayals like David Halberstam's *The Coldest Winter: America and the Korean*

War. Hollywood's perennial promise to make a Korean movie to match *Band of Brothers* remains unfulfilled.[25]

It was not all that much different in the other nations. The Commonwealth nations, especially Great Britain with its long military tradition, tended to make more fuss about its returning troops, acknowledging the National Service contribution, but both Australia and Canada took a long time to begin any recognition or to attempt to capture the history of their involvement. The same was true for New Zealand. France was involved with another war and had already become disillusioned with events in Korea and hardly acknowledged the end of that conflict. The Republic of Korea celebrated what many considered to be their salvation but once the external war was over the political confrontation expanded and it was several years before they were strong enough or economically prepared to begin remembering. They began making films of the war in 1963 with *The Marines Who Never Returned* and have continued at a slow pace, but they have almost no distribution in any other part of the world. The war novel *War Trash* (2004) by Hai Jun has gained some popularity.

It is perhaps most obvious in the United States, which was so deeply involved, but the normal literary and artistic responses to this major event are just not there. There is an unexplained absence of Korean War plays, art,[26] music, or sculpture in the culture of most nations that took part, and a seeming disinterest in most functioning galleries for displaying photographs from that war. Coffee table books, still being produced in the hundreds about World War II, have never been on the market. Try and find any information about the "other nations" on the Internet and you will discover what is there is very limited and of questionable value.

Philippines producers made a film during the war—*Korea* (1952)—and one or two after, focusing on the experiences of their own men, but again they are almost never available outside the country. Colombia produced a theatrical work, *The Barren Mount*, which criticized war in general and the Korean War in particular. But surprisingly little has been produced, or fostered, to keep this particular memory alive.

Time will determine how well any of those involved will be remembered. But they were there. Whatever their reasons, whether they were totally invested in the peace keeping role of if they simply provided token contributions chiefly for the diplomatic appeasement of the U.S., they made a difference. As tensions between North Korea and the world continue, some have to wonder if war were to break out there again, what would be the alignment of nations, now that the world has changed so much?

Three years of war had left the boundary line pretty much the same as it had been in 1950.

Notes

Preface

1. Gary L. Huey, "Public Opinion and the Korean War," in Lester H. Brune (ed.), *The Korean War: Handbook of the Literature and Research*. Westport, Connecticut: Greenwood Press, 1999, p. 409.

2. Clay Blair, *The Forgotten War: America in Korea, 1950–1953*. New York: Times Books, 1986; Malcolm Cagle and Frank A. Manson, *The Sea War in Korea*. Annapolis, Maryland: United States Naval Institute, 1957.

3. William Stueck, *Rethinking the Korean War: A New Diplomatic and Strategic History*. Princeton: Princeton University Press, 2002, p. 1.

4. Bevin Alexander, *Korea: The First War We Lost*. New York: Hippocrene Books, 1986, p. x.

5. We sometimes have more information from North Korea than from South Korea since the ROK lost so many of its papers in the back and forth fighting.

Introduction

1. Bruce Cumings, *Origins of the Korean War, 2 Volumes, 1947–1950*. Princeton, New Jersey: Princeton University Press, 1990. The emergence of the revisionist point of view was heralded by Joyce Kolko and Gabriel Kolko in *Limits of Power: The World and the United States Foreign Policy*. New York: Harper and Row, 1972, particularly Chapters 10 and 20–21. Also see I. F. Stone's *The Hidden History of the Korean War*, New York: Monthly Review Press, 1952.

2. President Truman did not go to Congress for a declaration of war and did not believe he should. Primarily he was afraid that Congress would discuss it for so long that it would be too late to act. Anyway, presidents before him had taken the same steps and he believed he had the authority to take such action without Congress.

3. Not really a coup, as the new government was formed by election according to the Czechoslovak constitution of 1920.

4. The airlift, which ended on 30 September 1949, managed, with the help of many nations, to deliver 2,326,406 tons of supplies.

5. Rosemary Foot, *The Wrong War: American Policy and the Dimensions of the Korean Conflict*. Ithaca, New York: Cornell University Press, 1985, p. 44.

6. Joseph Strumberg, "The Loss of China, McCarthy, Korea and the New Right," August 31, 1999. www.antiwar.com/strumberg/aticleid=3329.

7. "The Korean War, Document 68." www.shmoop.com/korean-war/politics.html, p. 1.

8. The assumption on the part of the West was that North Korea could not muster the political autonomy or the military necessities to execute such a large maneuver. According to Kathryn Weathersby, it was Stalin who made the decision in 1949 to invade South Korea, finally going along with Kim Il Sung after their third request. He made this decision assumedly without talking to Mao, according to Weathersby. "The Soviet Role in the Korean War," in William Stueck (ed.), *The Korean War in World History*. Louisville: University Press of Kentucky, 2004, pp. 61–92. The situation is well explained by saying that Kim Il Sung should be seen as the "initiator and Stalin the facilitator." Ibid., p. 66.

9. The National Security Council is a part

of the executive branch of government. It was formed in 1947 by President Truman to advise the president on matters of national security and foreign policy.

10. Truman Papers, June 28, 1950, Center for the Study of the Korean War.

11. The details of the document were considered so secret that it was not declassified until 1975.

12. It is hard to believe that at this point the American people would have shared this point of view. While there is no doubt they saw the Soviet Union looming over their future, there would have been little interest in militarizing the American society, nor in preparing for World War III.

13. As quoted in Max Hastings, *The Korean War*. New York: Simon and Schuster, 1987, p. 58.

14. For consideration of the political restraints on the president's power see Paul G. Pierpaoli, Jr., *Truman and Korea: The Political Culture of the Early Cold War*. Columbia: University of Missouri Press, 1999.

15. Foot, *The Wrong War*, p. 49.

16. I am indebted to Kathryn Weathersby for identifying this point of view. See her "The Soviet Role in the Korean War," in William Stueck's *The Korean War in World History*, p. 71.

17. William Stueck, *The Korean War: An International History*. Princeton: Princeton University Press, 1995.

18. Papers of George M. Elsey, June 28, 1950. 2 of 3, Harry S. Truman Presidential Library and Museum, Independence, Missouri.

19. Westwood, Connecticut: Praeger Press, 2000.

20. William Steuck, *The Korean War in World History*, and Steuck, *Rethinking the Korean War: A New Diplomatic and Strategic History*. I am indebted to him for his scholarship and insight in both these excellent works.

21. *The World and Democracy*, December 7, 2010. www.youtube.com/watch?v=vjtvzhy P21s.

22. This figure includes Mao Tse-tung's son, who was killed in a bombing raid.

Chapter 1

1. Department of the Army, *United States Army in the Korean War*, 4 Volumes, Washington, D.C.: Government Printing Office, 1961–1972, p. 72.

2. Evacuation was considered on several occasions. But the concern was not only facing a defeat in Korea, but the fact that the loss of a major number of troops would leave Japan unprotected and vulnerable to attack.

3. James I. Matray, "Myths of the Korean War," *The Journal of Conflict Studies*, Vol. 22, No. 1, Spring 2002.

4. In this instance the PRC was playing the same game of hidden commitment and announced that it was not declaring war, but simply allowing Chinese volunteers to assist a favored neighbor.

Chapter 2

1. John Edward Wilz, "Korea and the United States, 1945–1950," in Stanley Sandler, *The Korean War: An Encyclopedia*. New York: Garland, 1995, p. 175.

2. General MacArthur did not like having CIA agents in his area of command and limited their activities as much as possible.

3. Darian Cobb, "The Moral Exception: The UN and the Korean War," paper delivered at the annual Conference of the Center for the Study of the Korean War, February 2000, at the center.

4. Reinhold Niebuhr, Protestant theologian and advisor to presidents.

5. Both became members on 17 September 1991.

6. American Soviet specialist George Kennan agreed with Stalin on this point, that it was in fact a civil war, but he asserted that while America had every right to intervene in order to protect its interests in the area, the issue should not have been taken to the UN seeking sponsorship.

7. S/RES/83 (1950) Secretary's Papers, Harry S. Truman Presidential Library and Museum.

8. This is not the whole story by any means. The Soviets were afraid that seating the PRC in the UN would put it in too close contact with the West, but did not want to vote against it due to its long traditional friendship. It was easier to walk out in protest and not take any action.

9. Behind this discussion was the already leaked fact that the United States intended to act alone if necessary. See Ian C. Gibbon, "UN Security Council Resolution of June 27, 1950," in Matray, *The Dictionary of the Korean War*, p. 500.

10. Editors, "UN Offensive Across the Thirty-eighth Parallel." In Matray, *Historical Dictionary of the Korean War*, p. 488.

11. As quoted in Foot, *The Wrong War*, p. 93.

12. So, in 1953, the nations accepted a four kilometer-wide buffer zone much like that proposed by Great Britain, but after tens of thousands more deaths.

13. Foot, *The Wrong War*, p. 91.

14. As quoted in Stueck, *The Korean War: An International History*, p. 163.

15. Escott Reid, p. 163.

16. United Nations Papers, 25 October 1952, Harry S. Truman Presidential Library and Museum.

17. Neither the United States nor North Korea had ratified the Geneva Convention of 1949 on prisoners of war, but both sides had agreed to abide by its stipulations.

18. These quotes are found in Foot, *The Wrong War*, pp. 216–217.

19. Operation Everready was a plan, formulated by Washington and Eighth Army early in the war, to overthrow President Rhee and replace him with a military government more willing to work with the UN. It is some indication of the lack of trust that existed between the partners who were at war with a common enemy.

20. Kathryn Weathersby, "The Soviet Role in the Korean War: The State of Historical Knowledge," in Stueck, *World History*, p. 75.

21. Malenkov came to power after Stalin's death and a victory over Lavrenti Beria and Nikita Khrushchev, all of whom vied for power. After taking office he promoted a new policy to cut Cold War tensions, reduce military spending, and provide his citizens new incentives.

22. Wheland, *Drawing the Line*, p. 369.

23. At the time MacArthur was in his seventies and had not been in the United States for more than a dozen years.

24. Ronald H. Cole, et al., *The History of Unified Command, 1946–1993*. Washington, D.C.: Joint History Office of the Office of the Chairman of the Joint Chiefs of Staff, 1995.

25. James F. Schnabel, *U.S. Army in the Korean War: Policy and Direction; The First Year*. Washington, D.C.: Office of the Chief of Military History, 1973, pp. 46–48.

26. In contrast to the American approach, the Russians, north of the 38th parallel, had come prepared for the occupation with well-trained Korean speaking administrators.

27. Bruce Cumings, *The Origins of the Korean War, Volume II: The Roaring of the Cataract*. Princeton, New Jersey: Princeton University Press, 1992; Jin Chull Soh, "Some Causes of the Korean War of 1950: A Case Study of Soviet Foreign Policy in Korea (1945–1950) with Emphasis on Sino-Soviet Collaboration." PhD dissertation, University of Oklahoma, 1963; Allan Millett, *Understanding is Better than Remembering: The Korean War 1945–1954*. Manhattan, Kansas: Kansas State University, 1997.

28. Rhee, when he was president of the Korean government in exile, had been released over questions of ethics and procedure.

29. Hickey, *The Korean War*, p. 11.

30. Wiltz, "Did the United States Betray Korea," pp. 243–270.

31. A.W. Cordier and W. Foote (eds.). *Public Papers of the Secretaries-general of the United Nations, Vol. 1, Trygve Lie, 1946–1953*. New York: 1969.

32. While the Truman administration said it had consulted all diplomatic sources and there was approval for the appointment of the general, there was some disapproval almost from the beginning of the war. The commander made occasional reports to the UN and received suggestions, but there was little oversight. See Hastings, *The Korean War*, p. 79.

33. The agreement was never put into a formal document but to Rhee's credit he allowed it to happen. See Appleman, *South to the Naktong, North to the Yalu*, p. 112.

34. Department of State Publication 4263, Document 100, *U.S. Policy in the Korean Conflict: July 1950 to February 1951*, p. 47.

35. Statement by the President, July 8, 1950, "I am directing General MacArthur, pursuant to the Security Council resolution, to use the United Nations flag in the course of operations against the North Korean forces concurrently with the flags of the various nations participating." George Elsey Correspondence File, 8 July 1950, Harry S. Truman Presidential Library and Museum.

36. This was the case with British Naval officers coming into already organized American commanded task forces.

37. David Halberstam, *The Coldest Winter: America and the Korean War*. New York: Macmillan, 2008, p. 482.

38. Blair, p. 79.

39. T.R. Fehrenbach, *This Kind of War: The Classic Korean War History*. Washington, D.C.: Brassey's, 1994, p. 272.

40. "A Treaty of Peace, Amity, Commerce and Navigation," signed at Chemulpo, Korea, 22 May 1882, agreed, among other things, to "mutual assistance in case of attack." State

Department, *Treaties and Conventions Concluded Between the United States of America Since July 4, 1776.* Government Printing Office, 1889, p. 216.

41. In Dean Acheson's speech to the National Press Club, 12 January 1950, he outlined the U.S. defensive position and left out South Korea. Many have seen this as a go ahead for Joseph Stalin, but recent information suggests this is probably not true. He was, in fact, simply describing what already established policy was. See James I. Matray, "Dean Acheson's Press Club Speech Re-examined," *The Journal of Conflict Studies*, Volume 22, Number 1, Spring 2002. He discusses Acheson's speech and how it portrayed American policy. The Soviet strategists must certainly have noticed that the U.S. had not only removed the occupation troops from Korea, but the Marines from the Shantung peninsula in China. U.S. military forces were obviously withdrawing from the Asian mainland.

42. "Pertinent Papers on the Korean Situation, January 1953," Harry S. Truman Presidential Library and Museum.

43. Ibid., July 14, 1950.

44. Stueck, *The Korean War: An International History*, p. 198.

45. "Tabulation of Replies," ibid.

46. The papers of George Elsey, 12 July 1950, Harry S. Truman Library and Museum.

47. Ibid., 5 July 1950.

48. Chen Jian, "In the Name of Revolution," in Stueck, *Rethinking the Korean War*, p. 111.

49. James Matray, "Revisiting Korea: Exposing Myths of the Forgotten War." *Prologue*, Volume 34, Number 2.

50. As quoted in Steuck, *Rethinking the Korean War*, p. 96.

51. Historian Bruce Cumings points out that this was not an off-hand remark but was rather a well calculated probe.

Chapter 3

1. Princeton University Press, Princeton, 1995.

2. *Congressional Record*, 1950, 10996.

3. Steven Casey, *Selling the Korean War: Propaganda, Politics, and Public Opinion in the United States, 1950–1953.* Oxford: Oxford University Press, 2010, p. 90.

4. The army's assistant chief of staff for plans and operations.

5. As quoted in William Stueck, "Arab-Asian Peace Initiatives," in James I. Matray, *Historical Dictionary of the Korean War.* West-

port, Connecticut: Greenwood Press, 1991, pp. 20–21.

6. See discussion of India in Chapter 7.

7. See Japan in Chapter 7.

Chapter 4

1. As quoted in Appleman, *South to the Naktong, North to the Yalu.* Washington, D.C.: Office of the Chief of Military History, Department of the Army, 1961, p. 115.

2. Ibid., 48. There is more to this; see the Republic of China in Chapter 8.

3. Hastings, *The Korean War*, p. 238.

4. Robert O'Neill address to the Australian War Memorial Anniversary, 11 November 2003. www.awm.gov.au/events.

5. Forbes, Cameron. *The Korean War: Australia in the Giant's Playground.* Sydney: Pan Macmillan, Australia, 2010.

6. Australian War Memorial page. www.awm.gov.au/exibigtions/korea/faces/saunders.

7. Belgium rotated its troops through the war with the 1st, 2nd and 3rd Belgium Battalion serving in order.

8. Official number, www.korean-war-medals.com/belgium. The veterans' monument in Korea, however, records 97 killed, 350 wounded and five missing in action.

9. The offer also included the Turkish Brigade as a part of the Commonwealth force.

10. "Memoir," located at the Center for the Study of the Korean War, Independence, Missouri.

11. John Blaxland, "The Armies of Canada and Australia: Close Collaboration?" *Canadian Military Journal*, Volume 4, Number 4, August 2002.

12. Stueck, *The Korean War: An International History*, Chapter Nine, footnote 24. Foreign Broadcast Information Service (FBIS), 27 July 1953.

13. Some sources have reported as many as six frigates being sent. This is probably not the case since official records indicate the Colombian navy had only one frigate at the time.

14. Participants' Correspondence File (H), Center for the Study of the Korean War.

15. James I. Marino, "Korean War: Battle on Pork Chop," *Military History*, April 2003.

16. Les Peate, "From Bogota to Old Baldy: Colombia's Contribution," *Esprit de Corps*, June 2004.

17. An excellent account of Ethiopian soldiers at the Battle of Pork Chop Hill is found in S.L.A. Marshall, *Pork Chop Hill.* New York: William R. Morrow, 1952.

18. Alex Last, "An Ethiopian Hero of the Korean War," BBC News, 24 September 2012.

19. Participants' Correspondence File (S), Center for the Study of the Korean War.

20. James A. Huston, *Guns and Butter, Powder and Rice: U.S. Army Logistics in the Korean War.* Selinsgrove, PA: Susquehanna University Press, 1989, p. 318.

21. Nationalarchives.glov.uk/cabinet papers/Korea-entry.

22. Hickey, *The Korean War,* p. 93.

23. Robert Weller, "Korean War: French Bayonets," *Huffington Post,* 28 June 2010.

24. Ibid.

25. The olive oil, especially prepared, was delivered from home and distributed by the U.S.

26. "Luxembourg in Action," unpublished manuscript located at the Center for the Study of the Korean War.

27. For a more detailed account see Belgium's contribution in Chapter 4. The Luxembourg unit was involved in rotation at the time but several members of the unit remained behind and fought with the Belgium unit at this battle.

28. Ralph Romono, Participants' Correspondence File (R), Center for the Study of the Korean War.

29. Korean Augmented Troops, United States Army.

30. The force also included former members of the Waffen SS whose prison terms were remitted and citizenship restored in return for volunteering.

31. They are best remembered by veterans primarily for the fact the canteen served a ten-cent shot of gin. Les Peate, "The Van Heutsz Create a Tradition: The Dutch Contingent in Korea." *Esprit de Corps,* August 2004, http://findarticles.com.

32. The Netherlands' military histories include few references to its military forces in Korea.

33. Originally called the Cooperation Economic Development in South and Southeast Asia, it was founded in 1950. It was an organization that fostered economic and social cooperation among the member states.

34. Michael Hickey, *The Korean War: The West Confronts Communism.* New York: The Overlook Press, 2000, p. 55.

35. Persons of Polynesian-Melanesian background.

36. Rokdero.com/2008/05/07/heroes-of-the-korean-war.

37. In Korean the words for "four" and "death" are pronounced the same, thus the number 4 is not used in South Korean unit designations.

38. *Times,* 25 October 1950, p. 5.

39. Quoted in Hastings, *The Korean War,* pp. 94–95.

40. Foot, *The Wrong War,* p. 135.

41. Hickey, *The Korean War: The West Confronts Communism,* pp. 92–94.

42. www.korea50.army.mil/history/factsheet/allied.shtml.

43. Hickey, *The Korean War: the West Confronts Communism,* p. 93.

44. Ibid., p. 129

45. "The Turkish Brigade in Korean War," http://changingturkey.com.

46. *Turkish Times.* Tallarmeniantale.com/korea

47. Ibid.

48. www.korea-war.com/turkey.

49. Participants' Correspondence File (F), Center For the Study of the Korean War, Independence, Missouri.

50. Stueck, *The Korean War: An International History,* p. 185.

51. www.korean-war.com/turkey.

52. Ibid.

53. Ibid.

54. The standby C rations that were first available, most left over from World War II, included pork and beans, wieners (pork) and beans, sausage and gravy, bacon and eggs, and pork gravy.

55. www.korean-war.com/turkey.

56. The Papers of Dean Acheson, 24 July 1950, Memorandum of Conversation, Ambassador Jooste of the Union of South Africa, Harry S. Truman Presidential Library and Museum.

57. Quoted from Elizabeth Schafer, "South African Forces," in Stanley Sandler, *The Korean War: An Encyclopedia.* New York: Garland, 1995, p. 320.

58. Joint Chiefs of Staff to CINCFE, 29 June 1950, Harry S. Truman Presidential Library and Museum.

59. As quoted in Hastings, *The Korean War,* p. 70.

60. Stueck, *The Korean War: An International History,* p. 320.

61. His decision, during the armistice negotiations, to allow some American prisoners to remain unaccounted for has suggested to some just how little he understood about what was happening in Asia.

62. Clark led a survey mission to determine conditions at the port of Inchon prior

to the landing. The team was also able to light a lighthouse in Flying Fish Channel that helped direct the invasion force.

63. Cagle and Manson, *The Sea War*, p. 362.

64. In the United States the temperance movement joined forces with a body of evangelical women and lobbied Congress to deny liquor to the American fighting man, a policy only temporarily followed.

65. 1871.

66. Even at this early date the U.S. was concerned that Syngman Rhee, if he had heavy weapons and tanks, would initiate an invasion of the North.

67. By far the best presentation of the military involvement is found in Gordon L. Rottman, *Korean War Order of Battle: United States, United Nations, and Communist Ground, Naval, and Air Forces, 1950–1953*. Westport, Connecticut: Praeger, 2002.

68. *Universal Peace Federation* magazine, 11 May 2010.

Chapter 5

1. See Japan in Chapter 7.

2. Participants' Correspondence File (Q), Center for the Study of the Korean War.

3. As quoted in Huston, *Guns and Butter*, p. 325.

4. India also sent a medical unit to North Korea, see Chapter 5.

5. Hereafter the term *Quisling* has been used to mean coward, betrayer, and traitor.

6. www.koreanwar.org/htm/units/un/neatherlands.htm.

7. *Swedish Wire*, 23 June 2010. www.swedishwire.com/opinion/5126-koreans-president-thanks-you-people-of-sweden-ol.

8. Neither German nor South Korean sources have been able to shed much light on this.

Chapter 6

1. Memo, Office of the Secretary of State, 6 October 1950. UN Documents, Command and Staff College, Fort Leavenworth, Kansas. The primary sources for the extent of the contribution are located in hundreds of UN documents dealing with logistics.

2. Choi He-suk, "22 More Nations Recognized for Support in Korean War," *The Korea Herald*, May 10, 2012. www.my.news.yahoo.com/22-more-nations-recognized-support-korean War-053003081.htm.

3. Richard Miller, Jr., *Funding Extended Conflicts: Korea, Vietnam and the War on Ter-*ror. Westport, Connecticut: Praeger Press, 2007.

4. For more information about this see Paul M. Edwards, *Between the Lines of World War II*. Jefferson, North Carolina: McFarland, 2010, Chapter Nine.

5. Brazil also offered troops for the conflict. See Chapter 8.

6. Kim Chum-kon, *The Korean War, 1950–1953*. Seoul, Korea: Kwangmyong, 1973, pp. 505–5.

7. Ethiopia sent a significant contingency of troops to fight in Korea, see Chapter 4.

8. Monrovia was also the name of Monroe's illegitimate son born of the slave Liberia Thurmont. "U.S. Department of State: History" http://www.history.state.gov/milestons/1830–1860/Liberia.

9. Kim Chum Kon, p. 367.

10. Ibid., p. 371.

11. Paul M. Edwards, *Historical Dictionary of the Korean War*. London: Scarecrow Press, 2010, p. 220.

12. Ibid., p. 373.

13. Ibid., p. 374. The Philippines also provided armed forces; see Chapter 4.

14. Kim Chum-kon, *The Korean War, 1950–195*, p. 381.

15. Kim Chum-kon, p. 383.

Chapter 7

1. This is another area in which there is still some controversy. Some scholars using Russian documents have suggested that the planes first appeared in November 1950 while others citing Chinese sources claim it was January of 1951. See footnote 24 in Stueck, *The Korean War in World History*, p. 124.

2. James L. Stokesbury, *A Short History of the Korean War*. New York: William Morrow, 1988, p. 223. John Foster Dulles harrumphed when he heard this, saying, "Neutralism is immoral."

3. *The Telegraph*, www.telegraphindia.com.

4. As quoted from Hastings, *The Korean War*, p. 134.

5. Bipan Chandra, *India After Independence*. New Delhi: Viking, 1999, p. 153.

6. "Japanese Peace Treaty," as found in Matray, *Historical Dictionary of the Korean War*, p. 195.

7. Appleman, *South to the Naktong, North to the Yalu*, pp. 58–59.

8. Suggested by Michael Schaller, "The Korean War," in Stueck, *The Korean War in World History*, p. 172ff.

9. *People's Daily On Line*, 8 December 2010.

Chapter 8

1. "Status of United Nations Offers of Aid for the Korean War," Harry S. Truman Library and Museum, R Files.

2. Ibid.

3. Despite the drop in shipping that followed the postwar demobilization of the fleet, the military did not anticipate a shortage of merchant ships.

4. It was not much of a revolution, as only one man and one donkey were killed.

5. Edward Marolda, "Invasion Patrol: The Seventh Fleet in Chinese Waters," Navy History Heritage Command, www.history.navy.mil.

6. MacArthur memorandum, 1 August 1950, Harry Truman Files on the Korean War, Center for the Study of the Korean War.

7. The State Department was well aware that MacArthur often initiated foreign policy without checking with the government.

8. Hickey, *The Korean War*, p. 67.

9. There are several cases in the records of clandestine activities during the war in which the Nationalist Chinese were involved.

10. Li Yi, "Chiang's Offer of Chinese Troops," found in James Matray, *Historical Dictionary of the Korean War*, p. 83.

11. He apparently had suggested that if taken they would become an "albatross around our neck." Li Yi, Ibid., p. 84.

12. Joint Chiefs of Staff to Douglas MacArthur, June 30, 1950. UN Documents, Command and Staff Library.

13. One can only wonder at what the United States would have done if the Soviet delegation had vetoed the resolutions. The evidence seems very strong to suggest that America had every intention of continuing its involvement regardless of the United Nations decision.

14. Nationalist China was reported as a co-conciliator in at least two CIA directed operations during the war. See Edwards, *Unusual Footnotes to a Forgotten War*, 2012.

Conclusion

1. The response reminds one of General Ferdinand Foch's beliefs that the British idea of minimal British contribution in 1914 was one British soldier, and make sure he gets killed.

2. Concept identified and quote taken from Steuck, *The Korean War in World History*, p. 70.

3. Bevin Alexander, *Korea: The First War We Lost*. New York: Hippocrene Books, 1986, p. 482.

4. As a personal aside I remember a significant number of Americans in my outfit who were proud to be there with, or close to, troops from these nations. This was especially true of the Turks since everyone believed the Chinese were afraid of them and would not attack if they were nearby.

5. Marguerite Higgins, *War in Korea: Report of a Woman War Correspondent*. New York: Doubleday and Company, 1951, p. 83.

6. Ibid., p. 84.

7. Stokesbury, *A Short History of the Korean War*, p. 193.

8. While the Marines tend to believe they were the only ones involved in the fight and retreat from the Chosin Reservoir, for the sake of perspective it is important to remember that not only were Army forces there but troops of "other nations" as well.

9. James Steward, *Airpower: The Decisive Factor in Korea*. Princeton, New Jersey: D. Van Nostrand, 1957, 1973.

10. Following World War II a reorganization of the Coast Guard and a change in national policy allowed the service to fight in international wars under its own command.

11. In the first two years of the Korean War the rate of artillery fire was about the same as was fired in the World War II period between D-day and V-J day. The Air Force expended nearly twice as much as in all the theaters during the first two years of World War II. Huston, *Guns and Butter*, p. 162.

12. The authorized ammunition reserve in the Far East in June 1950 was 45 days, based on the expenditure in the Pacific in World War II. Ibid., p. 72.

13. Ibid., pp. 372–373.

14. Ibid., p. 314.

15. T. R. Fechrenbach, *This Kind of War*, p. 42. In a conversation with the author of this work, I challenged this because in my experience, in well over a year, I never heard such a remark. He stuck to his conviction.

16. In the peak year, 1952, 561,770 were inducted. In 1953 at the end of the war 59 percent of those in Korea were draftees.

17. Hickey, *The Korean War: The West Confronts Communism*, p. 164.

18. Ibid., p. 165.

19. Consulate General, People's Republic

of China, manuscript in possession of the Center for the Study of the Korean War.

20. Great Britain, with the help of other nations, had gone to war to preserve the right to sell opium. The Unequal Treaties were a series of treaties forced on the Chinese at the end of the 19th century that gave foreign government the power over areas of Chinese land and industry.

21. Ni Lexiong, *Asian Times,* 15 June 2001. www.atimes.com/koreas/cf150g02.

22. PRO: London W6216/728.

23. As quoted in Whelan, *Drawing the Line,* p. 154.

24. Brian Catchpole, *The Korean War.* New York: Carroll and Graf, 2000, p. 328.

25. In the files of the Center for the Study of the Korean War are at least six folders of correspondence with film makers who said they were working on films. None of these have appeared.

26. The painting by Pablo Picasso called *Massacre in Korea* (1951) is considered by many as being too violent to show.

Bibliography

Acheson, Dean. Papers. Harry S. Truman Library and Museum, Independence, Missouri.

British Korean Veterans Association. *The Morning Calm: Journal of the British Korean Veterans Association.* Hessle, North Humberside: The Association, 1940.

Department of State Publications. "U.S. Policies in Korea," 4263, Document 106. Harry S. Truman Library and Museum, Independence, Missouri.

Edwards, Paul M. Correspondence File (1953–1954), Center for the Study of the Korean War, Independence, Missouri.

Elsey, George. Papers. Harry S. Truman Library and Museum, Independence, Missouri.

Eighth Army Command Report. Allied Personnel and Ground Units in Korea, March 1953. G-4 Daily Memos of Important action. Archives of the Office of the Chief of Military History.

Joint Chiefs of Staff (microfilm); Command and Staff College, Fort Leavenworth, Kansas.

Judd, Walter H. Papers. Harry S. Truman Library and Museum, Independence, Missouri.

Letters File. "Nations Involved in the Korean War." Center for the Study of the Korean War, Independence, Missouri.

National Security Council Papers, 1950. Harry S. Truman Library and Museum, Independence, Missouri.

Notes from phone calls and e-mails to national embassies in New York, Chicago, New Orleans, and Los Angeles. Center for the Study of the Korean War, Independence, Missouri.

Participants' Correspondence (filed by alphabet); Center for the Study of the Korean War, Independence, Missouri.

Papers on the Korean Situation, January 1953; Harry S. Truman Library and Museum, Independence, Missouri.

The Pink Files. Select Truman Presidential Papers dealing with the Korean War. Center for the Study of the Korean War, Independence, Missouri.

United Nations. Documents, Microfilm File. Command and Staff College Library; Fort Leavenworth, Kansas.

United Nations. Papers, R File. Harry S. Truman Library and Museum, Independence, Missouri.

United Nations. "Status of United Nations Offers in Aid for the Korean War." Harry S. Truman Library and Museum, Independence, Missouri.

United Nations. "Tabulation of Replies, 12 July 1950." Harry S. Truman Library and Museum, Independence, Missouri.

Wolfgeher, Paul. Papers [collection of public relations and propaganda items prepared during the Korean War]. Center for the Study of the Korean War, Independence, Missouri.

Electronic

The Korean War. http://korean-war.com.
North Korea. http://Kwanan.com//v//019.

U.S. Navy Historical Center. http://history. navy.mil/index.

Veterans History. http://www.theforgotten-victory.org.

General

Alstedter, Christie. "Problem of Coalition Diplomacy: The Korean Experience." *International Journal*, Volume 8, Number 4, Autumn 1953, pp. 256–265.

Blanton, Stephen Dwight. "A Study of the United States Navy's Minesweeping Efforts in the Korean War." master's thesis, Texas Tech University, 1993.

Caridi, Ronald J. *The Korean War and American Politics: The Republican Party as a Case Study*. Pennsylvania: University of Pennsylvania Press, 1968.

Carter, Worral Reed. *Beans, Bullets, and Black Oil*. Washington, D.C.: Department of the Navy, 1953.

Catchpole, Brian. *The Korean War 1950–1953*. New York: Carroll and Graf, 2000.

Cooling, Franklin. "Allied Interoperability in the Korean War." *Military Review*, Volume 63, Number 26, June 1983, pp. 26–52.

Danzik, Wayne. "Coalition Forces in the Korean War." *Naval War College Review*, Volume 47, pp. 243–261.

Edwards, Paul M. *To Acknowledge a War: The Korean War in American Memory*. Westport, Connecticut: Greenwood Press, 2000.

Eisenhower, Dwight D. *The White House Years: Mandate for Change, 1953–56*. New York: Doubleday, 1963.

Fehrenbach, T.R. *This Kind of War: The Classic Korean War History*. Washington, D.C.: Brassy's, 1963.

Goodrick, Leland. "Collective Action in Korea." *Current History*, Volume 38, June 1960, pp. 332–336.

Hastings, Max. *The Korean War*. New York: Touchstone, 1987.

Hickey, Michael. *The Korean War: The West Confronts Communism, 1950–1953*. London: John Murray, 1999.

Higgins, Marguerite. *War in Korea: The Report of a Woman Combat Correspondent*. Garden City, New York: Doubleday, 1951

Higgins, Rosalyn. *United Nations Peacekeeping 1946–1967: Documents and Commentary*, Volume II. Oxford: Oxford University Press, 1970.

Higgins, Trumbull. *Korea and the Fall of MacArthur*. Cambridge: Oxford University Press, 1960.

Hispanics in American Defense. Washington D.C.: Department of Defense, 1963.

"History of the Korean War: Inter-Allied Co-operation During Combat Operations, 1952." Headquarters Far East Command, Military History Section, Dean Historical Center.

Huston, James A. *Guns and Butter, Powder and Rice: U.S. Army Logistics in the Korean War*. Selinsgrove: Susquehanna University Press, 1989.

James, D. Clayton. *Refighting the Last War: Command and Crisis in the Korean War, 1950–53*. New York: Hardcover Free Press, 1992.

Khrushchev, Nikita. *Khrushchev Remembers*. New York: Little, Brown, 1971.

Kim Chull-Baum (ed.). *The Truth About the Korean War*. Seoul, ROK: Eulyoo, 1991.

Kipper, P.M. "Supplying United Nations Troops in Korea." *Military Review*, Volume 33, Number 21, April, 1953.

Lyons, Gene. *Military Policy and Economic Aid in the Korean Case, 1950–1953*. Columbia: Ohio State University Press, 1961.

Matray, James I. (ed.). *Historical Dictionary of the Korean War*. Westport, Connecticut: Greenwood Press, 1991.

Millett, Alan. *The Korean War*. Falls Church, Virginia: Potomac Books, 2007.

Portway, D. *Korea: Land of the Morning Calm*. London: George Harrap, 1953.

Roehrig, Terence. "Coming to South Korea's Aid: The Contribution of UNC Coalition." *International Journal of Korean Studies*, Volume 15, Number 1, Spring-Summer 2011, pp. 381–415.

Rottman, Gordon L. *Korean War Order of Battle: United States, United Nations, and Communist Ground, Naval and air Forces, 1950–1953*. Westport, Connecticut: Praeger, 2002.

Rovere, Richard H., and Arthur M. Schlesinger, Jr. *The MacArthur Controversy and American Foreign Policy*. New York: Noonday Press, 1965.

Sandler, Stanley. *The Korean War: An Encyclopedia*. New York: Garland, 1995.

Schnabel, James F. *Policy and Direction: The First Year.* Washington, D.C.: Office of the Chief of Military History, United States Army, 1972.

Stokesbury, James L. *A Short History of the Korean War.* New York: William Morrow, 1988.

Stone, I.F. *The Hidden History of the Korean War.* Turnstile Press, 1952.

Stueck, William. *The Korean War: An International History.* Princeton: Princeton University Press, 1995.

_____, (ed.). *The Korean War in World History.* Lexington: University Press of Kentucky, 2004.

Thorne, Christopher. *Allies of a Kind.* E-Book: Hamish Hamilton, 1978.

Westas, Odd Arne. *Global Cold War.* London: Cambridge University Press, 2007.

Argentina

Lewis, Colin. *Argentina: A Short History.* London: Oneworld, 2002.

Lewis, Daniel K. *A History of Argentina.* Hounasville: Palgrave Macmillan Press, 2003.

Shumway, Nicholas. *The Invention of Argentina.* Berkley: University of California Press, 1993.

Westover, J. *U.S. Army: Combat Support in Korea.* Washington, D.C.: Department of the Army, 1955.

Australia

Bartlett, N. *With the Australians in Korea.* Canberra: Australian War Memorial, 1954.

Brown, Colin H. *Stalemate in Korea and How We Coped: The Royal Australian Regiment in the Static War of 1952–1953.* Loffus, NSW: Australian Military History Publication, 1997.

Trembath, Richard. *A Different Sort of War: Australia in Korea 1950–1953.* Melbourne: Australian Scholarly Publishing, 2003.

Belgium

Belgium Can Do It Too! The Belgium-Luxembourg Battalion in the Korean War. Brussels: Royal Museum of the Army and of Military History, 2011.

Bolivia

Dangi, Benjamin. *The Price of Fire: Resource Wars and Social Movement in Bolivia.* Edinburgh, Scotland: A.K. Press, 2007.

Lehman, Kenneth D. *Bolivia and the United States.* Athens: University of Georgia Press, 1999.

Canada

Bercuson, David J. *Blood on the Hills: The Canadian Army in Korea.* Toronto: University of Toronto Press, 2002.

McGuire, F.R. *Canada's Army in Korea.* Ottawa: Queen's Printer, 1956.

Melady, John. *Korea: Canada's Forgotten War.* Toronto: Macmillan of Canada, 1988.

Peate, Les. *The War That Wasn't.* Ottawa, Ontario: Esprit de Corps Books, 2005.

Wood, Herbert F. *Strange Battleground: Official History of the Canadian Army in Korea.* Ottawa: Queen's Printer, 1966.

Chile

Collier, Simon, and William F. Sater. *A History of Chile 1808–1996.* Cambridge: Cambridge University Press, 2004.

Sater, William F. *The Grand Illusion: the Prussianization of the Chilean Army.* Lincoln: University of Nebraska Press, 1999.

China (Nationalist)

Crozier, Brian, with Eric Chou. *The Man Who Lost China: The First Full Biography of Chiang Kai-shek.* New York: Scribner, 1976.

Manthrore, Jonathan. *Forbidden Nation: A History of Taiwan.* Hounasville: Palgrave Macmillan, 2008.

Roy, Denny. *Taiwan: A Political History.* Ithaca, New York: Cornell University Press, 2002.

Colombia

Danley, Mark H. "The Colombian Navy in the Korean War." *Naval War College Review,* Volume 47, Autumn 1994, pp. 25–39.

Peate, Les. *From Bogota to Old Baldy: Colombia's Contributions.* Ottawa: Scott Taylor, 2004.

Costa Rica

Blake, Beatrice. *The New Key to Costa Rica.* Berkeley, California: Ulysses Press, 2009.

Yasher, Deborah J. *Demanding Democracy:*

Reform and Reaction in Costa Rica and Guatemala, 1870–1950. Stanford, California: Stanford University Press, 1997.

Cuba

Gott, Richard. *Cuba: A New History.* New Haven, Connecticut: Yale University Press, 2004.

Suchlicki, James. *Cuba from Columbus to Castro and Beyond.* Dulles, Virginia: Potomac Books, 2002.

Denmark

Derry, T.K. *A History of Scandinavia: Norway, Sweden, Denmark, Finland and Iceland.* St. Paul: University of Minnesota Press, 2002.

Jespersen, Knud J. *A History of Denmark.* Hampshire, United Kingdom: Palgrave Macmillan, 2004.

Ecuador

De La Torre, Carlos (ed.). *The Ecuador Reader: History, Culture, Politics.* Durham, North Carolina: Duke University Press, 2009.

Rudolph, James D. *A Country Study: Ecuador.* Washington D.C.: Government Printing Office for the Library of Congress, 1969.

El Salvador

Haggarty, Richard A. (ed.). *El Salvador: A Country Study.* Washington, D.C.: Government Printing Office for the Library of Congress, 1988.

Williams, Philip, and Knut Walter. *Militarization and Demilitarization in El Salvador's Transition to Democracy.* Pittsburg: Pittsburg State University, 1979.

Ethiopia

Shordiles, Kimon. *Kagnew: The Story of Ethiopian Fighters in Korea.* Kagnew, 1954 (published in English).

Zewde, Bahru. *A History of Modern Ethiopia, 1855–1991.* Athens, University of Ohio Press, 2001.

France

Gahide, J.R. *La Belgique et la Guerre de Coree.* France: Bruxelle, 1999.

Kenneth E. Hamburger. *Leadership in the*
Crucible: The Korean War Battles of Twin Tunnels and Chipygong-Ni. College Station: Texas A&M Press, 2003.

Greece

"13th Flight of the RHAF in Korea." http://koti.welho.com/msolanak/koreaengl.html.

Clogg, Richard. *A Short History of Modern Greece.* Cambridge: Cambridge University Press, 1986.

Department of the Army. *The Greek Expeditionary Force in Korea, 1950–1953,* 1956.

Iceland

Derry, T.K. *A History of Scandinavia: Norway, Sweden, Denmark, Finland and Iceland.* St. Paul: University of Minnesota Press, 2002.

Whitehead, Por. *The Ally Who Came in From the Cold: A Survey of Icelandic Foreign Policy 1946–1956.* Reykjavik: University of Iceland Press, 1998.

India

Chan Wahn, Kim. "The Role of India in the Korean War." *International Area Studies Review,* 2010, pp. 21–38.

Gupta, Alka. *India and UN Peace-keeping Activities: A Case Study of Korea 1947–1953.* New Delhi: Radiant Publishers, 1977.

Rao, P.V. Narasimha. "Nehru and Non-Alignment." *Mainstream,* Volume 57, Number 24, 30 May 2009.

Varma, Shanta. "A Hero of Indian Foreign Policy: V.K. Krishna Menon," *Lucknow Journal of Social Science,* Volume 4, Issue 1, 2007.

Iran

Abdo, Genève, and Jonathan Lyons. *Answering Only to God: Faith and Freedom in Twenty- first Century Iran.* New York: Henry Holt, 2003.

Ward, Steven. *Immortal: A Military History of Iran and Its Armed Forces.* Washington, D.C.: Georgetown University Press, 2009.

Israel

Eytan, Walter. *The First Ten Years of Diplomatic History of Israel.* London: Weidenfield and Nicholas, 1958.

Sachar, Howard M. *A History of Israel.* New York: Knopf, 1976.

Italy

McCarthy, Patrick. *Italy Since 1945.* Oxford, England: Oxford University Press, 2000.

Smith, Dennis Jack. *Modern Italy: A Political History.* Ann Arbor: Michigan University Press, 1997.

Japan

Akagi, Kanji. "The Korean War in Japan," *Journal of Korean Studies,* Volume 24, Number 1, June 2011, pp. 175–184.

Rees, D. *The Korean War: History and Tactics.* London: Obis, 1984.

Vardaman, James M. *History of Japan Since 1945: From MacArthur to the Information Society.* Berkeley, California: Stone Bridge Press.

Lebanon

Salibi, Kamal. *A House of Many Mansions: The History of Lebanon, Reconsidered.* London: Ibtauris, 1988.

Salibi, Kamal. *The Modern History of Lebanon.* Delmar: Caravan Books, 1977.

Liberia

Cassell, C. Abayomi. *Liberia: A History of the First African Republic.* New York: Macmillan Press, 1970.

Nelson, Howard D. *Liberia: A Country Study.* Washington, D.C.: Government Printing Office for the Library of Congress, 1985.

Luxemburg

Reid, Andrew. *Luxembourg: A History of the Celts to the Present Day.* United Kingdom: AuthorHouse, 2005.

Mexico

Kirkwood, Burton. *The History of Mexico.* Westport, CT. Greenwood Press, 2000.

Russell, Philip. *The History of Mexico from Pre-Conquest to Present.* New York: Rutledge, 2010.

Netherlands

Dupuy, Ernest, and Trevor Dupuy. *The Encyclopedia of Military History from 3500 to the Present.* London: Jane's Printing, 1980.

Schaffsma, M.D. *The Dutch Detachment of the United Nations in Korea.*

New Zealand

Hopkins, G.F. *Tales from Korea: The Royal New Zealand Navy in the Korean War.* Auckland, Australia: Reed, 2000.

McGibbon, Ian. *New Zealand and the Korean War,* 2 Volumes. Auckland: Oxford Press, 1986.

_____. "New Zealand's Intervention in the Korean War, June-July, 1950," *International History Review,* Volume 11, May 1989, pp. 272–290.

Nicaragua

Derry, T.K. *A History of Scandinavia: Norway, Sweden, Denmark, Finland and Iceland.* St. Paul: University of Minnesota Press, 2002.

Kinzer, Stephen. *Blood of Brothers: Life and War in Nicaragua.* New York: David Rockefeller Center for the Study of Latin America, 2007.

Norway

Pedersen, L.U. *Norge I. Korea.* Oslo, 1991.

Surhorn, Lambert M., and Marian Tennoe. *NORMASH.* www.morebooks.de. Betascript, 2010.

Pakistan

Aya, Harish Chandra. "The Korean War and U.S. Pakistani Relations," *International Studies.* Volume 9, Number 3, January 1967, pp. 332–339.

Gopswmi, B.N. "Pakistan and the Korean Crisis," *Indian Yearbook of International Affairs 15–16,* 1966–67, pp. 538–557.

Paraguay

Federal Research Division, Library of Congress. *Paraguay: A Country Story.* Washington, D.C.: Department of the Army, 1990.

Peru

Beebe, Henry S. *The History of Peru.* New York: Forgotten Books, 2012.

Hunefeldt, Christine. *Brief History of Peru.* New York: Facts on File, 2004.

Panama

Ealy, Lawrence O. *The Republic of Panama in World Affairs, 1903–1950.* Westport, Connecticut: Greenwood Press, 1986.

Philippines

Polo, Lily Ann. *A Cold War Alliance: Philippine–South Korean Relations 1948–1971.*

Villasanta, Art. "The Glory of Our Fathers." *Philippine Expeditionary Force to Korea (PEFTOK): 1950–1955.* http://peftok.blogspot.com/.

Sweden

Derry, T.K. *A History of Scandinavia: Norway, Sweden, Denmark, Finland and Iceland.* St. Paul: University of Minnesota Press, 2002.

Jurgensen, Peter. "The *Jutlandia* Expedition 1951–1953," *Maskinmestern,* Number 9, September 2000 (printed in English).

Thailand

Snit Satyasnguan. *The Thai Battalion in Korea.* Bangkok: Toppan, 1956.

Turkey

Brown, Cameron S. "The One Coalition They Craved to Join: Turkey in the Korean War." *Reviews of International Studies,* Volume 34, Number 1, January 2008, pp. 89–108.

General Staff. *The Battles of the Turkish Armed Forces in the Korean War, 1950–1953.*

Howard, Douglas Arthur. The History of Turkey. Westport, Connecticut: Greenwood Press, 2001.

Kinzer, Stephen. *Crescent and Star: Turkey Between Two Worlds.* London: Farrar, Straus, Giroux, 2001.

Ozselcuk, Musret. "The Turkish Brigade in the Korean War." *International Review of Military History,* 1980, pp. 253–272.

Uruguay

Safi, Julian. *Uruguay.* Diffusion: Vilo, 1979.

Union of South Africa

Moore, Dermont Michael. *South Africa's Flying Cheetahs in Korea.* Johannesburg: Ashanti, 1991.

United Kingdom

Carew, John. *Korea: The Commonwealth at War.* London: Cassell, 1967.

Farrar, P.N. "Britain's Proposal for a Buffer Zone South of the Yalu 1950," *Journal of Contemporary History,* Volume 18, 1983.

Farrar-Hockley, Anthony. *Official History: The British Part in the Korean War,* Two Volumes. London: HMSO, 1990.

Futrell, R.F. *The United States Air Force in Korea, 1950–1953.* Washington, D.C.: Officer of Air Force History, 1983.

Great Britain, Cabinet Office. *British Part in the Korean War: An Honourable Discharge.* London: Stationary Office Books, 1995.

Harding, E.D. *The Imjin Roll.* London: Gloucester, 1981.

Hoare, J.E. "British Public Opinion and the Korean War." *Papers of the British Association for Korean Studies,* Number 2, 1992.

Kahn, E.J., Jr. "No One but the Gloster." *New Yorker,* 26 May 1951.

MacDonald, C. *Britain and the Korean War.* Oxford: Basil, Blackwell, 1990.

McNair, Elizabeth J. *A British Army Nurse in the Korean War.* London: History Press, 2007.

Venezuela

Tarver, H. Michael, and Julia C. Frederick. *The History of Venezuela.* Hampshire, United Kingdom: Palgrave Macmillan, 2006.

Uzcategui, Rafael, and Chaz Bufe. *Venezuela: Revolution as Spectacular.* Tucson, Arizona: Sharp Press, 2001.

West Germany

Cooling, III, Benjamin Franklin. "Allied Interoperability in the Korean War," *Military Review,* Volume 63, June 1983, p. 26.

Index

Numbers in **bold italics** indicate pages with photographs.